What Lesbian Looks Like

Dyke Activists Take On the 21st Century

edited by Kris Kleindienst

Firebrand
Books
Ithaca, New York

This book may not be reproduced in whole or in part, except in the case of reviews, without permission from Firebrand Books, 141 The Commons, Ithaca, New York 14850.

Book design by Sunset Design
Cover design by Look At That and Sunset Design

Printed in Canada

10 9 8 7 6 5 4 3 2 1

Library of Congress Cataloging-in-Publication Data

  This is what lesbian looks like : dyke activists take on the 21st century / ed-
    ited by Kris Kleindienst.
    p. cm.
  ISBN 1–56341–116–4 (paper : alk. paper)—ISBN 1–56341–117–2 (cloth : alk.
    paper)
    1. Lesbians—United States—Political activity. I. Kleindienst, Kris, 1953–

HQ75.6.U5 T55 1999
306.76'63—dc21

                                                                99–051938

Acknowledgments

This book is obviously the work of many who have inspired and enabled me to bring it together, most notably, the contributors.

To Susan Raffo I am deeply indebted for her generous assistance at every level of this project—her sharp thinking, her fine example, and her belief in me.

I am profoundly thankful for the unconditional support of Barry, Lisa, and all the others at Left Bank Books, where I have been privileged to spend twenty-five years of my work life. They put up with, covered for, and otherwise endured when this project served no apparent purpose for the bookstore and at times even cost it.

I am grateful to Kathleen Saadat, who led me to Hedgebrook, a Retreat for Women Writers, where the idea for this book took shape, and to Hedgebrook itself, a remarkable place of transformation for me.

Renee White is a hero for keeping our household from disintegrating in the final stages of the book's process.

I am incredibly lucky to have the unconditional love of my mother, who bought me a decent chair in which to write, numerous breakfasts and lunches, and donated her excellent typing skills to the task.

Nancy Bereano has not only given me a lifetime of literature from Audre Lorde and Pat Parker to Minnie Bruce Pratt and Leslie Feinberg, but allowed me to carry this project through.

A special debt of gratitude is owed to those early organizers who shaped my life's work—Gail Pellett, Laura Ann Moore, Mary Beth Tinker, and Janice Gutman.

Linda Brantley has attended the labor and delivery of this book with a love that has sustained me and reminded me, at the most basic level, why I do this work.

And for Deke Law, who has loved and challenged me every step of the way to be more than I think I am, words will never be enough.

For my mother,
the first lesbian activist in my life

and for Deke

Contents

Introduction
Kris Kleindienst

I came out as a lesbian and a feminist at the same time. It was 1970. I was seventeen and waiting tables after high school part-time in a natural foods restaurant. Another waitress, a graduate student at the nearby university, would talk to me in-between rounds with the coffee pot about the feminist ideas she was studying. In those days, graduate students saw themselves as community organizers, and she was organizing me. She gave me Shulamith Firestone's *The Dialectic of Sex* and Robin Morgan's edited collection, *Sisterhood Is Powerful,* both recently published and practically the only books in print at that time on the subject of women's oppression. She tried out her nascent feminist voice on me and I was an eager student, hungrily swallowing this language of liberation that spoke to me, a woman.

My newfound feminism led me directly to gay liberation. This was a world I was introduced to by a friend of a friend, a working-class butch woman who took me to gay liberation meetings and taught me about politics and self-sufficiency through car repair classes. My lover at the time was a woman I met in high school. She lived in a collective of men and women, and I started spending a lot of time there. I practiced my fledgling politics, translating all the powerful ideas I was learning into my own language, my own voice. The women of the collective encouraged and supported me over long cups of coffee and Roberta Flack singing "Do What You Gotta Do."

The quantum leaps in my political awareness and in my personal life that year were inextricably bound. Feminism framed my thinking and lesbianism claimed my heart. I was equally passionate about both. I can't imagine where I would be now had I not been exposed to those people at that time—chance occurrences, perhaps, fleeting interactions with women who profoundly affected the course my life has taken. It was as if I turned eighteen and the book that was to be my life was laid open for me. I wrote my life as a lesbian, a feminist, and an activist with the language those women gave me.

I have been primarily a cultural worker—writing journalism for gay newspapers; starting a women's music production company; and, for most of my life, running a bookstore, where I have been able to offer information that has the power to change and even at times save lives. Through the bookstore I have had many encounters with lesbians at crisis points in their lives: coming out to parents, surviving abusive lovers, leaving husbands, breaking up with a lover, arriving new in town. They come to the bookstore searching for something real to them, something that helps. Like the waitress and mechanic did for me, I have told them what I know, given them what I can. In this way something that seems as simple and insignificant as a single conversation can have profound effects.

Twentysome years after I came out I joined a lesbian and gay anti-racist focus group. We were a mixed-race group that coalesced after the events in Oregon and Colorado showed us (once again) that we needed to do our homework around race if we were going to garner widespread grassroots support against the Christian Right. As we were casting about for materials to read, I found myself photocopying a speech given by Mab Segrest in 1993 at the National Gay and Lesbian Task Force Creating Change Conference. "Our failure to understand race is killing us," she wrote. Mab, a white lesbian, dared to go public, dared to own the racism in our queer ranks, dared to challenge our movement to examine itself. It was the kind of leadership that lesbians have often taken in the feminist and gay liberation movements. Her speech inspired me and gave me courage to take my own self-examination to the next level. It provided a partial theoretical framework for my political activities.

Yet if I hadn't been fortunate enough to have a lover who attended the particular conference where the speech was delivered, and who subsequently tracked it down when it was printed by a progressive funding agency, I wouldn't have been exposed to what was for me a pivotal piece of analysis. Like so much of the best thinking currently being done in this country, Mab's speech sank into a kind of obscurity, only available to the small number of us who already knew about it. That not only excludes both any would-be queer activist without the time and money to travel to conferences or access to people who do, but most of the lgbt community. This seems a terrible waste of precious human resources.

Over the years I have been challenged and inspired by the work of other lesbian writers and organizers whose speeches, articles, and informal conversations cut to the heart of what progressive political and cultural work could be. Their thought has been born of experience—direct action, grassroots organizing, personal experience of oppression(s). Their work and life examples are based on a firm commitment to sound theory and solid practice: social justice-based theory and multi-issue, liberation-based practice. Some of this work and thinking has significantly influenced the very language many of us use, become part of the paradigms upon which our efforts are based. The influence is sufficiently pervasive that we often are unaware that a lesbian is responsible for articulating the idea in the first place.

With some exceptions, however, the thinking and work coming from lesbian activists is almost completely inaccessible, either because it hasn't been published anywhere, or has been published only once in a small-circulation journal, or because it hasn't ever been written down. Sometimes we get lucky and an Urvashi Vaid or Suzanne Pharr publishes a book. And yes, anthologies are coming out at a rapid rate, often with compelling and useful themes. What I realized I wanted, though, was a collection that covers a broad range of issues, the many issues being addressed today by lesbian activists, a collection that delivers some of the best thinking on these issues.

This book, then, seems to me a necessity. As I reflect on the individuals who first exposed me to the ideas of liberation and the lively environment of political argument that was subsequently created in the feminist and lesbian presses of the time, I take to heart those gifts and seek to carry forth this vision of grassroots activism. *This Is What Lesbian Looks Like* collects the words of lesbian activists who inspire me now, individuals who seek to move our collective thinking further, who challenge us to do the work we do with integrity and in a spirit of true democracy. I wanted a book I could hand to people and say, *Here it is, read this.*

There is another reason I wanted to do this book. In 1997, Nancy Bereano, Firebrand Books' founder, publisher, and editor, sent out a letter saying, "We're not crying wolf," which bravely called attention to the fact that we are not supporting our lesbian presses and that they, in particular Firebrand, may not survive. Having been a bookseller for twenty-five years, I am well aware of the serious threat to a free press—

and to democracy itself—the corporate takeover of publishing and bookselling presents. The body count of independent bookstores and presses continues to grow. When we lose them, we lose these resources forever. They will be inordinately difficult to replace and certainly are not compensated for by the entities that have destroyed them.

When I was faced with that warning letter from Firebrand, I panicked. I could not imagine losing the press that brought us Dorothy Allison, Claudia Brenner (and her story of fatal antilesbian hate violence on the Appalachian Trail), Leslie Feinberg, Jewelle Gomez, Judith Katz, Audre Lorde, Pat Parker, Minnie Bruce Pratt, and so many more. Books by these authors are not ones that would have been touched by mainstream presses. They are not books that chain bookstores have any regard for, though they are always happy to shelve them in the lesbian section (for a month or so) to siphon off business from the local women's bookstore. They are not books I could have easily lived without.

Thus, as much as I am giving this book to the world, I, along with the two dozen generous contributors herein, am giving this book to Nancy, to Firebrand, in hopes that we can use what we know how to do to sustain this important press.

Having committed myself to do this project, there were several structural questions for me to answer. First, why do we need an anthology of lesbian activists, why not a queer collection? Because, unfortunately, the mixed anthologies remain almost exclusively male, and often attempt to be "balanced" politically, including the words of conservatives alongside those of progressives. I have made no such attempt here. The voices in this book are decidedly liberationist because that is what has fed me and that is what I believe offers the most hope for the most people. *Balance* is irresponsible at best, cowardly at worst, built on a false notion that objectivity is possible and preferable, somehow more credible. Writers and editors should own their political assumptions, should take obvious positions on issues.

Second, who exactly is a lesbian activist? I have sought to use terminology in the least restrictive ways. I view the lexicon of identities as a tool for describing our varied experiences, not as a system of delimiting labels that can be intended to exclude. Hence, the term *lesbian* is large here: it encompasses bisexual as well as male-to-female and female-to-male-identified people. These are people for whom lesbian has played some part in their identities, a part they claim.

We have outgrown the way we defined lesbian when I came out in 1970, and this is a good thing. In the seventies some attacked the previous decade's butch/femme prefeminist women as not being "real" lesbians. In the seventies we didn't allow bisexual women in lesbian space. In the seventies there were few if any women of color in the pages of our mags. In the seventies only previously married women brought children into lesbian relationships. In the seventies we couldn't imagine the many-gendered realities of human existence. Thirty years later we see the effects of our best work, sometimes in spite of ourselves, and we are occasionally unprepared for what it looks like. But we better be ready to welcome those shifts in the tectonic plates of our community or lgbt organizing will cease to have revolutionary potential.

There are voices missing here, voices of the intersexed, Native voices, voices under twenty-one. I will not, as I have seen others do at this juncture, dismiss these omissions with the self-serving caveat that I could not pretend to have expertise in these areas and so I did not cover them; or that I tried to include them and they did not/would not respond; or that time and space simply did not permit. No. Time and space never permit the disenfranchised. This is no excuse for poor organizing. I take responsibility for the absences, which, in effect, become silences. I apologize to my readers, some of whom may not find themselves in these pages when they thought they would. I tried, but not hard enough. I fell back on closer-in political and friendship circles as time and work constraints tightened.

The decision to work for justice is not accidental, but access to the resources to do so can be. It has been my good fortune to have access to an abundance of those resources, most definitely including the voices given expression in these pages. In passing them along here, it is my hope that someone, somewhere, waiting tables in a restaurant, fixing her car by herself, slogging through winter weather to a queer organizing meeting once a week, or just looking for answers to questions that don't get addressed anywhere else, will pick up this book and be inspired to take the next step.

St. Louis, Missouri
May 1999

This

essay is a slice out of Dorothy Allison's family life, an example of the "queered" family that Jenifer Fennell talks about in her essay, "Changing Everything." Dorothy has been shaking up preconceived notions through her writing for years: notions about sex, about class, about violence, about family. Not because she likes to shock, but out of sheer necessity, for the sake of survival in a hostile world. She simply speaks truths that have too long remained unspoken. In this snapshot of her life (written in 1998), she does not talk about the hostile world "out there," but about those within the queer community who find her path to happiness confusing, discomforting, even threatening. Have we, as a community, been in a defensive posture for so long that we can't give ourselves permission to find solutions—sometimes very queer solutions—that speak to the core issues in our lives?

Mama and Mom and Dad and Son

Dorothy Allison

This past December, Dan and I took our son, Wolf, to the uniquely San
Francisco performance of the Dance-Along Nutcracker. A portion of
the audience of adults and children had come dressed to dance in glit-
tering outfits, toe shoes, and holiday corsages. For everyone else there
were things you could rent: tutus, tiaras, clip-on bow ties, feather head-
dresses, and, of course, magic wands trailing long strands of multicol-
ored ribbons. At five, our boy was leery of anything that might make
him look silly, so while he grinned at the grown-ups sorting through
the stack of costumes, he carefully placed the tiara on my head, passed
a bow tie to Dan, and claimed only a couple of magic wands for himself. When the conductor invited the audience to dance, Wolf just
leaned into me and waved his wand in the air.

The evening featured dancing interludes alternated with holiday music
and comedy routines. The audience applauded the performances but
at every opportunity leaped to their feet to dance, and some of them
had clearly been practicing. Couples spun in classic pas de deux. A line
of men and women with linked arms did jetés with great style. Wolf got
so excited he kept jumping up to watch. Women in worn Danskin tights
were up on their toes next to ferocious drag queens in outfits so tight
they could barely sway to the music. A tall man with gorgeous white
hair and dressed in a respectable business suit tied a tutu to his hips
and did a series of fast, tight spins. It was too much for Wolf. Waving
his wand he pulled me to my feet and tugged me to the back of the room.
His dancing involved more hopping from one foot to the other than
anything else, but he did it with enthusiasm and a great happy smile.
Dan kept our seats for us, holding in one hand the tiara that wouldn't
stay on my head once I started moving around.

Wolf and I had been up and down a half a dozen times before I realized that the two men in the aisle in front of us were scowling each time

Originally published in *Harper's Bazaar* (March 1998).

we got up. Had Wolf or I bumped them? They were two nicely dressed older men, sitting so close that they had to be intimates. I took more care the next time we got up, but as we stepped to the end of the aisle, I looked directly into the face of the man who had been frowning and saw the look in his eyes. Something worse than contempt or resentment burned there. It was a look of hatred. "What's the problem?" I asked Dan while Wolf waved two magic wands in the air to conduct the orchestra. Dan gave a rueful shrug. "I think they think we're straight," he told me in a subdued whisper.

I looked to the front of the hall. My partner, Alix, Wolf's biological mom, was playing clarinet in the band and wearing a wide red strip of tinsel wrapped around her neck and shoulders. She caught my look and beamed at me, taking the chance to give one quick wave to Wolf. Excited, Wolf bounced up on his toes and jumped on my lap. Reflexively, I hugged him and watched as the two men took seats farther away. One of them looked at me fleetingly before tugging his chair around so that he couldn't see us. There was no mistaking his expression. He did not want us there.

The Dance-Along Nutcracker is not, strictly speaking, a lesbian and gay affair, though the band that performs is the San Francisco Lesbian/Gay Freedom Band. Families come to the Dance-Along, all kinds of families. I looked like many of the other moms—lumpy sweater with Kleenex in the pockets, hair pinned back so it wouldn't get in my way, and the telltale shadows under my eyes of a woman who works at home but rarely gets enough sleep. The only thing that distinguished me from the three other mothers in our aisle was that they were sitting with female partners, while mine was up front in the band. I was sitting with Dan, Wolf's biological dad, and we were comfortable enough with each other to giggle and hug and pass Wolf back and forth from one lap to the other.

We might have been an old married couple, a heterosexual married couple, and I had a moment in which I was tempted to run up to the orchestra and give Alix a big sloppy kiss, and another in which I felt like I should pull away from Dan. Maybe if I'd worn my leather jacket I wouldn't have earned that icy stare of indignant revulsion. I felt ashamed of myself, as if I had done something dishonest or betrayed some dearly held conviction about who I was and where I belonged. But who was

I and where did I belong? I was with my family in a setting that welcomed all members of the community.

Our son is a deliberate creation. He was named for Alix's uncle Michael, with Wolf added after I complained that I didn't want him to sound like some stockbroker. "Well, what do you want to call him?" Alix said, teasing me. "Wolf?" "Why not?" I replied, and so he has been. The name suits our strong-minded, independent child so much, now we can imagine no other. His father, Dan, was a gift to us from my best friend, Bo, a writer who was fighting the ravages of AIDS. When Bo discovered that Alix and I were planning to have a child, he pushed us to speak to his lover, Dan. Dan met all our criteria—a healthy, HIV-negative, feminist, gay man who understood both our desire that our child's father be a part of all of our lives and our fear that he might suddenly become an interfering, bossy, traditional patriarch. He also thought carefully before he committed himself to helping us out, though I don't think any of us fully understood how completely our lives would change the day Wolf was born. I remember Dan coming to the hospital late and giving me a quick hug before rushing back home. Bo was not well. For the next two years until his death, there were few times when he was, but through everything we shared the joy of this new marvel we had all helped to birth. By the time of Bo's death, we had begun to feel ourselves a family, and we did everything we could to comfort one another.

It was during the long months of mourning Bo that Alix, Dan, and I became truly close. Dan was all raw nerves and hurt. He would drive up to where we were living every few weeks and sit in back of the house with a book in his lap. He got little reading done. Wolf kept climbing up on him, demanding attention. Small boys understand grief in a different way than adults. They pull us back to life insistently. Wolf pulled us all back and closer together. Gradually, we discovered that we were more alike than different, that we all believed that the most important thing you could give a child was love and security, and that no matter how hard Wolf tried he could not manage to manipulate us against each other. We learned that we shared the same passions and interests, that all of us needed a great deal of peace and quiet, that we would all rather read books than go dancing, and that each of us had a weakness for young people in trouble. All of us had been at one time young people in trouble.

Dan came more and more often and stayed longer. Eventually we sent Wolf down to stay with him for a weekend, then another. Dan's fear was that he would overstep what he saw as the boundaries we had established. Our fear was that our demanding lives would swamp his. Gradually we learned that none of that was happening. We had fallen into a relationship of genuine respect, and our son was thriving. When Wolf turned four, Dan took care to be at the birthday party and stay over. I remember watching him clean chocolate frosting off Wolf's chin, his touch so gentle our boy closed his eyes and sighed happily. It reminded me of the way I had felt as a child when my mother would cradle me, that sense that no matter what happened in the world, this person loved me with her whole heart. "Look at that," I said to Alix. We both looked. A few weeks later, we started talking about what it might mean for us all to live together.

When Wolf was born, Alix and I lost some friends. There were women who simply did not want to have anything to do with the whole subject of children and childbirth. There were men who didn't object but just didn't want to hear about it. There were also friends of mine, other writers, who told me bluntly I had done the worst thing a woman writer could do—have a child at a point when I should be turning out novels every other year. Quite deliberately, Alix and I let all those people go, taking comfort in the many others who were delighted with Wolf and happy to offer us advice, baby clothes, and genuine support.

This summer, after almost two years of feeling it out, we moved from Guerneville down to San Francisco and began to live with Dan. We told our friends we were going to find out what it meant to make our own design of a happy family: mama and mom and dad and son. Alix is completing a music degree. Dan commutes to work across the bay. I write and travel too much. Most important, Wolf is completely happy that we are all living together. When we can manage it, we all go to his school functions together, and our boy cheerfully introduces us to his friends, blithely unaware that his three parents are not the norm. It is a family life made simpler by the fact that we are all grown-ups, that Dan and Alix have been so many years sober, and that I've worked hard not to pass on the heritage of family violence that marked my childhood.

I have spanked my son exactly once in his life—when he ran into the road as a car was coming. And once I had him safely in my arms, I promptly sat in the grass and cried. Afterward, Alix and I tried to explain to Wolf that when I was a girl I was beaten by my stepfather, that I had cried because I never wanted him to fear being beaten by anyone. "You didn't hurt me, Mama," he told me solemnly. I hugged him tight. He will have to be a lot older before I explain more to him, tell him that because of what was done to me as a child, I can never have children, that the limp that is getting worse began then, that the reason some nights I do not sleep is not only because I like to work late. Alix and Dan and I agree. We are raising a boy in such a way that it will be hard for him to understand the world in which I grew up. The nights I can't sleep I think about that with great satisfaction—that and how happy my life has become. Though few people would understand, I think what truly distinguishes our little family is our shared sense of humor. In a world full of difficulty, we laugh more than I would ever have believed possible when I was a girl.

What I have also, perhaps naively, found surprising is how many people have expressed concern at what we are doing. It is not the approach we are taking to the concept of family that bothers most people, but the logistics of our multilayered relationships. Yes, it took a hard search to rent a house we could afford where we could each have our own room, and we give one another a great deal of respect and privacy. But I don't think our daily lives are so much more complicated than most people's. We share housework, cooking, and shopping, try to live within our budget, and rarely entertain. We are private people and would be even if we did not live together. Alix and I are careful not to try and matchmake for Dan, though we keep telling him that you never know when true love might come along. Neither Alix nor I believed in the concept when we found each other. Love is completely unpredictable; family is infinitely more simple. At least we think so.

Some of our friends are still unsure. Those who know Dan agree that he is a great father and a sweet guy, but living with him? Isn't that going a bit far? I have no doubt Dan has had people express similar concerns to him. If lesbians and gay men start living together and raising children, what will it mean? To which I always reply, "Exactly. What will it mean?" One of my old friends recently told me that she was sorry, but she just never thought about inviting Dan to any events to which she invited Alix and me. Wolf, she had always welcomed, but the gay male partner of a lesbian couple confused her. It was something new to think about. It would take her time to sort it all out. She's not the only one.

I understand a lot more about the complications these days. Alix and I will have been together ten years come next September, just a few weeks after Wolf turns six. Sometime in the next few years, we hope to buy a house with Dan. We have already rewritten our wills and named each other as guardians should anything happen. We're exploring what it will mean to have all of us recognized legally as Wolf's parents, something that appears to be even more difficult than having me adopt while Alix retains her rights as Wolf's birth mother. The adoption process seems to be based on the idea that there is no birth father to claim the rights that I have assumed. But along with our shared sense of humor goes a hard-nosed pragmatism. If it were necessary to keep Wolf safe, either of us would happily marry Dan, but it is less the law than everyday life that concerns me: people who stare at us because they cannot quite categorize us as easily as they would like, gay men who sneer at what they read as our heterosexual guise, lesbians who get angry when we bring "male energy" into women-only situations, or even the mailman, who simply wants to know who belongs to this household after all.

I write books about families in trouble. It is my territory, the landscape I understand and care about passionately. I write about girl children who are not kept safe by their mothers, sisters who are raised to hate and resent each other, loving relationships broken by violence, and women who can endure but not forgive. These days I find it remarkable that while I write about these broken families, I am part of such a strong and loving one. After our long, hard childhood, my sisters and I talk on the phone about our own children and laugh at the notion that we have somehow come to this place of safety, this sense of family that is not broken. When Alix and I moved in with Dan, their reaction was the same. Why not? We've all done more difficult things.

I never use the word *dysfunctional*. I don't believe in it. I know we are all human and flawed and capable of failing ourselves and those we love today but winning them back tomorrow. Put simply, I believe in forgiveness. I believe in the power of determination in the face of despair, the way we might, if we try hard enough and long enough, heal our own hearts. Mine is not an empty faith. It is hard-won and stubborn. I can put my arms around my son and feel the strength of it, touch Alix's arm and know she believes it too, and now I can look over at Dan and see how he sees it. This is what a family looks like, all of us holding on to and trusting each other.

Dorothy Allison *is the author of two novels,* Bastard Out of Carolina, *which was one of five finalists for the 1992 National Book Award, and winner of both the Ferro-Grumley Award and the Bay Area Book Reviewers Award, and* Cavedweller *(both from Dutton).* Bastard *was also made into a movie directed by* Anjelica Huston *in 1996. Dorothy is also the author of the award-winning collection of essays, speeches, and performance pieces,* Skin: Talking About Sex, Class & Literature, *and* Trash, *a collection of short stories, as well as a collection of poetry,* The Women Who Hate Me *(all from Firebrand). She makes her home in northern California, where she lives with her partner Alix Layman, and her six-year-old son,* Wolf Michael.

Leon A. Borenstein

The *relationship of choice to agency in our lives as political animals is subtle and challenging. Can we build a movement for progressive social change structured on a biology-as-destiny argument? Where does that put a disabled lesbian? What about a disabled lesbian activist? Does one have agency in a life that sometimes allows neither the room to be gay nor the ability to move freely in the physical world? Do you "choose" to be an activist if your motive is fighting for your life? Victoria Brownworth turns her activist writer's lens on her own life to examine the sometimes painful intersections of the gay liberation movement with disability rights.*

A Chronology of Consciousness: The Politics of Visibility

Victoria Brownworth

My lesbian self was born on the eve of the Stonewall Rebellion. As a high school freshman, my lesbian sensibility sang out within the sound-proofed cocoon of the music practice rooms in my all girls' school. There, in that muted and ethereal light, I found upperclasswomen eager to teach me all they knew.

While I learned these covert lessons of lesbianism at the hands and lips of girls just a few years older than I, girls whose lesbianism slipped off them as easily as an unbuttoned blouse after they left the darkened safety of those cushioned rooms, in a different queer territory a battle for lesbian visibility and gay liberation raged through the streets of Greenwich Village. In the sweltering heat of a New York summer, lesbians, gay men, and drag queens broke bottles, hurled rocks, and generally disrupted the peace of those who had tried to enforce their silence and invisibility one too many times.

The sound of breaking glass, splintering wood, and voices raised to shrieks carried the ninety miles from New York to Philadelphia, insinuating itself into my teenage consciousness as stealthily as my first lover unfastening my pajamas in the middle of the night during a ninth-grade sleepover. The resonance of that world splitting open on the streets of New York, the shock waves of the tidal moment in which gay liberation had surged forth also washed over me, catching up my newly discovered lesbianism.

Somehow the visibility, the tangibility of the moment crystallized an identity I hadn't known for certain I possessed. Somehow being aware of those women and men in New York meant that I could no longer skulk along the pink marble hallways of my high school on my way to one or another secret tryst. Visibility and identity had become inextricably linked for me during that week of rioting in New York we now observe as Gay Pride. I could not—would not—be one of those hidden, quaking, fearful lesbians like the other girls I knew and loved. I could not, would not shed my lesbian skin like a snake, slithering back into the safe, comforting warmth of heterosexual privilege. I was one of them, part of that militant crowd refusing silence, refusing to be sent back into the shadows, out to the margins. Still a child, I had found my mentors; later I would know I had also found my calling.

The synchronous nature of the emergence of my own lesbian identity and that of the militant lesbian and gay liberation movement resonates for me still. I feel a sense of privilege at having been born at just the right historical moment to enjoy the immense power of the dawning of the movement that swept me up young and early. My youth and naiveté combined with the urgency of those raised voices in New York to jettison me from any closet in which I might have hid. I came out so early I didn't know what coming out was, what the ramifications were, what damage visibility might wreak on my young life or my future. I was soon to learn.

One cold, gray winter afternoon, my lover's mother intercepted us as we were leaving school for the day, dragging her daughter by the arm. The three of us rode in silence to the neat row of barracks-like housing in the working-class neighborhood where they lived. As we entered the house in which I had spent so much time, I realized my lover's mother had rearranged it as though it were a crime scene; all that was missing were the klieg lights and yellow police tape.

Carefully arrayed on the spotless formica table in the kitchen were letters I had written, mostly quick scrawls torn from spiral notebooks and stuffed into a locker while going from one class to another. Some were longer, written on pale blue note paper and scented with the perfume I used as a teenager, a light lemony fragrance that reminded me of summer. Other "evidence" was laid out on the dining room table, with still more spread over the plastic slip-covered sofa.

These items were more damning. Underground newspapers, antiwar leaflets, invitations to meetings of radicalesbians and Daughters of Bilitis, a tattered paperback of *The Price of Salt* pilfered one night from a baby-sitting job, an even older copy of *Beebo Brinker,* a photomontage of female nudes I had made in art class as a gift. The customarily bare surfaces, on which I had rarely seen more than a coffee cup or an ashtray, were now thick with things far more shocking to my lover's mother and her sensibilities than domestic clutter.

I remember thinking how it must have taken hours to arrange everything with the care and precision of a curator. She would have gone to my lover's tiny bedroom and opened the drawers one by one, removing each item. She would have examined the closet for other contraband, searched hiding places—under the mattress for the diary, in the guitar case for the paperbacks, behind the rack of clothes for the montage. Stopped in the doorway, perhaps, for a final inventory.

The three of us stood silently, surveying the intricacy of the exhibit as one would on entering a museum. Then my lover's mother began to speak, quietly at first, but with an underlying tone of rage. She picked up various pieces and declared them Communist (the leaflets), pornographic (my montage), filthy (the novels), sick (letter after letter). All the while she gripped my lover's arm hard enough to make the wool of her sweater taut beneath her fingers.

She began to talk about me, telling her daughter how I had damaged her life, tainted it in the eyes of our mutual Catholic God, her family, and any prospective husband. I, she asserted, played the field, dating boys while her daughter sat home waiting for my phone calls. I, she accused, was merely toying with her daughter, experimenting with perversion while her daughter's immortal soul was placed in jeopardy. An inexplicable paradox: a mother fighting for her daughter's soul as if immersed in some biblical drama, yet furious that her daughter may have been badly treated by the very infidel she yearned to exorcise from her daughter's life. I had, she declared, led her daughter to the mouth of hell but never crossed the threshold myself, secure in my ability to "pass"—an ability I didn't yet know I had, a concept she intuited rather than understood, even as she articulated it through the drama of her diatribe against me.

My lover cried; I did not. I remained silent, fury building. How long had we stood there? How long had we traversed the soft green carpet, from kitchen to dining room table to living room sofa, examining the displays? Minutes, perhaps more, but with the interminability that accompanies any interrogation.

I stayed just a bit apart from them: close enough to my lover to exude what I hoped was some measure of silent support; far enough away from her mother to avoid having my own arm secured in her steely grip.

Suddenly, the clock stopped ticking for me. Perhaps it was the accusations of my alleged betrayal, or my inability to bear the sight of women crying. Perhaps it was an understanding that the tone in my lover's mother's voice had edged closer and closer to real violence. Or perhaps it was more visceral—an inchoate knowing rising up in me. Analytical thought had all but ceased as we stood outside the high school, a chill wind whipping our long hair into our mouths and eyes, and had stopped utterly as we rode, silent, in the car.

Now, however, one small series of thoughts was edging around the corners of my mounting anger: I was taller than either of these women. I was an athlete. I was stronger. I didn't have to listen to this anymore. I would not listen. It would stop. I would make it stop.

This epiphany eclipsed everything else.

With one dramatic sweep of my arm all the carefully exhibited letters and other bits and pieces of an adolescent love affair were scattered like big handfuls of confetti onto the spotless green carpeting. I pried her mother's fingers from my lover's arm and pulled her away, to me, my arms encircling her. The voice that came up out of my throat was calmer than what I was feeling, but it came, nevertheless. *Stop it,* I demanded of the mother. *That's enough,* I asserted, my own increasing rage limning my words.

When she flew at me, screaming at me to take my sick, disgusting hands off her daughter, I pushed my lover behind me and slapped her mother hard in the face. My lover screamed.

Until that day, I hadn't quite committed to my lesbianism. Despite the meetings and the marches, despite the overt expressions of my lesbianism, I must have intuited that I could cross back over the heterosexual threshold if I so chose, that lesbianism and heterosexuality were equal options to be weighed.

Why did I strike back? Was it the terrible invasion of my adolescent privacy? The defamation of my character? The refutation of my steadfastness as a lover? Or was it an unconscious realization that to lie about the bits and pieces of my life, presented with such obsessive precision, would be to betray myself in a way far more damaging than anything my lover's mother could do to me?

The days that followed became the most defining ones of my young life. My lover's father called my parents that evening. The word *assault* was used, the word *molestation*. My lover, the older upperclasswoman, was presented as a child led astray by a juvenile criminal—me. The next day my lover's mother played curator once again, this time for the principal of our school. My lesbianism was the exhibit, the indictment irrefutable. In a scene seemingly borrowed from Lillian Hellman's *The Children's Hour*, I was deemed a "bad moral influence" on the hundreds of other girls at my school, among them the upperclasswoman who had first undone my pajamas, among them the teacher with whom I conjugated more than French verbs, among them the coterie of lesbian teachers who had walked those halls for decades after they, too, had stolen kisses across a piano bench in the velvety recesses of the music practice rooms. My father was called to the school and told my "proclivities" made me too risky for the school to retain.

I was expelled.

The other girls and women who had taught me all I knew about lesbianism remained while I was thrown out of the school my mother and grandmother had attended. My lover whispered a tearful *I'm sorry* as she hovered outside the principal's office, but she never spoke in my defense. No one did.

Thirty years after Stonewall, nearly thirty years after I was expelled from high school, most queers believe our sexual orientation is predetermined, a genetic trait like blonde hair and blue eyes. Lesbians and gay men repeatedly assert: *Why would anyone choose to be lesbian/gay? Such a difficult life, still fraught so many years after the scene of that defining civil rights action, would never be chosen. We must be born queer. That's the only explanation.*

This negation of choice removes us from any responsibility for our sexual orientation. It allows us to be tolerated by our families, our religions, the heterosexual society in which we live and work. *We can't help ourselves. Sexual orientation, like race, is an accident of birth*, we argue, demanding pity as well as civil rights.

With no solid evidence to support this genetic theory, I remain skeptical of its validity, my skepticism fueled by my own experience. As I stood that cold winter afternoon with the artifacts of my lesbian life arrayed before me, I had a preview of what life as a lesbian would be like. I saw the scrutiny, anger, disgust, fear. Yet even as I acknowledged those things, even as my heart pounded wildly in my chest, even as my face flushed as hot and red on that chilly winter day as if it were high summer, even as I, a sworn pacifist, raised my hand to strike a woman more than three times my age, I chose lesbianism.

It was 1990 when the fatigue first came over me. A bone-numbing exhaustion I cannot describe because it was like nothing I had ever experienced. With it came blurred vision, headaches, pain in my head, neck, back, arms. Numbness and tingling in my extremities. Legs so weak I could barely walk. Some symptoms would temporarily abate, but then return, lasting far longer each time. Finally, they never went away again. My balance shifted. I felt as if I were navigating the deck of a ship in high seas. I fell repeatedly, my legs giving out under me without warning. A broken wrist, broken ankles, a dislocated knee, a dislocated shoulder, cracked ribs, a facial fracture—all the result of falls on the unsteady deck of my own life.

Recognition of my serious debilitating illness happened slowly, even as doctors and specialists arranged tests, prescribed medications, pronounced diagnoses. Acknowledging my disabled status came only after I could no longer walk more than a few feet before falling. I had been in a wheelchair for over a year when I lost my vision. My denial had somehow managed to incorporate the wheelchair; it could not incorporate blindness.

There was no actual moment when I realized I was a lesbian, no sudden moment of discovery of my lesbian identity, and no concomitant revolt against it. My acceptance of my own lesbianism, as revealed to me by other women, was one of the few passive experiences of my life. I never really questioned the rightness of my lesbianism; any conflicts I have had over my sexual orientation have come from social pressure to be straight, not from an internal desire to be so.

The realization that I was disabled, that I would not recover, came as a tremendous, unwelcome shock. I struggled against acceptance of my disabled status, much as I suppose many gay people struggle against acknowledging their sexual identity. But all such struggles are ultimately as futile as they are painful.

Activism is often an accident of timing. I was fortunate to have awakened to my lesbianism at the same time the queer nation was being jolted awake by Stonewall. There was no such fortuitous confluence for my acknowledgment of my disability. In fact, there were no supports in place at all.

How, in my carefully constructed, politically conscious activist life, a life in which I had friends of many races, ethnicities, religions, and classes, had I managed decades without a single close friend who was disabled? Why, when I had compiled and contributed to many anthologies, striving for racial and ethnic balance, had I never commented on the lack of representation of disability? Why, when I had been one of the leading AIDS reporters since the beginning of the epidemic, had I not acknowledged other aspects of disability within my own community? How, when my own lover was disabled for years because of chronic illness, did I manage to write repeatedly about her disease, in both the mainstream and queer press, and never mention the word *disability?* Why, when I had already spent several years in a wheelchair, when I was too weak and ill to travel, when I was too debilitated to even leave my house for more than a few hours at a time, did I continue to deny the extent of my own disability?

As I became more disabled I found myself pushed further and further to the margins of what I had called community—a community I had spent over a quarter century helping to build, a community in which my name, my work, my activism was well-known. My wheelchair has kept me from many venues: wheelchair accessibility, given lip-service in the early days of the movement, is often absent now. My physical weakness makes it impossible for me to spend more than a few hours sitting up. My illness has exacerbated my asthma and makes me sensitive to environmental factors like smoke and perfume, things that did not affect me dramatically before. There is no queer venue where neither is in evidence.

When my most recent book was published, the local queer bookstore asked me to have a celebratory booksigning. I explained that I could not attend because the store, which I have supported for two decades, is not accessible—lots of steps and landings, the only bathroom located on the second floor at the top of a steep flight of stairs. The owner, whom I have known as long as the store's been open, merely said, "Well, maybe next book." As if my disability were a momentary inconvenience rather than a way of life. As if I were the inaccessible one, not the bookstore.

Where is the consciousness that infused the early days of our movement, the consciousness that led us to include one group after another? How have we allowed such a large segment of our society to be denied access to the comforts of community? Disabled lesbians aren't just shunted to the back of the community bus. They cannot even board it. What does it mean that I cannot—literally—cross the threshold of many venues in my own community? If I am disallowed entrance to community, does that mean I am not wanted within that community? Even if I am not intentionally or maliciously denied access, as I often am as a lesbian in the straight community, the end result of my exclusion is the same.

Visible for so many years, I cannot accept invisibility now. I learned early that visibility forces change. Though I had already chosen my lesbian path before I learned of Stonewall and the radical lesbian groups born out of that political conflagration, these other activists were, in their visibility, my mentors. Once mentored, one mentors others.

I know how to be a lesbian activist because I have been one all my adult life. Disability activism is more difficult. I navigate a territory for which there is no map. Catapulted into the newly demarcated landscape of lesbian visibility when I was very young, I learned the topography early, sought out the maps and charts, became a geographer of that world. How do I become a geographer of this new world and cross the border between queer community and disabled community? How do I make the community in which I have always lived accessible to its disabled members? How do I open the disabled community to its queer members? And where, as a disabled dyke, do I belong? Where is *my* community?

As I look for images of disability, for writings by disabled writers, for a history of disabled life, I find a crushing similarity between these early days of disability rights activism and the early days of queer activism. Just as I had searched the library shelves as a teenager for models of lesbianism and found none to which I could relate, I have found little within existing disability literature to help me model myself as a disabled woman, a disabled lesbian.

Disability sneaked into my life unexpectedly, uninvited, unwelcome. Unlike my lesbian identity, my identity as a disabled woman feels awkward, like getting into a garment that doesn't fit properly. And I lack the tools to make the necessary alterations.

That discomfiture must also be made visible, because tales told of disability are all of heroic acceptance, miraculous cures, tear-jerking sentimentality, triumph over adversity. Disability remains something the nondisabled shudder over while mouthing the words, *There but for the grace of god go I;* something to use as a marker for what they believe they can or cannot do, as in, *I could never live like you,* or, *I would kill myself if I thought I'd have to spend life in a wheelchair.* These are insults. As we have heard the repeated refrain, *Who would choose to be queer?,* the disabled hear a similar chorus: *How can you live like that?*

When Karen Thompson waged her legal fight to bring home her lover, Sharon Kowalski, who had been severely brain-damaged in a car accident, the queer community saw a battle for lesbian and gay rights. Any one of us could have been Thompson, we said, deprived by homophobic family members from being with the person with whom we shared a relationship, home, love. None of the public discourse imagined what it was to be the now brain-damaged Kowalski, deprived not just of her health and wholeness, but of the familiarity of her lover.

When we envision this battle from the perspective of the nondisabled partner, Thompson, we dismiss Kowalski and her personhood—lesbian or not—as definitively as the courts did when they gave custody of Kowalski to her homophobic parents rather than her lesbian lover. In this line of thinking, Thompson was incredibly brave and noble to take on the costly and time-consuming battle of caring for a partner who would never be the same again. Every time this was stated, every time this was written in the queer press, however, Kowalski became a little less human, a little more "vegetable." And once the fight was won, once Kowalski was indeed "home" with Thompson, the queer community withdrew. Queer support held for a fight against homophobia; no such support was there for disability rights.

For decades I have been asked by straight people why I flaunt my lesbian identity. I am now asked why I must make an issue of my disability. As if to say, must you call attention to it by trying to get in where you have been deliberately excluded by thick curbs, a flight of stairs, a too-small door, bathrooms that won't accommodate your chair? Just as I have been asked why I don't simply pass for straight, I am asked to pass for invisible by nondisabled society, both straight and queer. Disability reminds the nondisabled that they may be one chromosome, one car accident, one faulty gene away from this body that no longer resembles the one that wasn't disabled.

Why must I flaunt my disabled state? Because so many people—even those within my own community who pride themselves on their inclusivity—simply "forgot" that the deaf need signers, the cripples need ramps and bathroom access. Because I am a disabled dyke in a nondisabled straight world, in a nondisabled queer community yearning for assimilation, for as few differences between "us" (queers) and "them" (straights).

Disability, like lesbianism, is supposed to be silent, embarrassed, ashamed, self-loathing, repentant. We are supposed to accept our Otherness but never expect those who aren't Other to accept us. As a lesbian I shun assimilation, abhor "tolerance." Assimilation is only as good as the people in power at any given moment. Tolerance is mistaken—dangerously—for justice. Disabled, I also shun these things. Experience has taught me we protect ourselves not with silence and invisibility but with resounding presence. I learned that the day the exhibit of my lesbian life crashed to the floor of my lover's house, the day I was barred from my high school.

I am wary of tolerance. Assimilation looks strangely similar to the closet to me. I have had the opportunity to pass for straight my whole life and have chosen not to. Why should I subvert who I am to make others comfortable? The nondisabled may choose to see only my wheelchair. But I choose not to be silent, I choose to flaunt.

I can still block the path of their ignorance with my political presence, trip them up in their presumptions about disability with the words I continue to wield as effectively as I did before I became disabled. The shape and demeanor of my presence may have altered through disability. My politics have not. While I may have lost the use of my legs and the strength of my arms, I have not lost the power and intensity of my writer's voice. The nondisabled may not see me, but that does not, cannot, make me invisible.

We disabled dykes can rage in our art, writing, and political action at the unfairness a nondisabled world foists upon us. We can refuse to pretend contentment with our lot. We can demand efforts be made to alter the status quo so that we are included. We can protest lack of access to our own lives. My books get into stores; why can't I? We can create new models for ourselves and for those others who may one day be disabled.

As lesbians cross over that so-called bridge to the twenty-first century, we had better be damned sure the signposts are encoded in Braille, the signatories are sign language-literate, and the bridge itself has ramps and is wide enough for wheelchairs. There can be no true community, no true civil rights, if so many of us are left on the other side.

When we commemorate the moments that have defined our queer history, delineated the markers of our queer struggle, we will only have reason to be proud if our quest for inclusivity is indeed inclusive—if the disabled who have been forced into the margins of our already marginalized community have been made as vital a part of that community as everyone else. Thirty years after the Stonewall Rebellion, thirty years after queers refused to scurry back into the dark little holes to which straight society had relegated them, one in six of us remains in a ghetto not of our making. And our rebellion is at hand.

Victoria A. Brownworth is the author of seven books, including the Lambda Literary Award finalist and winner of a Myers Center Study of Human Rights Award, Too Queer: Essays from a Radical Life (Firebrand), and Film Fatales: Independent Women Directors (Seal). She is the editor of seven books, including the Lambda Literary Award finalist, Night Bites: Vampire Stories by Women (Seal). She is an award-winning journalist and Pulitzer Prize nominee whose writing has appeared in many national publications, including Ms., the Village Voice, the Nation, OUT and the Advocate. She is a columnist for several magazines, including Curve, and has written screenplays for several award-winning short films, including the Naiad Press/Northern Arts Video winner for Best Lesbian Experimental Film, but would you take her back?

Tee A. Corinne

If

Carol Queen's essay is the theory, then Karen Bullock-Jordan's most certainly is the practice. Some may find her unashamed celebration of transgressive sexuality to be "too much information," but it is precisely the suppression of this information that perpetuates a culture of ignorance, silence, and lies. Karen's essay represents the voice of a generation of women who benefited from the efforts of the women's movement to free women from oppressive sex roles and take back our bodies and our sexual agency. After all, what did we think a world where women were unashamed of themselves would look like? Karen articulates, in addition, an oft-overlooked aspect of antifemme and antifeminine critiques—that this criticism is actually misogynist in nature. She not only takes back female sexuality from the shackles of shame-based patriarchy, she liberates femme. Her voice is beautiful in its celebration of freedom.

Girls Just Want to Have Fun
Karen Bullock-Jordan

I am a thirty-one-year-old midwestern black, single, SM/leatherdyke, polyamorous Scorpio femme. I am a progressive lesbian feminist sex radical, an activist and organizer. I am an outsider, an outlaw. I've been part of the queer community for a little over a decade. I've been active in the movement for about six years. I've watched the movement move closer to the right and become more conservative, more assimilationist. I've seen the increasing desexualizing of lesbians and gay men (I am purposely not using the term *queer* here). Bisexual, transgendered, kinky, nonmonogamous, and polyamorous folk have been pushed to the fringe as they've become more and more vocal and visible. Our organizations, and many spokespeople, have moved away from talking of "sexual liberation" to begging for civil rights crumbs. Much of the time this is done by pretending that we are all just like everyone else, or that only those of us who are like everyone else are deserving of respect and freedom. That leaves most of us out.

I'm a feminist because I believe that women have equal capabilities as men and should have equal access to institutions and power (at the same time that I want to reform those institutions and change the very meaning of power). I'm a feminist because I believe that current gender roles are repressive and limiting to both women and men. I'm a feminist because I believe the role of family in society needs to change, that the definition of family needs to broadened, and that the very real work of motherhood needs to be valued like any other work. I call myself a radical feminist because I believe that we must change the roots of thought in our society that lead to inequality, rather than just ending the symptoms—equal pay will not solve our problems and reproductive rights means more than access to abortion. Finally, and most importantly, I'm a feminist because I believe that every woman, regardless of race, class, religion, or sexual preference* should receive from society the support and resources she needs to reach her full potential—mental, intellectual, physical, spiritual, and yes, sexual.

I'm purposely using the term *preference*. While many people may have a sexual orientation, many others—straight and queer—may not. The sexual liberation movement did not always use the term

I'm a sex radical because I am committed to actively challenging belief systems about sex and sexuality that are oppressive and demeaning to both women and men. I do this through taking part in protests, through speechifying, teaching, and writing, and in one-on-one conversations. The view that sex and sexuality are personal and private matters is extremely dangerous. Shame about and ignorance of sex and sexuality are responsible for a long list of ills. Shame and ignorance cause some women to succumb to the facade of a heterosexual life. Shame and ignorance keep some women from knowing about their bodies, placing them at the mercy of the woman-hating medical industry. Shame and ignorance keep some women from even knowing what their vaginas look like. Shame and ignorance prevent some women from knowing how to orgasm, from knowing if they've ever had an orgasm. (Men, I can tell you, don't have that problem, and to borrow Susie Bright's line—That's not biology, honey, that's oppression.) Shame and ignorance keep some people in unhappy sex lives (straight and queer). The belief that sex is private contributes to an increase in venereal disease, AIDS cases, and unwanted teen pregnancy. Being a sex radical doesn't mean having kinky sex, being promiscuous, or having few rules. As Pat Califia writes in her introduction to *Public Sex* (Cleis), you can still be a sex radical "even if you prefer to get off in the missionary position and… believe there are only two genders."

Lesbian feminists play a critical role in changing the dominant culture because of our status as outsiders. We will always be outsiders, no matter what kind of sex we have or don't have, no matter how silent or vocal we are about it, simply because we are women who love—and make love to—other women. We must constantly use our minds, voices, words, and bodies to push society to broaden its scope of ideals, mores, and behaviors.

Transgression and Desire

The question of gender is multilayered. Gender is no more individual than race is. Both are social constructs derived from some formation

---

orientation, and I believe its coinage and usage was part of the strategy that moved us into a civil rights framework, the idea being that if we fuck others of the same sex because we are oriented that way, then we are more deserving of civil rights. Choice has been completely discounted. In my opinion, the *orientation* argument seems to be little more than *Don't be mean to us poor homosexuals. We can't help it.* It is important to also argue for the right of an individual to *choose* homosexuality if that makes sense to them. I *chose* to be a dyke (because I love women and, honestly, the sex is better), and it's the best decision I ever made!

For a wonderful discussion of sexual orientation and sexual preference, see *Closer to Home: Bisexuality & Feminism,* edited by Elizabeth Reba Weise (Seal Press, 1992).

of biological factors, and are used primarily to divide the world into the haves and the have-nots, the worthy and the worthless, the oppressor and the oppressed. The expression of gender, however, can be an individualized experience, can give one a unique way of moving in the world.

To illustrate just how complex these expressions can be, I will share this story:

A few months before my divorce from my partner of eight years, I had a fun-filled few days away. I got on the plane afterward with an incredibly sore body, a huge grin on my face, and a loosening of my old ideas about gender and how it relates to my desire. I had spent that weekend playing with five individuals from the SM/leather community who live all over the gender spectrum: an old-school butch top who had a breast reduction; a woman who is not androgynous, but who is completely both butch and femme and moves seamlessly between the two expressions based on the whims of her desire; a grad student who identifies as neither butch nor femme, but feels that she is perceived as butch in the non-SM lesbian world because of a lack of performance of femme, and as femme in the SM lesbian world because of a lack of performance of butch; an FTM (female-to-male transsexual) who'd just had chest surgery, and whom I'd met years before when sie was one of the hottest little butches I'd laid eyes on; and a butch switch, born intersexed, whose top personas are all male, but who bottoms as a little girl.

I am a dyke attracted to opposites, to dissonance, to complexity. I am a woman who desires other transgressively gendered women. Femmes can be transgressively gendered, and I consider myself to be so, but I am primarily attracted to butches. On the rare occasion that I'm attracted to another femme, I'm never sure if I want to *do* her or *be* her.

By transgressively gendered, I mean women who challenge gender roles, expectations, and boundaries; women who are aware of both the limits and the potential of gender; women whose expression of their gender identity challenges the very essence of what it means to be a female-bodied person; women who take what works for them personally from a range of gender expressions and compile them into a whole, the rest be damned.

By dissonance, I mean "masculinity" in the female body, "femininity" in the male body. "Masculinity" in men and "femininity" in women alternately bores, depresses, or enrages me. By this, I do not mean that

I don't like other femmes. I feel *femininity* and *femme* are separate, although related. I am, as I have said, attracted to the opposite gender expressed by those of the same sex.

Femmes

I'm of the generation that benefited from the work of the early feminist movement. I was lucky enough to come out in a time and place where I was not subject to ostracism or pressured to change because I embraced femme. I missed out on most of the mud-slinging and accusations by other lesbian feminists for my public pursuit of pleasure.

My femme identity is complex. It is informed by my race, my class, my generation, my erotic desire, the region where I grew up, my family history, and a host of other environmental and possibly genetic factors. My gender expression has many faces. I'm aggressive, opinionated, take up a lot of space, am courageous, intimidating, logical, protective, independent. I'm also reticent, painfully shy, nurturing, emotional, and intuitive. Some days I feel like a housewife, others like an Amazon warrior; some days like a bimbo, others like an earth mother; some days like a grand diva, others like a quintessential femme fatale.

My self-identity has changed over the years since I've been a dyke. When I came out, I went the andro route, or attempted to. I disguised and underplayed my femaleness. I even did a brief stint as a stone butch. I stopped shaving my legs and pits, stopped wearing makeup, jewelry, and heels, and started wearing more men's clothes. Then I got involved in the skinhead scene. This was back in the days when skinhead meant cool-anarchist-or-artist-who-wears-black-and-chrome, has-tattoos-and/or-piercings, and-listens-to-thrash/punk/ska/hardcore music, as opposed to the current meaning of punk as young-white-kid-who-feels-disenfranchised-and-has-turned-to-neofascism-as-the-answer. I adopted a punk femme aesthetic: heavy black eyeliner, chrome jewelry and accessories, ripped fishnets, miniskirts, and combat boots. This lasted until I broke up with my similarly attired butch girlfriend and I adopted a more mainstream feminine look. I was frequently mistaken for straight by the butch girls I cruised in nonqueer settings.

Then I met the woman who became my life partner, another butch who perceived me as femme. Our circle of friends was mostly butch/femme couples. At the time I did not identify as femme. I said, "I *do* femme, or I *play* femme, but I am not *a* femme." I was suffering from internalized femme phobia. I thought of femme as weak, passive, and timid, even though all the femmes I knew and respected were anything but. If pressed, I would say I was a butchy femme. Older white femmes went out of their way to tell me I was a femme in denial, but their definition of femme didn't fit for me. I was told things like: the femme interprets the world for the butch, and the butch for the world; a femme's desire is invoked by the butch's desire for her; the butch controls the sexual journey, interpreting the femme's sexual needs and taking her where she needs to go. These definitions did not sit well with me.

My life partner introduced me to the SM/leather scene. I came out as a switch, although I primarily topped. As my confidence in my topping abilities grew, my top personas became increasingly femme. I started identifying as a femme top, although in the non-SM lesbian world, I still resisted femme as an identity.

There have been many women, both butch and femme, who've helped me in my journey to femmedom. There are two significant highlights in this journey. The first was hanging out with a sweet young drag queen in San Diego while there on business. He let me borrow a long wig when we went out clubbing. Although the rest of my aesthetic that night was not particularly high femme, I felt larger than life. Hyperfemme. I moved differently all night and sensed a different kind of power emanating from me, one that I usually only feel when in SM spaces. I decided I was a drag queen trapped in a lesbian's body.

The second highlight came when I was courted by a young novice butch bottom boychick women's studies major who identified as transgender and had a life-long desire and appreciation for femmes. As we wooed one another with words over the phone and by e-mail, the conversation naturally turned to desire. In the midst of typing her a long note about my primary desire for butches, I wrote that I was seldom attracted to femmes and when I was, I always wanted to fuck them but could never imagine a femme fucking me. I confessed my dilemma, wondering if I was still suffering from internalized femme phobia, or if I was simply overanalyzing my desire. I was typing at a high rate of speed, not stopping to think about what I was typing, but simply letting it flow from my unconscious, when I wrote, "Why do I assume that a femme wouldn't know how to fuck me? I'm a femme who likes to fuck and I know that I do it well." I paused and read what I had just written. It felt as if a thunderbolt had hit me. I had just called myself a femme. I was stunned. It was 3:00 A.M., and my butch wife of six years was asleep with the flu. "Honey, honey," I cried, in the midst of an epiphany, "I just called myself a femme!" She opened one eye and croaked, "Uh-huh, and your point is...?," rolled over, and went back to sleep. I was in a state of shock for months and went around telling everyone I knew that I had just discovered I was a femme. The responses of my butch friends and various playmates ranged from choking on their food to loud guffaws of disbelief at my disbelief.

Although femme is now my core identity, it still involves a high level of performance. Like a drag queen, I'm constantly interpreting and reinterpreting female gender, taking what works, leaving the rest, and putting my own special twist on it. For me, femme is "interactive performance art." In order to get the most enjoyment from and the best articulation of my gender expression, an understanding and appreciative audience is required. That audience can be receptively flirtatious butches, or similarly outrageous power femmes, but they must share a sense of humor and a flexibility of thought.

Butches

I am a femme who desires, worships, needs butches. I'm attracted to women whose gender identity is as equally complex, if not more so, than my own. I desire a woman with female genitalia, who may experience her sexuality and her gender identity as "male." She may not always be comfortable with that incongruency, may at times seriously consider transitioning, but always decides to remain a woman. She can experience sexual pleasure through her female genitalia (with or without the use of dildos), and feels more or less at home in her body. She does not fit society's idea of what a woman should look like, think, feel, do, or desire, but is all-woman nonetheless.

A more specific, complex butch who really trips my trigger is the "fag butch," a queer female-bodied person whose gender expression is similar to that of a stereotypical homosexual male in dress, manner, and style. She will often be cruised by gay men who mistake her for one of them. She is not offended by this, but rather gets a sexual charge from it, a charge she may or may not bring into bed with her. To me, having the courage to live out there as a woman-who-society-says-wants-to-be-a-man-who-society-says-wants-to-be-a-woman speaks to a complicated sexuality, one that can match my own.

I don't perceive the women I am attracted to as more "masculine" than me. They are my complements, the flip side to my inner being. I strongly reject the idea that aggressiveness, courage, or sexual prowess are masculine qualities. These are qualities that I have, and there is nothing whatsoever "masculine" about me. I do support my sisters' right to explore and self-define as they see fit, but I must admit that I cringe whenever I hear women talk about getting in touch with their masculine side. I have yet to understand what that means. Part of the problem is that we have limited language to talk about gender. Right now, I have no other choice but to use the words *male* and *masculine*, although I don't believe that they alone can convey the complexities of that gender.

The two women who had the greatest impact on my coming to, accepting, and celebrating my femme identity are both butches. My ex-partner of over seven years is a slightly older fag-butch, petite Asian/Pacific Islander dyke daddy, who is larger than life. My ex-girlfriend (these relationships overlapped) is a slightly younger beautiful towering white fag-butch-boy, who made the chickenhawks drool whenever we were in a gay bar. I have become more of a girly-girl because of the affirmation, love, and respect of these butches and others like them. In a society that devalues women, this validation is in direct proportion to the denigration my femaleness receives from the straight world.

Sex

Sex serves several important functions in my life. It's a form of communication. There are things I can tell someone I love or like with my body that words simply are incapable of expressing. Sex is also a religion for me—a doorway both into and out of my body, a way to commune with god (however I choose to define her). Sex is also just great fucking fun (pun intended)! It's one of my hobbies. I find it is easier to learn than knitting, requires less strategic thought than chess or backgammon (though not always!), and needs no special equipment besides latex and lube (I'm not speaking here primarily of SM/leather activities, which often require more in the way of props, although as any good practicing pervert knows you can always make those yourself, or appropriate everyday items).

I am also a very erotic and sensual person. Every interaction I have with the world, every interpretation of my senses, is colored by eroticism. I possess a lot of sexual energy, a veritable force field that emanates from my pores and creates an almost tangible presence. I can focus it on one person, but I can't shut it down, and it's almost beyond my control. It simply is. It shows up in the way I talk, in the way that I move, in the way that I laugh, in my stare. I am all-woman and I am many women. I'm the insatiable slut. I'm the Amazon conqueror, taking whom I will, leaving depleted butches strewn in my wake. I'm the uppity bitch who needs to be put in her place. I'm the bratty girl who never minds. I'm the demon who cares nothing for your pain and gets my jollies from breaking you and making you cry. I'm the strict but caring mommy who knows what's best for you and only hurts you for your own good. I'm the sarcastic ice queen whom you worship, knowing you will never melt my heart no matter how you try. I'm the woman who knows exactly who you are, what you need, and how to give it to you. I'm the woman who knows exactly who I am, what I want, how to get it, and what to do with it once it's mine. I'm the confident sexual femme who silently, but not so subtly, asks, *Do you have what it takes to sate me? Are you woman enough to try?*

My sexual identity is complex. I like to be fucked. I like to be overpowered and controlled. I've found that there is great power in sexual receptiveness, and I don't see receptiveness as passivity. I take in my butch's energy and give her something that transforms us both. This is true whether I'm being fucked in the traditional sense or being serviced as a top.

I also like to control, to dominate, to bend others to my will. I like to strap on a dildo and fuck my butches. It's my penis, another sex organ, but in no way do I experience any part of my identity or sexuality as male. I never feel masculine or butch when I'm fucking or packing. I'm a chick with a dick, one that knows how to use it. I like to go out packing in public, but only when I wear high femme fashion.

I prefer my butches to fuck me, although I could never be with a butch who didn't want to get fucked. I've often said that my hips aren't decorative, they're functional, and a different dynamic is at work when I'm fucking someone. I control the sexual journey, taking her where she needs to go, or where I need her to go, in the manner I want her to get there. When I'm fucking a butch, there is a special emotional technique of fucking her cunt or ass without denying her or compromising her butchness. It becomes an even more delicate challenge to fuck a fag-butch while respecting her inner fag.

What Next?

The desexualizing of homosexuality is a short-sighted strategy in the gay movement's struggle for civil rights protections. In the end, if we are to win "tolerance" and "acceptance" only by agreeing to silence our joy of sex, then the revolution will have failed. Homophobia is closely linked to erotophobia. What frightens, enrages, and confuses our enemies is not our love of those of the same gender or sex, but the sexual expression of that love or lust. There are no laws against emotional love between those of the same sex, only against fucking them.

If we are to truly change society, we must combat the discomfort, fear, and confusion about sex, sexuality, and gender that is ultimately at the root not only of the oppression of queers, but of women as well. In order to have a truly effective movement, we must not downplay our sexuality. Rather, we must remember that sex, sexuality, and desire are wonderous mysteries, gifts to be celebrated, gifts that give us the power to transform ourselves and our world.

__Karen Bullock-Jordan__ is a lecturer, writer, and organizer on sexuality and politics. She has been published in feminist and queer periodicals, and given workshops and presentations at universities and numerous conferences. She is the former director of the OutWrite Conference and a former staff member of the National Gay and Lesbian Task Force. In her spare time, she avidly searches for sexy, articulate, humorous, kinky (or corruptible), political, gender transgressive butches who know how to properly appreciate a fierce feminist femme.

I was barely eighteen years old when I encountered Leslie Cagan and her leftist organizing. She was living in St. Louis with a collective of organizers from New York. I don't even remember what they were in town to do; probably it was antiwar work. I spent very little time in their house and only ran into them from time to time at antiwar events, but Leslie's presence made an impression on me. It was clear to me she was a lesbian, but here she was doing "important leftist organizing." My own youthful activism at that point had included a variety of progressive issues—antiwar, students' rights (high school), runaway youth, antiracism work. But I had just come out, just discovered feminism, and still wasn't sure how all these pieces fit together. I did seem to understand one thing from the example of the New York House: First you rent a big, dilapidated place and fill it with folks who are working on your issue. Then you do stuff. My house was the dyke house (we called it "women's" then) and my stuff was mostly dyke stuff, because after I came out I retreated from the sexism, ageism, and homophobia in the Left that I knew. Almost thirty years later, I'm finally getting around to asking Leslie to tell me about how she "does stuff" as a lesbian and a leftist. Her story is an important contribution to the history of progressive organizing in late-twentieth century America.

This Dyke's a Leftie—This Leftie Is a Dyke
Leslie Cagan

Venceremos Brigade, 1969

In November 1969 I traveled to Cuba as part of the Venceremos Brigade, a contingent of 211 students and other young people who openly defied the U.S. government's ban on travel to the island. It was an amazingly positive experience, and when I came home I continued to work in the organizing committee for the Brigade. In the early fall of 1970, a little more than a year after the Stonewall riots, we put together a fundraising event which was to be held at a theater in the Chelsea neighborhood of Manhattan.

When we arrived at the theater the evening of our event, there was a great deal of confusion. A gay group was also there for an event they had organized for the same place, at the same time. It turned out that the folks in charge of the theater had made a big mistake and double-booked for the evening. There was a fair amount of back and forth—we were here first, no we were here first—and I don't even remember what the final resolution of the matter was. But there was one exchange that has stayed with me all these years.

One of the men active with the Venceremos Brigade and I were trying to figure out what to do. I had known Allen for several years, and in 1968 we had both been part of the U.S. delegation to the World Youth Festival in Bulgaria. At that festival, the U.S. delegation had an emotional meeting with the delegation from North and South Vietnam, during which Allen pulled out his draft card and burned it. Several other men followed suit, and in a matter of moments the ties we were starting to feel with the Vietnamese turned into lifelong bonds. As Allen and I stood in front of the theater that night two years later, one of the other Brigade activists approached us and said, "Let's get out of here, let's get away from those people." Without skipping a beat Allen replied, "I *am* one of those people!"

It resonated deep inside me. Several years earlier I had fallen in love and had my first relationship with a woman. Even though I was already active in the women's liberation movement and fully aware of Stonewall and the burgeoning gay movement, it would be almost two more years before I claimed my lesbian identity. When Allen said he was one of "those" people I felt my own anxiety. Was it possible to be an anti-intervention activist and a lesbian at the same time? Would I find a home in either community, or rejection from both?

Searching for a Home

Without dropping my interest in anti-intervention, peace, and social justice struggles generally, by the early seventies I had found my way into sexual politics. For the first time I understood my own life as an arena of political struggle, an expression of how power plays out. Throughout most of the 1970s I was deeply involved in the women's and the lesbian/gay movements. I was living in Boston, where both communities of activists were thriving, often overlapping.

In the feminist movement we fought to defend the right to abortion and full control over all aspects of our reproductive lives. Take Back the Night marches, self-defense classes, and safe houses were part of the growing struggle to end violence against women. At the new Women's Center in Cambridge we ran a school, teaching everything from auto mechanics to women's history. In the Boston Women's Union we deepened our analysis and I, like many other women, identified as a social-ist-feminist as we sought to connect our understanding of gender, race, and class oppression.

For gay activists, these were the days of Anita Bryant (spokesperson for the Florida orange growers, who had made terribly homophobic comments terrible enough to precipitate a national boycott of orange juice); the Briggs initiative (one of the earliest attempts by the right wing to pass antigay laws, this one by the California state legislature); the first gay pride marches; and a host of efforts to overcome our invisibility with speakers bureaus, publications, cultural events—you name it, we did it! As with feminism, the insights of the lesbian/gay liberation movement gave us new tools to think about the totality of our experience.

Nuclear Disarmament Demonstration, June 1982

In the late seventies I was involved with the Boston Mobilization for

Survival, the local affiliate of a national network of groups working for nuclear disarmament, an end to nuclear power and military intervention, and for cuts in military spending in order to meet basic human needs. I did this work as an out lesbian, and I was certainly not the only lesbian in town deeply committed to these struggles. From the very first discussions in the fall of 1980, a full eighteen months before the event, I was involved in planning the nuclear disarmament march and rally that would take place in New York City in June 1982. Early on we had a sense this would be big; little did we know it would turn into the largest demonstration, up to that point, in the country's history. About eight months before the demonstration, the coalition moved into high gear and began putting together a staff. With lots of experience in demonstration organizing, I moved to New York City and was the first person hired in what would become a thirty-two-person staff.

Not long after that a major internal dispute erupted over the political perspective that the demonstration would be articulating through its demands. Part of the struggle had to do with leadership of the coalition, particularly staff leadership. It was clear from the beginning that my skills and experience meant I was completely qualified to be the staff director. But as part of the internal struggle my role was questioned.

There was never a doubt about my qualifications, skills, or commitment to the project. Yet as the battle about the coalition's leadership unfolded, it became obvious that some folks had problems with an out lesbian being in charge. No one ever had the courage to tell me this directly—I learned it from a number of straight allies who had heard it from others. The fact that I am a leftist and that I was one of those who saw this demonstration as an opportunity to link the fight for nuclear disarmament to other struggles was another major concern. Some organizations in the coalition argued that we needed to stay singularly focused on nuclear weapons and not confuse people by bringing in other issues. I was in the camp arguing that by making connections we would strengthen our demands, more accurately reflect how issues are linked, and open space for more diverse constituencies to participate.

But what was the deal with my being a lesbian? After all, the gay movement had already been around for thirteen years and here we were in New York City—didn't everyone know at least one lesbian or gay man? The fear was that having a lesbian in a visible leadership position might alienate people. Their "logic" ran along these lines: the threat of nuclear disaster was so great that our movement could not take the chance of losing potential supporters, which having a lesbian in charge might risk.

The internal fight over the content of the demonstration's demands, who would serve in the coalition's leadership, and the issue of my role was brutal, and made all that much harder since some issues—my lesbianism, for instance—were not addressed openly and directly. Once again I wondered: Can I be both a lesbian and an antiwar activist? Can I find a home in both communities? The good news in all of this was that I was not alone. A solid group of straight people stood with me, arguing that my qualifications were what mattered most.

The compromise was a three-person staff leadership team: I was in charge of outreach and logistics, a man (ironically, a very closeted queen) was in charge of financial matters, and another woman was to handle the rally program. In fact, because I had much more experience than either of these two people, I served as the overall coordinator. In the end, we saw one million people in the streets of New York on June 12, 1982, and I marched proudly wearing my pink triangle.

Anniversary of Historic Civil Rights Demonstration

August 1983 was the twentieth anniversary of the historic 1963 civil rights march, the march where Dr. Martin Luther King, Jr. gave his stirring "I Have a Dream" speech. Because of the success of the nuclear disarmament demonstration a year earlier, I was called upon to help with this march and rally. In the months leading up to it I represented the National Mobilization for Survival in the national coalition, and worked with the New York organizing committee. The last few weeks before the march I went to Washington, D.C. and served as the special assistant to the march coordinator, and again, never hid the fact that I am a lesbian.

As the final plans for the day's speakers list were being made, it was clear there was no out gay person included. How could this be: a major civil rights event and no one to address gay oppression or the struggle for gay civil rights? An all-out lobbying effort by African American lesbians and gay men, including a sit-in at the offices of the national chair of the rally, Rep. Walter Fauntroy, pushed the national leadership of the black civil rights community to move beyond its homophobia to acknowledge the existence of African American lesbians and gay men. At a press conference several days before the rally, the leadership of this nation's black civil rights movement, including Coretta Scott King, announced they would no longer tolerate discrimination against people because of their sexual orientation.

I was fortunate to be included in several conference calls of the national leadership when this issue was discussed, and I heard how people struggled and eventually got to a better place. I found myself in a challenging position: I was participating in the calls in my capacity as a special consultant to the effort, not as part of the leadership. How much should I say, when should I speak, how do I share my thoughts while respecting the leadership? It is in moments like these that we figure out what is essential to say and what can wait for another time. I said what I had to and hoped people would take what I offered to heart. At the eleventh hour the various efforts to include a gay speaker paid off and Audre Lorde was added to the program.

As she took the microphone at the rally I was again engulfed in a sea of emotions: proud that I had played a part in this history-making movement, horrified that the cheers which greeted her were matched with homophobic name calling.

Speaking at a Jesse Jackson Rally

In the spring of 1988 the Jesse Jackson presidential campaign came to New York City. In the fall of 1987 I had become involved with the national Gays and Lesbians for Jackson committee, working to ensure the campaign's inclusion of gay issues and to activate gay people in the campaign. As part of the campaign's activities in New York, Jackson was scheduled to appear at a series of neighborhood rallies.

I was suggested as a speaker from the gay movement during the planning for one of them. As I was to find out later, there were objections because, as one person said, "She's an antiwar activist." (This seemed particularly ironic given my own history as reflected above.) Having been part of rally planning committees many times, I knew exactly what must have been happening: a list of issues or constituency groups needed to be represented and it was certainly easier to think in small specific categories than to find people who might present a more comprehensive, connecting approach.

I spoke at the Jackson rally that day, and as a lesbian I addressed the need to support a candidate who was as committed to peace abroad as he was to social justice at home.

Linking Struggles

In the six years leading up to Stonewall, the nation had experienced nothing less than: the historic civil rights march in 1963; the murder of Goodman, Chaney, and Schwerner, three student civil rights activists killed during Freedom Summer the next year; the Free Speech movement at Berkeley; the bombing death of four young black girls in a Birmingham, Alabama, church; scores of demonstrations, including massive marches on Washington against the Vietnam war; the assassinations of Malcolm X, John Kennedy, Robert Kennedy, and Martin Luther King, Jr.; major riots in virtually every major city of the country; the explosion of youth culture with its music, drugs, and "sexual revolution"; the murder of students in antiwar protests by the National Guard at Kent State (Ohio) and Jackson State (Mississippi); the birth of the second wave of feminism.

The gay liberation movement emerged in the context and climate of a strong, national social change movement—at a moment when massive numbers of people were demanding and fighting for their social, economic, and political rights. Many of us, and I realize I'm talking about a specific age-defined group here, came to gay activism via other movements. Our ability to embrace our sexuality was strengthened by our passion for social justice. We realized there was something about this notion of liberation that resonated with our own experience, that we could apply it to issues of sexuality and the dynamics of interpersonal relationships. We understood that sexuality is central to identity, one of the core elements of the human experience, not a secondary or back-burner issue.

But whether we are gay activists having passed through other social change movements, or our activism in the queer movement expands to involvement in a range of struggles, many of us share a belief that our fight is not isolated or separate from the struggles of other people seeking justice, equality, and freedom.

To some degree this has to do with the fact that simply because we're lesbians doesn't mean we have no other interests. We live in different locations, have different jobs, read different books, like sex in different ways…and we also are drawn to activism around different issues.

In no small way, the reality that we are of different ethnicities, classes, and cultural backgrounds gives shape to the choices we make about our activism. Our political energies don't just randomly fall into one struggle or another but are expressions of our historical and present context. This also means that even when we work on the same issue we might very well have different analyses and take different approaches to the work.

I don't know what would have happened, or where we would be today, for example, if every lesbian activist had only done political work in the queer movement. I believe it's a good thing that this isn't the case, that we *are* everywhere. It's far better, I believe, that we bring the reality of our lives into other struggles, sharing our lives with other people. And conversely, that we use what we have learned elsewhere in our own movement.

Or, put another way, I don't believe in separatism as a political strategy. Given the daily bombardment of negative images, inaccurate representations, varieties of discrimination, and hate-filled assaults on us, I can understand the appeal of separatism. At the same time, there is something extremely compelling about the richness of the diversity of human experience. Life is more exciting—certainly more challenging—when we interact with people who are different from us and when our presence forces them to interact with us.

While I'm not a separatist, autonomy makes a lot of sense to me. This is what I mean by autonomy: the coming together of people who experience the same oppression in order to deepen their understanding of that oppression, and to develop strategies for fighting against it. If we seek to confront and change the present hierarchies of power and control, then we need a movement that builds on the rich, diverse experience of our people. A movement strong enough to contest for power (in all of its expressions) must be constructed with a foundation based on the unity of diverse constituencies. To be a lasting movement, each of those constituencies must come to the table with its greatest strengths intact. Autonomy makes sense as a critical part of a process that brings us together, making us individually and collectively stronger.

Here's an example: In 1969 there was a major demonstration against the Vietnam War being planned in New York City. Women involved in the newly activated women's liberation movement convened a meeting to discuss our relationship to this march. Everyone opposed the war. The issue was how to best express that opposition. Two positions emerged. One was to not participate in the antiwar demonstration but to plan our own event, a women's event opposing the war. This was the separatist position. The other position was to march as a women's contingent within the march, using banners and signs and chants to make our statement as women about the war. This was autonomy at work. In either case, of course, we would need to meet as women to more fully develop and articulate a women's perspective on the war. The difference was what we then did with our analysis and what action we took.

Another example: In the mid-seventies I was at a conference where an African American organizer made a presentation about the need for reparations based on the work slaves did as they cultivated Southern crops. He talked about the ties of black people to the land, especially in the South. As he sat down, a Native American took the microphone and reminded him that indeed that very land had once been the home of Native peoples and they, too, had a claim on it. The African American said yes, of course, and in this moment everyone in the room understood that we must find common solutions to the complex problems we face. It was clear that both people spoke the truth as it was understood within their constituency. But had those people been separatists, they would never have found their way into that room, into that discussion with one another. The possibility of finding a collective solution, the possibility of unity, was dramatically improved because each brought to the table the insights and strengths of their own struggles.

Our experience as lesbians, including my own personal experience in social change movements, varies from the terrible to the terrific. There are times when I've felt all alone, like the only lesbian in the world. Coming out is a recurring experience as we do our best to make sure our colleagues/comrades/fellow activists never forget that we are lesbians. There have been moments when I've felt like I should have my head examined: social change activism is hard enough, why do I need to do it with people who just don't seem to get it about being queer?

And then there are the times when it's been hard to know if I'm up against homophobia or just plain old-fashioned sexism. In 1989 I served as the field director in the mayoral campaign of David Dinkins. (He won the election that year and became the first African American mayor of New York City.) After the grueling but successful primary campaign there was some reshuffling of staff assignments, and by any standard it would have made sense to elevate me to be one of the campaign's co-directors. But strong resistance by one of the men in a key campaign position, someone whose position in the staff hierarchy I would equal, forced the campaign manager to back off. With only six weeks to election day I had to make a decision: do I spend my time and energy fighting for the correct job title, or do I do the work necessary to win this campaign? I decided to focus my energies on making sure that I did the best job possible, even though my ability to do so was somewhat hampered by the sexist assignment of an inappropriate job title. While this unfolded, and for months after, I reviewed what had happened and why. Homophobia was most probably at play here as well, but at its core the single most important factor was sexism.

When it's working, when the people we do politics with get past their homophobia (and sexism), we all have the opportunity to build meaningful, respectful relationships with people we might otherwise not have known. As much as we help people learn more about our experience, we can't help but learn about theirs. We end up knowing more about the world we live in and, therefore, more about our own reality as lesbians. Sometimes it's rocky, but just as often we become politically and personally stronger, having a greater appreciation for the richness of the human experience.

What about the people in the other movements we are a part of: do they get as much out of it as we do? Those who move through their homophobia become more sensitive and politically stronger, I think. They are challenged to consider the centrality of sexuality; sometimes they even question or explore their own sexuality. Those who know that social change theory is more powerful when it's open to incorporating new insights will often expand their political analysis (and hopefully their practice) as they learn more about us, our oppression, our fight for liberation. And when you consider what we are up against, how profound the changes are that we desire, not doing this has to be understood as a major weakness in progressive politics.

Unfortunately, some traditional leftists refuse to let new ideas or social movements affect their thinking. Lesbians (and gay men) have been players in every social movement in this nation's history. Yet all too often our sexuality has been hidden. Even in this very post-Stonewall era, queers still strive to find their rightful place in other movements for social and economic justice. While many aspects of our lives as lesbians have improved in the past three decades, and we are now more welcome as out lesbians in a wide range of progressive/left movements than we used to be, the struggle for sexual liberation is not always understood as a central component of an all-encompassing theory of social change. There still seems to be an attitude that it's great if queers want to do the work, but what does "their" issue have to do with.... Fill in the blank.

What's most important is not whether individual left activists are changing, but whether progressive and left organizations are taking up our issues, standing with us as allies, and incorporating our insights into their analysis and our struggles into their agendas. The picture is complex and uneven. Some social change activists have made tremendous advances, while others seem stuck in nineteenth-century leftist texts which they believe give them the only road map for understanding the world.

Yes, lots of progressive/left organizations will sign a statement or endorse our activities, but how many are really out there on the front lines with us? How often do you hear about a nonlesbian progressive group mobilizing in support of a lesbian mother struggling to keep her children? How many leftists have integrated sexual politics into their analysis or expanded the ways they articulate what it is we are struggling to change?

At the same time, how many gay groups are seriously engaged with other constituencies and their struggles? It was exciting to see the Audre Lorde Project (a queer people of color center) and the New York City Lesbian/Gay Antiviolence Project participate in the fourth annual Racial Justice Day demonstration in Spring 1998. But part of what made their participation stand out was that fact that in a city with a tremendous queer community, these were the only two visible lesbian/gay/bisexual/transgender groups involved.

Indeed, there is still very little cross-over or solidarity when it comes to the details of day-to-day political organizing. Those of us active in other movements find a great deal of resistance in the queer movement when we seek to raise issues like reproductive rights for women, or foreign policy concerns, or affirmative action and the assaults on immigrants. The National Gay and Lesbian Task Force, for example, took quite a bit of heat when it opposed the 1991 Gulf War, even though many lesbians and gay men were involved in the work to stop that war.

I, for one, don't want the issues of the lesbian/gay/bisexual/transgender movement to be only addressed by queers—the fight for sexual freedom should be on the agenda for all social change activists. In the same way, the queer movement should not ghettoize itself by limiting the issues we will address.

As hard as it sometimes is to be an out (to say nothing of outspoken) lesbian in other movements, it can be just as hard, just as frustrating, just as isolating to be committed to a full progressive/left agenda within the gay movement. Developments over the past few years have made this even more difficult with the "corporatization" of our movement. There was a time when we fought for gay liberation, when we sought to undo the structures of control and domination, when everything was open to questioning and we struggled to create new models for all aspects of life. Now, so much of the gay community's energy goes into figuring out how we can be more acceptable to the mainstream, how we can be integrated into the structures of this culture without rocking the boat or making demands for fundamental change.

Several years ago, during the fight to end discrimination against lesbians and gay men in the military, I found myself in a heated (although very friendly) debate with a lesbian acquaintance. We agreed that wherever discrimination exists it must be challenged and stopped. I argued that while I do not want to see queers discriminated against in the military I think we need to address some of the problems with the U.S. military as an institution: the interventionist role it has played in virtually every corner of the world since World War II; the way it's used to prop up dictators; how it drains so much of this country's resources that might instead be used to meet everyone's basic human needs. She argued that we should not raise all of these other concerns because people would only be confused; we need to stay focused on the core issue at hand. I countered by saying that I believe people are smart enough to understand more than one item at a time; our movement should articulate its demands in the most contextualized way possible. She argued the beauty of simplicity and the importance of not getting off track; let's win one step at a time.

Neither of us won the argument, and I took her up on her offer to be her guest at the upcoming high-dollar fund-raising dinner for the Campaign for Military Service (the major national gay organization working on this issue at the time). She knew that I would probably hand out leaflets or wear an antimilitary button, something to raise my concerns. I did both.

I was blown away by the event. The dinner was held on the Intrepid, a retired aircraft carrier that now sits on the Hudson River as a museum of war planes and other weapons of mass destruction. The backdrop to the stage was the largest U.S. flag I have ever seen, anywhere, but that was to be expected. What I had not counted on was the overwhelming presence of "patriotic" symbols: hand-held fans for each of us decorated with a flag (it was a very hot summer night), little toy soldiers at each of our place settings (each one red, white or blue), the selection of songs by the New York City Gay Men's Chorus—obviously chosen for their patriotic message.

I tell this story because it reminds me, in much the same way that the present discussion of gay marriage does, just how far the lesbian/gay/bisexual/transgender movement has drifted away from the initial aspirations of the gay liberation movement. Is our goal now to be accepted within the parameters of this culture, to be treated fairly by the institutions of this society, to be allowed to sleep with whomever we desire as long as we don't rock too many boats or challenge too many structures? Yes, I want to be accepted, and I want to be treated fairly, and I want to be able to sleep with whomever I choose…but I want much, much more.

Still Searching for Home

Having said all of this, what keeps social change activists, leftist lesbian activists like myself going? Why do I keep doing this work? Believe me, I wish I knew the answer! It's one thing for an organizer to do the educational and inspirational work necessary to motivate others to take some action. It's quite another to know what it is that keeps people engaged for years, for whole lifetimes. In fact, people engage in political activism for a host of reasons and in many different ways. If there was one usual or regular way this happened, the work of social change activists would certainly be a lot easier since all we would have to do is figure out the magic formula and duplicate it. But it doesn't work that way.

Some people move primarily, if not exclusively, out of self-interest—their political involvement is in direct proportion to the intensity of the experience of oppression. For others the key to activism is consciousness or an articulated understanding of oppression.

At the same time, there are moments when people—and sometimes these are massive numbers of people—initially move into activism out of their solidarity with others. Consider, for example, the movement against the war in Vietnam. Yes, there were those who faced the draft, but what about the women, and men too old for the draft, who worked just as hard to end that war? Or what about the many, many people not in high-risk groups who are engaged in a daily battle against the AIDS epidemic?

Whatever the initial push into activism, one factor is almost always present: a belief that change is possible and that your involvement can help make a difference.

Just look at the history of the queer movement. For decades small numbers of lesbians and gay men bravely worked to end discrimination based on sexuality as the Mattachine Society, the Daughters of Bilitis and a few other organizations of the pre-Stonewall days offered opportunities for gay activism. Compared to what would explode after Stonewall, the gay movement was tiny. But it's not as if lesbians and gay men were not oppressed. Far from it! Actually, in this instance the level of political activism did not equal the intensity of the oppression.

Stonewall pushed a higher degree of consciousness amongst lesbians and gay men. As queer people around the country read the news, many could not help but wonder why other gay people were fighting with the police for three consecutive nights. Why were some lesbians/gays ready to say enough is enough to the police harassment, to the daily assault by the mainstream culture? What do those queens in Greenwich Village have to do with my life?

Beyond that, Stonewall sent a message loud and clear that it was time for a change, that we could fight back, and that we—out lesbians and gay men—could make a difference. This sense of possibility, coupled with an expression of community, gave birth to our movement.

On a more personal note, part of what keeps this dyke going dates back to my childhood. I had grown up in an activist family and it was at home that I first learned the values of justice and equality. It was good to care about others, and even better if I could use my time, energy, and skills to help make peoples' lives better. I came of age, politically and socially, in the culture of activism of the sixties. My generation experienced an intensity of involvement which, for many of us, laid the foundation for our lives' work. And part of it comes from feeling like I know too much to turn back. Both the women's movement and the gay movement added a personal connection to my already developing commitment to social change, helped me understand that my own freedom was directly tied to the struggles of people around the world.

This brings me back full circle. I can't imagine, as a proud lesbian, as a dyke, not being involved in other movements for social change, just as I can't imagine not being part of our queer movement. I'll end here with one more story related to Cuba.

In 1997 I headed up the organizing of the U.S. delegation to the World Youth Festival held in Havana, Cuba. In the end we sent over eight hundred young people to participate in a week's worth of political discussion, cultural activities, sports and educational events with the more than eleven thousand others who came from over one hundred twenty countries. As the organizing effort gained momentum in this country different organizations committed themselves to sending participants, and a few groups ended up with sizeable contingents. Working in partnership with the Venceremos Brigade (the same organization mentioned at the beginning of this essay) was a group called Queers for Cuba. This time around, there was no question but that lesbians, gay men, bisexuals, and transgender people would all be welcome. Indeed, there was complete acceptance of the idea that a truly representative delegation of young people from this country had to include queers. I was proud that I, an out lesbian, had played a role in helping us get to this day.

Leslie Cagan *has been a tireless organizer since 1967. From the Vietnam War to racism at home, from nuclear disarmament to lesbian/gay liberation, from fighting sexism to working against U.S. intervention, Leslie's coalition and organizing skills have put hundreds of thousands of people in the streets in many of the country's largest mobilizations, including the October 1987 Lesbian/Gay Rights March on Washington. During the nineties, Leslie coordinated the National Campaign for Peace in the Middle East (educating and mobilizing against the Gulf War), directed the Cuba Information Project for seven years, and coordinated logistics for Stonewall 25 in New York City. Her writing has appeared in three anthologies published by South End Press, Z magazine, and other publications. She currently coordinates the CUNY (City University of New York) Is Our Future Coalition (defending public higher education), co-chairs the Committees of Correspondence, is on the board of the Astraea National Lesbian Action Foundation, and the steering committee of the Same Boat Coalition. In the spring of 1999, Leslie was the coordinator of a major demonstration against police brutality in New York City.*

As

*we head into the twenty-first cen-
tury, the movement for lesbian, gay, bisexual, and transgender
rights stands at a crossroads. Is there one lgbt movement? Who
speaks for it? Who has the resources and who determines how to use
those resources? Who sets the agenda? Should predominantly white
lgbt organizations stop pretending and own up to their predominantly white (and predominantly middle-class) concerns? As a
black lesbian who has worked for the largest (predominantly white)
lgbt organization, the Human Rights Campaign (then the Human
Rights Campaign Fund), and now works for the National Black
Lesbian and Gay Leadership Forum, Mandy Carter has seen our movement from both sides. And what she has seen concerns her. She uses
the Millennium March as a springboard to discuss these larger
issues.*

The Emperor's New Clothes, or How Not to Run a Movement
Mandy Carter

The Millennium March has been one of the most hotly debated issues to come along in the lgbt community in years. I have stood opposed to it since the Metropolitan Community Church (MCC) and Human Rights Campaign (HRC) first went public with their intentions in February 1998. The march was poorly conceived at the beginning and continues to get worse—bad process, bad content, bad context. It isn't even a march. It is a rally on the Mall in Washington, D.C., a rally without specific political demands, without democratic representation or community accountability. The process of creating this event from the top down has put into perspective some of the central questions facing our movement today around the haves and the have-nots, and the principles and values upon which we organize.

I have watched this process unfold from the beginning when Robin Tyler first pitched the idea for another national march during the 1997 National Gay and Lesbian Task Force's (NGLTF) annual Creating Change conference in San Diego. NGLTF declined because it was already involved in its own national effort, Equality Begins at Home, an effort to have coordinated marches in all fifty state capitals in 1999. Robin then took her idea to both HRC and MCC, and they ran with it.

Five people got together in the beginning: Robin Tyler, Troy Perry of MCC, and David Smith, Donna Redwing, and Elizabeth Birch of HRC. They selected themselves to plan this march. In order to give the march credibility, they contacted eight other national lgbt organizations and basically said: (1) there would be a march, (2) they were going to press with this information on a deadline, and (3) you would have to commit now if you wanted to get on board. Those original eight—NGLTF, The National Black Lesbian and Gay Leadership Forum, Parents and Friends of Lesbians and Gays (PFLAG), the Gay and Lesbian Victory Fund, National Latina/o Lesbian, Gay, Bisexual, Transgender Organization (LLEGO), National Youth Advocacy Coalition (NYAC), National Center for Lesbian Rights, and the Gay and Lesbian Alliance Against Defamation (GLAAD)—all signed on under the pressure of deadline.

There was never a call for a meeting of these groups. No one had access to the press release in advance of it being made public. The first time anyone other than MCC and HRC saw anything in writing was in a February 1998 issue of the *Washington Blade*. And that's when things exploded. That's when the eight organizations learned they had signed onto an event sponsored by HRC and MCC; that the event would have no demands; that the theme of the march (since abandoned under pressure) would be "Faith and Family"; that, in fact, there would be no march, just one big rally on the Mall; and that the *lesbian/gay/bisexual/transgender* designation would not be in the name. It's too long, HRC and MCC argued; it could be a subhead.

Of particular interest to me is the involvement of the National Black Gay and Lesbian Leadership Forum. Then Executive Director Keith Boykin told me he got a call from HRC Executive Director Elizabeth Birch, who told him LLEGO had already agreed to participate, leading Boykin to believe that the Forum would not be the only organization involved representing people of color. He was eager to maintain the good relationship that the Forum had recently established with LLEGO. But Birch had been disingenuous at best. We later learned that Robin Tyler, who also made calls to get endorsements, was reading from a script generated by HRC, a script that left out as much as it put in. The tactic was a kind of violation of trust, since it is not unusual for national organizations to get last-minute calls from each other for endorsement on lobbying issues, etc. LLEGO had not, as some had been led to believe, been represented at the original table of five people. For many people of color opposed to the march, this remains a major point of contention. Why were they not at that meeting? If they had been included in setting the agenda, perhaps we wouldn't have the mess we have now. But that's exactly the point: the march convenors, assuming they already had a people of color organization on board, indulged in the "oversight" of meeting without them.

It wasn't a coincidence that five white people met via HRC and MCC and selected themselves to plan a national march, a march which they say will be the biggest one ever held, without once questioning who wasn't sitting at that table. I believe they were driven by their longing for power and the desire to control, tendencies bringing us directly to the bigger question of the state of our movement: the people who have the money and resources think they can set the national agenda because they can "afford" to.

Look at the numbers. The Human Rights Campaign has an annual budget of thirteen million dollars and sixty people on staff. The National Black Gay and Lesbian Leadership Forum has an annual budget of roughly one hundred thousand dollars with eight to nine people on staff. Which group is going to be in a better position to get things done? Why aren't those resources shared?

I served first on the board of directors and subsequently as a member of the staff of HRC (then the Human Rights Campaign Fund) for about three and one half years, from 1992 to 1995. Knowing it was a predominantly white organization, I had joined HRC because I believe in building bridges between the people of color lgbt community/movement and the white community/movement. I was led to believe this was possible at HRC. Ironically, this belief led me directly to the National Black Gay and Lesbian Leadership Forum.

In 1992, then-chair of the HRCF Board of Directors Randy Klose decided to have the HRCF board meeting in San Francisco to coincide with the Forum's annual banquet. Because it was a predominantly west coast organization at that time, and my work was primarily out of Washington, D.C. and Durham, North Carolina, I had only had limited contact with the Forum. To attend the Forum's banquet with 99.9 percent black folks, after being the only black person and the only person of color on the HRCF board, was astounding. It was a pivotal moment for me. I felt there was a possibility of moving beyond just having an HRCF table at the Forum's banquet. I thought there were real possibilities for the organizations to work together.

At the board meeting the next day, I said I believed that the table at the Forum banquet was the first real sign I'd seen that HRCF was serious about working with people of color. I said I was waiting for the next step. That was several years ago and HRC has, in fact, not worked with the Forum. While there are people of color on staff at HRC, they are primarily in mid-level administrative positions. To this day, there has yet to be a person of color in a directorship with the power to affect program decisions. It has not happened, and I don't think it can.

This experience and others like it have forced me to reconsider whether predominantly white groups are attempting to be more than it is possible for them to be. I'm beginning to think that groups like HRC need to be honest, need to fess up and say, *We're a predominantly white organization that works primarily with the white community*. Instead, HRC seems to want to position itself as the national representative organization, setting the agenda for the national lgbt movement.

But race *is* an issue in our lesbigaytrans community. And class is an equally pressing concern that is not being addressed. If organizations are willing to be honest about the nature of what they do and are capable of doing, perhaps coalition work between predominantly white groups and predominantly people of color groups can work. Until then, groups like the HRC will continue to make serious missteps in all of our names.

Take, for example, the controversy that erupted when Nike spokesperson Reggie White made derogatory comments about people of color and gay people before the Wisconsin state legislature. Reggie White, who is black, is a pro-football player for the Green Bay Packers, and a Christian minister. He later apologized for his people of color remarks but not his antigay ones. The gay community went after Nike for using an antigay spokesperson. The white Right jumped at the opportunity to drive a wedge between the gay and black communities, taking out a sixty-three-thousand-dollar ad in a July 1998 issue of *USA Today*, cleverly placing the gay community in an intolerant (read racist) position for its attacks on a black Christian minister.

What did HRC do? Certainly not work with mainstream African American organizations who had also complained about Reggie White's remarks. And certainly not join others in the boycott against Nike for the well-documented working conditions in its factories in Asian countries where wages were recently raised to twenty-seven dollars a month! No. HRC took out its own ad featuring white parents with their white lesbian daughter. It read, in part: "We are a typical American family, with old roots in the heart of America. We love our church, our community and the beautiful Minnesota countryside. We bike. We cross-country ski. We're Republican. We share wonderful times with both our daughters."

While I respect HRC for taking the initiative to run an ad, I will never forget that picture. In a single stroke, the HRC ad confirmed what the radical Right has been pitching to communities of color: gay equals white and middle class.

Another example of how white gay leadership in this country is missing opportunities to have persons of color take the lead is when it failed to make the connection between two brutal murders occurring in 1998. In Jasper, Texas, a black man, James Byrd, was dragged to his death from the back of a pickup truck driven by three white men, who later said they did it because James was black. In Laramie, Wyoming, a young white gay man, Matthew Shepard, was beaten and left to die, tied to a fence post by two straight white teenage boys. Both murders captured national attention. In the largely white gay and lesbian community, where numerous rallies and vigils were held for Matthew Shepherd, James Byrd was rarely mentioned. Yet in the black lesbian and gay community, many of us instantly thought and spoke of James Byrd upon hearing of Matthew Shepard's murder.

It makes me again suspect that there's a disconnect in the white-led gay organizations about the critical place of race and class in our movement. The lesbian and gay movement has been so single-focus that it fails to take into account the multiplicities of realities for lgbt people in this country. My being black and lesbian brings with it a different set of realities than those of someone who is white and therefore enjoys white-skin privilege.

In addition, the issue of class is generally ignored, like having an elephant in the living room that no one wants to admit is there. The loudest and most influential advocates for gay civil rights have white-skin privilege, and usually white male privilege, with the access to power and resources that usually accrue.

All-gay cruise ships were in the spotlight recently when there was resistance by the people of the predominantly poor and black island countries in which they were docking. Mainstream lgbt organizations decried this as antigay discrimination: after all, doesn't their dollar spend as well as the next tourist's? Yet the idea that white gay men could be up in arms about not being let off their boat to shop hit a sore spot in the black lesbigaytrans community. Quite frankly, I think it was the first time for some of those men that they understood what it meant to be discriminated against. Lgbt organizations did nothing to reach out to, or be respectful of, these impoverished black communities in other countries. When pushed, people in positions of power reverted, knowingly or not, to protecting their class interests.

I left HRC in 1995 for a couple of reasons. I was slated to be the HRC person working on the U.S. Senate race in 1996 in North Carolina, where a black progressive man, Harvey Gantt, was running against arch-conservative Jesse Helms. But then I found out that HRC intended to run an "independent expenditure" campaign. In this type of campaign you have no contact with the candidate or anyone else who has contact with the candidate. You raise as much money as you can and spend as much money as you want solely on the issues rather than the person. Essentially, HRC used the fear of Jesse Helms to fundraise all over the country without actually supporting Harvey Gantt's campaign. I could not do this in good conscience.

The other reason I left was that during the wave of antigay initiatives being brought by the white Right, I approached HRC with the need for developing a campaign to counter the Right's strategy of putting a wedge between the black and gay communities. Although I was given the go-ahead, the resources committed to this critical project were nominal compared to the money allocated for other ballot measure work.

I look back on my three and a half years at HRC with mixed feelings. On the one hand, HRC does amazing work on Capitol Hill, work that is recognized by everyone. Lobbying is what HRC does best because that was part of its original vision and mission. I learned firsthand how lobbying works and how to do it. It's a skill that can be taught. On the other hand, HRC's transition from its original stance to wanting to be more than a group that lobbies is problematic. HRC acts as if it speaks for the national movement now, setting the agenda.

Elizabeth Birch perhaps revealed more than she intended when she said in an interview with *Out* magazine in April 1998, "Imagine what you would have done if...you woke up and found that someone had handed you the movement. I'll bet you would have made most of the same decisions I've made." As if that wasn't enough, at a recent HRC dinner when someone yelled to her from the audience that she was the next Martin Luther King, Jr., she actually replied by saying thank you.

Enough said!

Working at HRC and doing my bridge-building work between white and people of color communities did take its toll on me. The contradiction between HRC's public posture of who it claims to represent and its actual track record are not unique to that organization. White, middle-class dominated lgbt organizations, locally and nationally based, must face up to the reality of what they are doing. The Millennium March, for all its problems, may actually be calling the question.

What is becoming more and more evident is that there is a need to have an autonomous, self-standing people of color lesbigaytrans community/movement that can work with predominantly white groups. In order to do this we need more trained and paid activists who are people of color and more organizations run by and for people of color. What was exciting for me recently was the People of Color Institute at Creating Change in November 1998. We talked about creating a national infrastructure for people of color and began to make plans for possible regional gatherings leading up to a national gathering in the next couple of years.

As we head toward the new century, our lesbigaytrans movement and community has tremendous potential for doing multi-issue, multi-racial, multi-ethnic organizing. Existing lgbt organizations have laid important groundwork fighting for legislative reforms and generally making gay issues visible. People of color are coming into our own as a distinct political voice, in part because of the blind eye of the other groups. What remains to be seen is how effectively we can build bridges between our communities for implementing lasting social change.

Mandy Carter is a consultant for the National Black Lesbian and Gay Leadership Forum, the only national organization dedicated to the nation's two and a half million African American gays and lesbians. She is also an Associate with Political Research Associates and an at-large member of the Democratic National Committee, where she serves on the DNC Gay and Lesbian Council. With awards from many human rights and community organizations to acknowledge her achievements, Carter currently sits on the boards of Southerners On New Ground, North Carolina NOW PAC, National Lesbian PAC, National NOW Lesbian Rights Committee, and Ladyslipper Music. She has worked in grassroots organizing for the last thirty years in almost every major geographical region in the country. She lives in Durham, North Carolina.

In
essence, Diana Courvant does with words what she talks about doing in real life: she strips herself bare in this essay to show us the answers to the questions too personal, too inappropriate to ask her to her face. Once living as an able-bodied man, now living as a disabled lesbian, she has been perceived in the world in a way that is almost always incorrect, frequently rude, and sometimes life-threatening. The extremes on the continuum of her identity were linked by nearly every sort of in between—feminine man, tall hairy woman, ambiguously gendered, and, as a therapist specializing in gender issues actually said, freak. Her shape-shifting gives her insights into the human condition that few of us will ever have. Her bravery in daring to "show it all" so that others may learn is incredibly generous.

Strip!

Diana Courvant

If you ever want power—strip.

Even now, I don't have the particular kind of courage and strength required in order to strip in a smoky, dimly lit club for men who like to exercise control from the shadows, too often using more than just imagination or money. But I live every day in a misunderstood body, and I have never had a day that taught me more confidence, more self-love, or more power than the day I stripped.

Five years before that day no one would have seen anything exceptional in my body. Being clean, white, tall and thin, I looked like the picture of an average American—an average American man. But that picture was one without a history.

As a four-year-old, I was convinced I would grow up to be a mother. As a seven-year-old, I fought urgently for girls to be admitted to boys' games. I took their exclusion personally, in a way that other children couldn't quite understand. But it was vital to me, almost visceral. Perhaps those feelings were even more important to me because I couldn't explain (or forget) them. In that sense, they were similar to the pain that had been in my joints for as long as I can remember. When I was young, that pain was dismissed, along with my visions of motherhood, as a phase.

But I never outgrew either.

With my first lover, a woman I met in high school, it was both eerie and wonderful to experience excitement in my breasts and nipples that seemed to come from above and within me at the same time. Closing my eyes, the boundaries of a body that would hold all those feelings shone whole and real on the backs of my eyelids.

My facial hair came in late, thin, blond, and patchy. Hating the ritual of shaving, I found the hairs easier to ignore. After a week or two, my skin itching, I would take them off, sometimes with a chemical hair remover, sometimes with a razor, but always with a mixture of unease and amusement at the idea of a beard on my face.

From *Adios, Barbie: Young Women Write About Body Image and Identity,* ed. Ophira Edut (Seattle: Seal Press, 1998).

As I began to work, to look for a career, I planned it around the vision of myself as a mother. Walking a sunny sidewalk, blond hairs on my chin, pregnancy plans rolling through my head, and pain ever-worsening in my knees, it hardly occurred to me that I might be seen as anything like an average man.

Over the next year, as I came to acknowledge my transsexual identity, others did begin to perceive me as less and less "normal," taking clues more from my new openness than from any changes in my body. Though I planned to go through electrolysis, then hormone therapy, and finally surgery, those steps all required more money and time. Instead, or in anticipation, I came out to each of my friends. Some were confused or denied my experience, thinking that because I had dated women, I couldn't be a woman. So, in coming out trans, I also had to come out as a lesbian. My best friend, a bisexual woman, was the most supportive. She bought me a labyris pin and gave me a copper pendant in the shape of a goddess. I wore both everywhere. And I named myself Diana.

I had long been depressed, but my self-image was improving. I used my rising energy to break out of unemployment and take a job conducting surveys over the telephone. Though it felt good to have energy and use it, and to work for the money I needed for my transition, I was nervous every time I met a new co-worker or spoke to a stranger over the phone. I knew that the discordance between my name and my body (or my voice) would conjure images of drag queens caricaturing femininity in sequins and heels, or grandmotherly church ladies who had worn beards and been called Jack or Robert well into their fifties.

Though I felt more whole than I had at any other time in my life, many would assume I must have a second, separate life filled with Cover Girl makeup and handbags matched with high heels. Actually, I had long preferred loose silk shirts or cotton tees in beige or gray worn over jeans or slacks. It was an androgynous look that felt comfortable to me, especially since most of my clothes were years old and broken in just how I liked them. Even if I had had the money for clothes, I would have spent most of it on new copies of favorite clothes that were pulling slowly at the seams. In a culture with a decades-long Barbie fetish, only my friends in the lesbian community could understand how I could claim a feminine identity without adopting dominant feminine beauty standards. Acquaintances or strangers would often ask why, if I was a woman, I wasn't wearing a dress. I wondered, but didn't ask, if they couldn't see all the other women on the street in slacks or shorts or sweatpants.

My unease at meeting new people often turned to outright fear when I was out in public. Though I was six-foot three, something in my body language would cause people who saw me from behind to call me Ma'am or Miss. If I turned around, my scattered, scruffy facial hair convinced most that they had made a horrible mistake, for which they would apologize abjectly, calling me Sir. Then, if introduced, my name would cause a second apology in less than a minute. Some took my androgynous looks and clothing in stride, but others would stare with hostility, as if I had intentionally caused their confusion and embarrassment. A political campaign against queers sparked threats and violence throughout Oregon. In the state capital, a lesbian and a gay man were killed by skinheads who threw a firebomb through their apartment window. My fear grew to the point where I could feel the eyes of anyone looking at me. Hypervigilant, I read each pair to discover whether I would disgust or offend them because I was not the Diana they expected. Would they hate me? Would I be seen as a freak?

It wasn't long before I found out. I began pursuing a medical transition to a body that for years had been my self-image. But I was required to get a psychotherapist's approval for each step: hormone therapy, changing the "sex" on my driver's license, sex reassignment surgery, and, eventually, recognition in a court of law. Because the entire process takes years to complete, I wanted to begin hormone therapy right away.

I sought out a therapist who advertised in a women's resource directory as a specialist in gender issues. A telephone call confirmed that she treated trans clients and that she recommended hormone therapy for some of them. Within the first hour of my initial evaluation, she told me that she wouldn't write the letter of recommendation I needed to begin hormone therapy until I had the money in the bank to pay for sex reassignment surgery. "Anyone," she went on, "with breasts and a penis is a freak." Well, there it was, and it was not very reassuring. Not only was I an official freak, but I was only going to get freakier.

Though I wasn't ashamed of being a trans woman, I began to realize the safety issues inherent in my growing visibility. Being a freak was dangerous. I didn't know how people would react to me—would their hatred and discomfort move them to violence? Never sure of the answer, I would vacillate between claiming my identity and withdrawing from other people, wanting to disappear. To hide, to blend in. Though any number of my friends were more comfortable in "dykey" clothes, they feel too butch for me. Sometimes, though, I wore the butchier clothes from my closet to remain anonymous. To remain safely androgynous.

Not that I felt safe even then: the gender police were always on patrol. How androgynous do you have to be to get harassed? Not very. Flat chested/small breasted? Wearing jeans and a T-shirt? Maybe a pair of earrings? Here they come. "You a fag?" "Dyke!" "Hey, babe, you tryin' to be a man?" I've heard it all. Twice. I could have gone crazy trying to figure out what makes a woman "normal" and what makes her a freak. When you play the gender game by everyone else's rules, you can only lose. So, I stopped listening to the taunts and the slime. If I was going to be a freak, at least I'd be my own freak, making my own choices.

Linen slacks, denim jeans, velvet dresses. I started wearing whatever I wanted. As electrolysis and hormones moved me further into androgyny, it became obvious that people had an incredible ability to ignore the obvious when deciding my gender. Labyris pins, height, breasts, facial hair—most people felt that they had to ignore something, since I had to be male or female, didn't I? But there were no tall bearded women, or breasted dykey men in American gender vocabularies. People would simply pretend that parts of me or my personality didn't exist, that they could still use simple categories to describe me. It was amazing how many familiar strangers—regular passengers or drivers on the buses I rode, grocery clerks in the neighborhood stores, servers in my favorite restaurants—were sure I was a man, when just as many were sure I was a woman. No matter how hard I worked to avoid getting tagged a freak, I realized the majority of people looking at me were working even harder.

But wearing whatever was in my closet, using whichever bathroom felt safest, every one of these choices painted me as a target. They were choices I was willing to make, chances I was willing to take...until the next time I was stalked home from the bus by a man with a vicious leer.

Those stalkings were society's unsubtle reminders that if you wear a target, someone will shoot at you. Sooner or later, someone will shoot.

In that respect, there was some good in my fading visibility as my joints deteriorated further and my pain increased. Single steps had become excruciating; no medication could help. So, I chose to walk with the help of a cane. Though thinking of myself as disabled came slowly, the cane made an instant difference in my visibility. Bus drivers would pull away from the curb without noticing that I was rising from the bench. Shoppers began to reach right in front of me to get bread or cereal off grocery store shelves. If I borrowed my housemate's electric scooter to carry home heavy things, like juice or peanut butter, I might spend ten minutes trying to get a store clerk to reach the top shelves for me.

One day, I was asked to wait by a busy pharmacist, even though I just wanted to drop off a written prescription before I started shopping. The next woman to arrive began to nudge the footrests of my wheelchair with her ankle, trying to push me away from the register. She wouldn't stop with a look from me; I had to say, "Excuse me!"

"Oh. Are you in line?" she asked with an expression of surprise I found difficult to fathom. I expected her to understand my place in line after that, but when the pharmacist came back, she placed her hand on me, leaned her weight painfully onto my shoulder, and handed her prescription right over my head. No one could have spun my world around faster. Used to a world that focused overtly on my androgyny, trying at various times to guess, assign, or punish my gender, I was completely unprepared for how quickly the same world could turn me into an inconvenient object. And it was all because the rubber I was using to move was on a tire instead of a pair of Nikes.

For the next two years, I was alternately perceived as a visible freak or a background object, though less and less the former. As my breasts grew and the sparse hair on my face diminished further, strangers stopped seeing me as male, or even androgynous, in spite of my height. A tall woman, I might still stand out in a crowd, but I presented a gender paradox only infrequently.

As my breasts and face changed, however, my disabling pain spread into my shoulders, arms, and hands. I set aside my cane in favor of bright purple crutches. Purple crutches are so rare—rarer still to see decorated with stickers or garlands—that they sparked conversation more often than dismissal. But this increase in visibility also brought with it some renewed attention to my freakishness.

For a time, life took on a deceptive normalcy. It became convenient, or perhaps just healthy, to forget that—despite new friendships, lessening street harassment, and mobility returning through crutches, wheelchairs, and drugs—my body remained freakish because I identified as, looked like, and was accepted as a woman, but I hadn't had sex reassignment surgery. The unnoticed truth was that my body had become more unusual, more directly challenging to American assumptions about gender, sex, and anatomy. I spent as little thought on it as possible, but my body, in its cultural challenge, still wore a target. Another episode of stalking and abuse on the way home from a bus stop left me shivering with the fear of how horrible the consequences might be if my stalker had attempted to rape me in my disabled, transsexual body. I was reminded of many rapes and abuses of trans men and women, and of the haunting but unverifiable estimates of how likely I was to be murdered because of my body.

Still, as society's perceptions of me became more and more consistent, I lost some of the need to cling strongly to an anchoring self-identity. I became more free to imagine how others might see me if they knew as much about me as I knew myself. Eventually, I realized, it was my self-perception that had begun to alternate more frequently between freakish and normal, or helpless and able.

Then came a summer conference, a radical women's gathering held in an empty, neglected building that had once been an athletic club. Several women had helped to build ramps to make some of the interior rooms accessible to me in the wheelchair I was using. But when I first tried the bathroom I found that the stall with the space and handbars I needed had no door. Since the bathroom itself had no lock, I knew that for four days I would feel unsafe. Every time I transferred from my wheelchair to the toilet or back again, I would be naked to any woman walking in the door. I used the bathroom and tried to leave my fear there, but it was with me as I was falling asleep that night, it stayed with me in my dreams, and was still with me when I woke.

I hated that fear and I hated the bathroom where my transsexuality and my disability conspired to make me vulnerable, to expose me, to put me at risk at a women's gathering, a place where I should have felt safe. If I could strip, I suddenly decided, then I wouldn't have to be afraid: there would be no additional reactions for me to fear. I felt like a freak, nonetheless, in spite of my decision. Leaving the gathering seemed easier than exposing my secrets, exposing the breasts and the penis of my transsexual body, something that I had never done—and have not done again, even for the woman who has become my romantic partner. If I hadn't believed so strongly that women's gatherings must be safe space for all women, I might have left, conceding to my fear and continuing to conceal my target-body. Instead, I announced to the gathering that I would teach a workshop on transsexual bodies and told my friends that I would strip. Maybe…probably…at least a little.

I spent the morning worrying that the whole idea was crazy enough, and threatening enough, that no one would show up. To keep the workshop from becoming too personal, I felt I needed at least eight or ten women to attend. Instead of eight or ten, there were eighty or ninety. Nearly every woman to attend any part of the gathering, as well as the few men there, came to the room that had once been used for aerobics to hear me talk about transsexual bodies, and to see me strip.

I started with my socks, throwing them backward over my head. For ten minutes or so I spoke about my feet, about the appreciation I have gained for them through conversations with a friend who lost hers in a train-hopping accident. My necklace was next. It was my goddess image with its own personal symbolic significance, and I spoke about wearing it in the early days of my transition as a visible symbol of my core self. Then I took off my shirt and spoke of growing breasts, of second puberty, of the hormones I will take every day for the rest of my life. When I removed my pants, I looked at my legs. They seemed both weak and strong to me. I spoke of the days when I had less pain and used a bicycle for transportation. I talked about how I would never lose the image of my legs swollen strong with blood after propelling me seven hundred miles in seven days. I spoke of the pain and how it changed from day to day. I spoke about what I still could accomplish using my legs and what was now out of reach.

And then I pulled my underwear past my knees, over my feet and off of my body. Using my wheelchair's arms, I stood. My testicles and penis, shrunken by estrogens, hung between my legs, while my breasts, firm and growing from the same hormones, stood out from my chest.

I introduced the room to my transsexual body, my disabled body, my woman's body. I realized, as I stood naked, that I was the freak my one-time therapist wanted to keep me from becoming. I told the gathering, "This is the body of a freak." And though I felt it—deeply, painfully, and genuinely—it was not the description of myself or my body that was written in the eyes watching me.

I spent over an hour answering any and all questions, naked in body and soul, before it was time for everyone to turn their attention to other workshops. Friends gathered my socks, thanked me briefly, and left me alone to dress. It wasn't until then that I noticed the mirrors that had been behind me for two hours as I had been stripping or naked. It occurred to me then that it might be years before I found out exactly how naked I had been. I went to the bathroom, giddy and giggling with the twinges of insecurity that I couldn't quite leave behind. In contrast to the intense fears that had been with me for a full day, I found those twinges more reassuring than frightening.

Returning home, I moved through a city of hundreds of thousands with a new confidence. No matter which of those hundreds of thousands of different interpretations of the stereotypes of gender or ability I might have to confront, I had stripped naked. I had stripped naked before women and men and been seen not as freak, not as an object, but as a woman, as a person, with a unique and human power.

Diana Courvant works with the Survivor Project, an organization dedicated to addressing the multiple issues and needs of domestic violence/sexual assault survivors who are trans or intersex. Although she lives in Portland, Oregon, some mystic force continues to bring people from Boston into her life. When not working or getting up at four in the morning to help her partner study for finals, she often daydreams of finding a pair of formal, glossy black crutches with no stickers or medical tape on them. Or at least finding the time to rehenna her hair.

Linda Kliewer

No

one unpacks the language of gender oppression as succinctly as Leslie Feinberg does. In a few short years, sie has already become the grandparent of trans liberation. Hir work has revolutionized the public conversation about gender, situating trans liberation issues within a progressive context alongside other anti-oppression struggles. This is important: if the Left in this country is permitted to categorize gay liberation as a private, personal concern, not an arena for struggle that has anything to do with "real" issues like jobs, housing, affirmative action, or disarmament, then the broader goal of gender liberation will most certainly be discarded along the way. But Leslie is working diligently to ensure that this doesn't happen. Hir grounding in socialist organizing only strengthens hir eloquent gender analysis. I have seen firsthand the broad sweep of lives—working class, poor, African American, as well as middle class and white—who hir words have touched. What follows is most of the introductory chapter of hir book, Trans Liberation: Beyond Pink or Blue, *an excellent introduction to hir thinking.*

We Are All Works in Progress
Leslie Feinberg

The sight of pink-blue gender-coded infant outfits may grate on your nerves. Or you may be a woman or a man who feels at home in those categories. Trans liberation defends you both.

Each person should have the right to choose between pink or blue-tinted gender categories, as well as the other hues of the palette. At this moment in time, that right is denied to us. But together, we could make it a reality.

And that's what this book is all about.

I am a human being who would rather not be addressed as Ms. or Mr., Ma'am or Sir. I prefer to use gender-neutral pronouns like sie (pronounced like "see") and hir (pronounced like "here") to describe myself. I am a person who faces almost insurmountable difficulty when instructed to check off an *F* or an *M* box on identification papers.

I'm not at odds with the fact that I was born female-bodied. Nor do I identify as an intermediate sex. I simply do not fit the prevalent Western concepts of what a woman or a man "should" look like. And that reality has dramatically directed the course of my life.

I'll give you a graphic example. From December 1995 to December 1996, I was dying of endocarditis—a bacterial infection that lodges and proliferates in the valves of the heart. A simple blood culture would have immediately exposed the root cause of my raging fevers. Eight weeks of round-the-clock intravenous antibiotic drips would have eradicated every last seedling of bacterium in the canals of my heart. Yet I experienced such hatred from some health practitioners that I nearly died.

I remember late one night in December, my lover and I arrived at a hospital emergency room during a snowstorm. My fever was 104 degrees and rising. My blood pressure was pounding dangerously high. The staff immediately hooked me up to monitors and worked to bring down my fever. The doctor in charge began physically examining me. When he determined that my anatomy was female, he flashed me a mean-spirited smirk. While keeping his eyes fixed on me, he ap-

From *Trans Liberation: Beyond Pink or Blue* (Boston: Beacon Press, 1998).

proached one of the nurses, seated at a desk, and began rubbing her neck and shoulders. He talked to her about sex for a few minutes. After his pointed demonstration of "normal sexuality," he told me to get dressed and then he stormed out of the room. Still delirious, I struggled to put on my clothes and make sense of what was happening.

The doctor returned after I was dressed. He ordered me to leave the hospital and never return. I refused. I told him I wouldn't leave until he could tell me why my fever was so high. He said, "You have a fever because you are a very troubled person."

This doctor's prejudices, directed at me during a moment of catastrophic illness, could have killed me. The death certificate would have read: *Endocarditis.* By all rights it should have read: *Bigotry.*

As my partner and I sat bundled up in a car outside the emergency room, still reverberating from the doctor's hatred, I thought about how many people have been turned away from medical care when they were desperately ill: some because an apartheid "whites only" sign hung over the emergency room entrance, or some because their visible Kaposi's sarcoma lesions kept personnel far from their beds. I remembered how a blemish that wouldn't heal drove my mother to visit her doctor repeatedly during the 1950s. I recalled the doctor finally wrote a prescription for Valium because he decided she was a hysterical woman. When my mother finally got to specialists, they told her the cancer had already reached her brain.

Bigotry exacts its toll in flesh and blood. And left unchecked and unchallenged, prejudices create a poisonous climate for us all. Each of us has a stake in the demand that every human being has a right to a job, to shelter, to health care, to dignity, to respect.

I am very grateful to have this chance to open up a conversation with you about why it is vital to also defend the right of individuals to express and define their sex and gender, and to control their own bodies. For me, it's a life-and-death question. But I also believe that this discussion has great meaning for you.

All your life, you've heard such dogma about what it means to be a "real" woman or a "real" man. And chances are you've choked on some of it. You've balked at the idea that being a woman means having to be thin as a rail, emotionally nurturing, and an airhead when it comes to balancing her checkbook. We know in our guts that being a man has nothing to do with rippling muscles, innate courage, or knowing how to handle a chain saw. These are really caricatures. Yet these images have been drilled into us through popular culture and education over the years. And subtler, equally insidious messages lurk in the interstices of these grosser concepts. These ideas of what a "real" woman or man should be straightjacket the freedom of individual self-expression. These gender messages play on and on in a continuous loop in our brains, like commercials that can't be muted.

But in my lifetime I've also seen social upheavals challenge this sex and gender doctrine. As a child who grew up during the McCarthyite, *Father Knows Best* 1950s, and who came of age during the second wave of women's liberation in the United States, I've seen transformations in the ways people think and talk about what it means to be a woman or a man.

Today the gains of the 1970s women's liberation movement are under siege by right-wing propagandists. But many today who are too young to remember what life was like before the women's movement need to know that this was a tremendously progressive development that won significant economic and social reforms. And this struggle by women and their allies swung human consciousness forward like a pendulum.

The movement replaced the common usage of vulgar and diminutive words to describe females with the word *woman* and infused that word with strength and pride. Women, many of them formerly isolated, were drawn together into consciousness-raising groups. Their discussions—about the root of women's oppression and how to eradicate it—resonated far beyond the rooms in which they took place. The women's liberation movement sparked a mass conversation about the systematic degradation, violence, and discrimination that women faced in this society. And this consciousness raising changed many of the ways women and men thought about themselves and their relation to each other. In retrospect, however, we must not forget that these widespread discussions were not just organized to talk about oppression. There was a giant dialogue about how to take action to fight institutionalized antiwoman attitudes, rape and battering, the illegality of abortion, employment and education discrimination, and other ways women were socially and economically devalued.

This was a big step forward for humanity. And even the period of political reaction that followed has not been able to overturn all the gains made by that important social movement.

Now another movement is sweeping onto the stage of history: trans liberation. We are again raising questions about the societal treatment of people based on their sex and gender expression. This discussion will make new contributions to human consciousness. And trans communities, like the women's movement, are carrying out these mass conversations with the goal of creating a movement capable of fighting for justice—of righting the wrongs.

We are a movement of masculine females and feminine males, cross-dressers, transsexual men and women, intersexuals born on the anatomical sweep between female and male, gender-blenders, many other sex and gender-variant people, and our significant others. All told, we expand understanding of how many ways there are to be a human being.

Our lives are proof that sex and gender are more complex than a delivery room doctor's glance at genitals can determine, more variegated than pink or blue birth caps. We are oppressed for not fitting those narrow social norms. We are fighting back.

Our struggle will also help expose some of the harmful myths about what it means to be a woman or a man that have compartmentalized and distorted your life, as well as mine. Trans liberation has meaning for you—no matter how you define or express your sex or your gender.

If you are a trans person, you face horrendous social punishment—from institutionalization to gang rape, from beatings to denial of child visitation. This oppression is experienced, in varying degrees, by all who march under the banner of trans liberation. This brutalization and degradation strips us of what we could achieve within our individual lifetimes.

And if you do not identify as transgender or transsexual or intersexual, your life is diminished by our oppression as well. Your own choices as a man or a woman are sharply curtailed. Your individual journey to express yourself is shunted into one of two deeply carved ruts, and the social baggage you are handed is already packed.

So the defense of each individual's right to control their own body, and to explore the path of self-expression, enhances your own freedom to discover more about yourself and your potentialities. This movement will give you greater room to breathe—to be yourself. To discover on a deeper level what it means to be yourself.

Together, I believe we can forge a coalition that can fight on behalf of your oppression as well as mine. Together, we can raise each other's grievances and win the kind of significant change we all long for. But the foundation of unity is understanding. So let me begin by telling you a little bit about myself.

I am a human being who unnerves some people. As they look at me, they see a kaleidoscope of characteristics they associate with both males and females. I appear to be a tangled knot of gender contradictions. So they feverishly press the question on me: woman or man? Those are the only two words most people have as tools to shape their question.

"Which sex are you?" I understand their question. It sounds so simple. And I'd like to offer them a simple resolution. But merely answering woman or man will not bring relief to the questioner. As long as people try to bring me into focus using only those two lenses, I will always appear to be an enigma.

The truth is I'm no mystery. I'm a female who is more masculine than those prominently portrayed in mass culture. Millions of females and millions of males in this country do not fit the cramped compartments of gender that we have been taught are "natural" and "normal." For many of us, the words *woman* or *man, ma'am* or *sir, she* or *he*—in and of themselves—do not total up the sum of our identities or of our oppression. Speaking for myself, my life only comes into focus when the word *transgender* is added to the equation.

Simply answering whether I was born female or male will not solve the conundrum. Before I can even begin to respond to the question of my own birth sex, I feel it's important to challenge the assumption that the answer is always as simple as either-or. I believe we need to take a critical look at the assumption that is built into the seemingly innocent question: "What a beautiful baby—is it a boy or a girl?"

The human anatomical spectrum can't be understood, let alone appreciated, as long as female or male are considered to be all that exists. *Is it a boy or a girl?* Those are the only two categories allowed on birth certificates.

But this either-or leaves no room for intersexual people, born between the poles of female and male. Human anatomy continues to burst the confines of the contemporary concept that nature delivers all babies on two unrelated conveyor belts. So are the birth certificates changed to reflect human anatomy? No, the U.S. medical establishment hormonally molds and shapes and surgically hacks away at the exquisite complexities of intersexual infants until they fit one category or the other.

A surgeon decides whether a clitoris is "too large" or a penis is "too small." That's a highly subjective decision for anyone to make about another person's body. Especially when the person making the arbitrary decision is scrubbed up for surgery! And what is the criterion for a penis being "too small"? Too small for successful heterosexual intercourse. Intersexual infants are already being tailored for their sexuality as well as their sex. Clearly the struggle against genital mutilation must begin here, within the borders of the United States.

But the question asked of all new parents, "Is it a boy or a girl?", is not such a simple question when transsexuality is taken into account, either. Legions of out-and-proud transsexual men and women demonstrate that individuals have a deep, developed, and valid sense of their own sex that does not always correspond to the cursory decision made by a delivery-room obstetrician. Nor is transsexuality a recent phenomenon. People have undergone social sex reassignment and surgical and hormonal sex changes throughout the breadth of oral and recorded human history.

Having offered this view of the complexities and limitations of birth classification, I have no hesitancy in saying I was born female. But that answer doesn't clear up the confusion that drives some people to ask me, "Are you a man or a woman?" The problem is that they are trying to understand my gender expression by determining my sex—and therein lies the rub. Just as most of us grew up with only the concepts of woman and man, the terms *feminine* and *masculine* are the only two tools most people have to talk about the complexities of gender expression.

That pink-blue dogma assumes that biology steers our social destiny. We have been taught that being born female or male will determine how we will dress and walk, whether we will prefer our hair shortly cropped or long and flowing, whether we will be emotionally nurturing or repressed. According to this way of thinking, masculine females are trying to look "like men," and feminine males are trying to act "like women."

But those of us who transgress those gender assumptions also shatter their inflexibility.

So why do I sometimes describe myself as a masculine female? Isn't each of those concepts very limiting? Yes. But placing the two words together is incendiary, exploding the belief that gender expression is linked to birth sex like horse and carriage. It is the social contradiction missing from Dick-and-Jane textbook education.

I actually chafe at describing myself as masculine. For one thing, masculinity is such an expansive territory, encompassing boundaries of nationality, race, and class. Most importantly, individuals blaze their own trails across this landscape.

And it's hard for me to label the intricate matrix of my gender as simply masculine. To me, branding individual self-expression as only feminine or masculine is like asking poets whether they write in English or Spanish. The question leaves out the possibilities that the poetry is woven in Cantonese or Ladino, Swahili or Arabic. The question deals only with the system of language that the poet has been taught. It ignores the words each writer hauls up, hand over hand, from a common well. The music words make when finding themselves next to each other for the first time. The silences echoing in the space between ideas. The powerful winds of passion and belief that move the poet to write.

That is why I do not hold the view that gender is simply a social construct—one of two languages that we learn by rote from early age. To me, gender is the poetry each of us makes out of the language we are taught. When I walk through the anthology of the world, I see individuals express their gender in exquisitely complex and ever-changing ways, despite the laws of pentameter.

So how can gender expression be mandated by edict and enforced by law? Isn't that like trying to handcuff a pool of mercury? It's true that human self-expression is diverse and is often expressed in ambiguous or contradictory ways. And what degree of gender expression is considered "acceptable" can depend on your social situation, your race and nationality, your class, and whether you live in an urban or rural environment.

But no one can deny that rigid gender education begins early on in life—from pink-and-blue color-coding of infant outfits to gender-labeling of toys and games. And those who overstep these arbitrary borders are punished. Severely. When those steel handcuffs tighten, it is human bones that crack. No one knows how many trans lives have been lost to police brutality and street-corner bashing. The lives of trans people are so depreciated in this society that many murders go unreported. And those of us who have survived are deeply scarred by daily run-ins with hate, discrimination, and violence.

Transpeople are still literally social outlaws. And that's why I am willing at times, publicly, to reduce the totality of my self-expression to descriptions like masculine female, butch, bulldagger, drag king, cross-dresser. These terms describe outlaw status. And I hold my head up proudly in that police lineup. The word *outlaw* is not hyperbolic. I have been locked up in jail by cops because I was wearing a suit and a tie. Was my clothing really a crime? Is it a "man's" suit if I am wearing it? At what point—from field to rack—is fiber assigned a sex?

The reality of why I was arrested was as cold as the cell's cement floor: I am considered a masculine female. That's a gender violation. My feminine drag queen sisters were in nearby cells, busted for wearing "women's" clothing. The cells that we were thrown into had the same design of bars and concrete. But when we—gay drag kings and drag queens—were thrown into them, the cops referred to the cells as bulls' tanks and queens' tanks. The cells were named after our crimes: gender transgression. Actual statutes against cross-dressing and cross-gendered behavior still exist in laws today. But even where the laws are not written down, police, judges, and prison guards are empowered to carry out merciless punishments for sex and gender "difference."

I believe we need to sharpen our view of how repression by the police, courts, and prisons, as well as all forms of racism and bigotry, operates as gears in the machinery of the economic and social system that governs our lives. As all those who have the least to lose from changing this system get together and examine these social questions, we can separate the wheat of truths from the chaff of old lies. Historic tasks are revealed that beckon us to take a stand and to take action.

That moment is now. And so this conversation with you takes place with the momentum of struggle behind it.

What will it take to put a halt to "legal" and extralegal violence against trans people? How can we strike the unjust and absurd laws mandating dress and behavior for females and males from the books? How can we weed out all the forms of transphobic and genderphobic discrimination?

Where does the struggle for sex and gender liberation fit in relation to other movements for economic and social equality? How can we reach a point where we appreciate each other's differences, not just tolerate them? How can we tear down the electrified barbed wire that has been placed between us to keep us separated, fearful and pitted against each other? How can we forge a movement that can bring about profound and lasting change—a movement capable of transforming society?

These questions can only be answered when we begin to organize together, ready to struggle on each other's behalf. Understanding each other will compel us as honest, caring people to fight each other's oppression as though it was our own....

Leslie Feinberg *is the author of* Trans Liberation: Beyond Pink or Blue, Transgender Warriors *(both from Beacon), and the now-classic* Stone Butch Blues *(Firebrand), winner of the American Library Association Gay/Lesbian/Bisexual Book Award and the Lambda Literary Award.*

Rebecca Dallinger

As *the lesbian daughter of a lesbian mother whose parenting tasks took place in the decidedly unlesbian-friendly fifties and sixties, I am deeply interested in the subject of this essay. I know what it feels like to be parented by a lesbian who has no support system. I know personally the costs of striving to imitate the dominant family model, failing miserably and being cruelly isolated by an indifferent, even hostile culture and community. Jenifer Fennell represents a different, younger generation of lesbian parents whose choices are seemingly endless, yet whose legitimacy is still practically nonexistent. She takes on the task of "queering the family" in this essay, and expands our understanding of what exactly is queer about our families in part by connecting them to other "illegitimate" families. In so doing, she establishes a political and social context for queer parenting that places the challenge of creating family squarely in the center of progressive organizing.*

Changing Everything, or How to Queer the Family

Jenifer Fennell

The question I've been handed here is this: what does it mean to parent "queerly" or to "queer" the job of parenting? On the surface, it's an odd question. I can imagine straight and gay people having a problem with the juxtaposition of those two words, if for vastly different reasons. Also, as with any question aimed at unpacking the nuances of contemporary lgbt life, it's filled with knotty race, class, and gender implications. To confuse things even more, it can be approached in any number of ways.

For example, are we talking about parents who just happen to be queer, or those for whom their sexuality defines their politics? Is it enough that queer people are choosing to raise children? Do lgbt parents automatically raise their children queerly, or does queer parenting require an awareness of a larger queer agenda? If so, who defines the agenda? Furthermore, who really cares about this issue anyway? I know some gay people for whom the question of parenting is an annoyance, something they've never considered and haven't missed. I've heard the view expressed that raising children is an inherently heterosexual concern and therefore irrelevant to queer life. For others, it's a middle-class preoccupation, an attempt at conformity, or a bizarre manifestation of the "we're just-like-you" mentality.

But the issue of parenting is important, and not just because lgbt people are jumping onto the baby wagon in record numbers. To begin with, there have always been gay and lesbian parents. Although in the past those people were usually folks who came out after having children in heterosexual relationships, the fact is that parents have never not been a part of the queer community. More significantly, the issue of how children are raised concerns everyone in a society. A culture that doesn't care for its children—as the U.S. by and large does not, despite all the profamily, prochild rhetoric—suffers the social consequences of young adults who are alienated and depressed.

Children are as much our responsibility as the straight world's, and many of us, including those who have no desire to raise children of our own, have children in our lives—nieces or nephews or cousins or the children of friends. These children benefit from the queer members of their families. We help teach them tolerance and show them, by our existence and our example, that their own lives could follow any number of paths. Additionally, unless they're wealthy, parents are frequently beleaguered by their responsibilities. All parents need time away from their children. The very notion of family should be overhauled to include networks of people that share in the burden and joy of raising children.

It seems to me that there are two main issues to consider in an analysis of queer parenting. The first is what it might look like to parent queerly, which requires a definition of queer that goes beyond sexual or gender orientation without losing sight of these things. The second follows from the first. If queer needs to be defined to include a progressive, cooperative political agenda, as I think it does, we will also need to analyze the ways in which some straight parents are effectively queered by our society's rules of exclusion. It is clear, for example, that certain types of people are held up as model parents, with skin tone, age, and access to money playing as big a role in this assessment as gender and sexuality. As a parent, you don't need to be gay to be stamped a sexual outlaw; you can lose your kids for being perceived as deviating from a variety of norms. At the very least you'll undergo intense and threatening scrutiny if you're poor, unmarried, a teenager, and/or dark-skinned, or, god forbid, all of the above, the ante being upped on your "lawlessness" the greater the number of "deviations."

Queers and Other Sexual Outlaws

I'm one of those people who had my children before I came out, and by then I'd already put up with twelve years of questions about my legitimacy as a parent, my right to mother my daughters. Naomi, my eldest, was born shortly after I turned seventeen. This was back in 1979, and though it's never been easy to be a single teenage mother in this country, I think it was a little easier then than now. Now we have a public conversation about teen mothers that utterly vilifies them. They are, according to conventional wisdom, shameful, sinful, sluttish, inherently bad mothers—a drain on the system in too many ways to count. The children of these mothers are reputed to be budding juvenile delinquents who will one day clog the courts and, finally, fill the prisons. And have you ever heard of a teenage mother who wasn't on welfare? In the public discourse, the two are simply inseparable. While these stereotypes were around when Naomi was born and people spent a lot of time looking at me like I was a walking statistic, the fact that I wasn't married didn't carry as much weight as it does today.

In 1979, teenage sex and sexuality, though always seen as a danger in this country, were not the targets they've become under the rise of the religious Right. Still, it wasn't easy. For the first six years of Naomi's life, I attended college, cleaned houses, and tutored writing students. Mostly we scraped by. Because both my parents died before I reached the age of eighteen, I received a social security check each month until I turned twenty-one as long as I stayed in school. It wasn't nearly enough to live on, but it helped. When that money ran out, I got a job in a restaurant and went to school at night. Things were going all right until the day my boss pinned me against a wall in his office and ran his hand up my thigh. When I threatened legal action, he threatened my life. Scared, I backed down and turned to welfare.

Like most women who find themselves with no money and no choice but some form of public assistance, I was desperate. The very last thing I wanted to do was go on welfare. Even then, welfare mothers were held up as the lowest of the low, the kind of scum you wipe off your feet. What was even worse was that the worker assigned to me told me I would have to drop out of school. The logic was simple: if I could arrange childcare for school, I could arrange it for work. It didn't matter that I was close to finishing a degree and the only job I could get would keep me mired in poverty. For nine months I lied on every form I filled out. No, I wasn't going to school. No, I had no way to find even minimal childcare. During the day when the caseworker might call, I was at home with my daughter. At night I went to school. I spent those nine months waiting to be found out and looking for another job.

A couple of years earlier, I had met a woman who announced to a crowd of people that she was a lesbian. I was intrigued. Here was a lesbian, a real lesbian! I'd heard of them before. I'd even seen two women—presumably lesbians—kissing on the lawn of a college campus when I was nine years old. But I'd never met anyone who called herself a lesbian, and there she was, this lesbian, wanting me. She got my telephone number about two minutes after I came running up to her to breathlessly congratulate her on her announcement. Within hours, that girl had me back in my apartment with my clothes off and the shower on.

I wasn't concerned. I had a boyfriend, and anyway, it was 1980, everyone was experimenting, and it didn't mean anything. It was just fun—and boy was it fun—until one day this woman and I were sitting on a blanket playing with my daughter in a park. Lori, the lesbian in question, got up, chased Naomi down, swung her round in circles, and then settled down on the blanket behind me, encircling me with her arms.

"You know," she whispered, "you're a lesbian, too."

Well, I looked around that park, and I looked at my daughter, and I looked back at this woman who had become my lover, and I thought, No way. No way in hell am I a lesbian. It was bad enough to be a teenage mother. It was bad enough to be poor. And later on it would be worst of all to be these things *and* on welfare. I was already a sexual outlaw, a woman who had broken too many rules of sexual behavior. How under all that strain could I possibly admit, even to myself, that I was a lesbian, too? I didn't. Lori was history. It was years before I could begin to allow my desire for women to surface, years more before I would find the courage to act on it.

In 1998 in Minneapolis it is often easier for me to tell people that I am a lesbian than it is to talk about having been a teenage mother, to admit that once, many years ago, I was one of those despised welfare mothers. But it's a part of my life I refuse to feel ashamed of, the same way I will not be ashamed of whom I love. The fact is the two realities are related—deeply, inevitably, inextricably related.

As a teenage mother, I was despised because I had refused to curtail my sexuality, because I wore it in and on my body, first in the form of pregnancy, and later when I carried my baby in my arms. As a mother on welfare, I was forced to answer a set of questions each month designed to monitor my sexuality: Was I pregnant? Had I had a miscarriage? Had I had an abortion? Had anyone moved into or out of my house? Refusal to answer even the question about miscarriage would mean a total loss of income, food stamps and medical assistance. As a lesbian, I'm denied many of the basic civil rights straight people take for granted. The commonality of what is under siege—then and now—is my sexuality and my right to express it how I choose.

The fact is that the attack on teenage mothers, poor mothers, and welfare mothers is an attack on sexual outsiders as well as an attack on the poor and on people of color. It's no coincidence that the image of a welfare mother that leaps to people's minds is of a black woman with several children. Black women have been stereotyped as aggressively and blatantly sexual. Intertwined with the efforts to destroy our social welfare system is a well-oiled and fabulously well-funded movement to restrict sexual freedoms. If poor mothers, black mothers, welfare mothers are first on the list, you can bet that lesbians are next.

Think about the rhetoric that has been employed to "end welfare as we know it." Welfare is blamed for the demise of the family, for the increase in crime rates (which, by the way, have not increased), for economic decline. It seems every problem we have in this country can be blamed on welfare. But why? The actual amount of money funneled to poor families through the AFDC program is negligible compared to, let's say, the space program. Clearly the issue is an emotional one, the product of great fears about what is happening, I would argue, to the image of the American family. Not the family itself, mind you, but the image. The average American family never resembled the Ward and June Cleaver model. And yet the image exerts great control over the public imagination. If we're going to talk about queer parenting, we're going to have to talk about queering—or "liberating"—the family.

Reinventing the Family

The precedent is set in lgbt culture for a fairly radical re-envisioning of family. Often outcasts from the families we were born into, queer people have ingrained in our culture a tradition of making family out of friends, lovers, and ex-lovers. These family networks are inherently a challenge to the largely dysfunctional idea that one's family is first the group of people one is born to, and later the group of people one helps create through marriage and childbirth. While it's not possible to fully discuss the problems with this model here, suffice it to say that the history of marriage in Western culture is fraught with physical, emotional, and sexual abuse. In part this is because of the way power has accrued to husbands and fathers, and in part because of the alienation people generally feel toward the idea of extended families—even though the latter can help alleviate the pressures of child-rearing.

My understanding of the importance of family networks is written deeply in my bones. My father died when I was eighteen months old. At fifteen, when my mother died, my fourteen-year-old brother and I were left profoundly alone. My mother had battled cancer for three and a half years prior to her death, and during that time Stan and I moved from one home to another, exhausting the small extended family network that could be called upon to help. Finally, we entered the foster care system, another institution that should be seriously examined. One thing's for sure: care is not its principal component.

After my mother died, I asked that I be allowed to stay the remaining three months before my sixteenth birthday at the home where I was living at the time of her death, and for legal emancipation after that. Stan, too young and in far too much trouble to be emancipated, remained in the foster care system where he was alternately ignored, abused, and exploited. He was seventeen when he got his first apartment and had already learned how to support himself by selling marijuana. Naomi was born eighteen months after my mother's death. In retrospect, it's completely clear to me that I became a mother in order to begin the process of recreating family for myself. What I wanted, of course, was a mother. My mother. Short of that, with no models and little connection to the people who were supposed to be my family—who lived, anyway, in distant parts of the state—I became a mother.

As Naomi was about to turn six, I met the man who is now father to both my children. He never did want to get married, though we discussed it for years because we knew his right to raise Naomi could be challenged if anything ever happened to me. Unlike gay men and lesbians, we could have taken advantage of the rights and benefits of marriage, but like many queer people we were put off by the sexism and heterosexism of the institution.

Capper, Alix's and Naomi's father, is important to this discussion because together he and I learned how to maintain family in the face of a huge and potentially destructive transition in my life. I don't use the word *destructive* lightly. Coming out remains one of the most difficult things I've ever done. For years, I was sure it could only mean dismantling the family I had so carefully put together. The pain I felt at the thought of losing my family was overwhelming. I'd already lost one family; I couldn't fathom losing another. But Capper knew with certainty before I did that I was a lesbian and, despite his pain, quite literally stood by me as I came into an acceptance of my sexuality.

Today, my family includes my daughters Naomi and Alix; Capper; Capper's lover, Michelle; Michelle's mother, Sandi, who was my dear friend even before Capper and Michelle fell in love with each other; Sandi's eighty-nine-year-old mother, Marie, who has just gone to live with Sandi; Michelle's brother, Zachary, and his girlfriend, Molly; my ex-lover, Lea; my friends, Susan and Raquel; and Scott, Heidi, Hannah, and Carlise, the family that lives next door to Capper. Together with my brother and aunt, who live in California (we live in Minnesota), these people form the core, the inner circle of my family life. I could call upon any of the adults in this configuration for any reason and I often do.

Most of the people I've just named in my large and slightly unwieldy family celebrate holidays and birthdays together, and, as the kids like to say, there's always room for more people. If it sounds like I'm bragging, I probably am. I've made sure that neither I nor my children will ever face the devastation of losing an entire family, but in order to do this I've had to totally redefine family to include people who are commonly excluded. It takes courage to maintain family connections in the face of relationship shifts. I don't think it's an overstatement to say that our survival depends upon our willingness to accept the fact that people change and that, despite the real pain of dealing with changes we may not want, we can continue to love them.

I have no trouble announcing that I have a queer family. Sure, there are several obviously queer people in it. Naomi is sure that lesbianism is in her future despite the fact that she likes boys; she calls it, lovingly, "the family curse." But it's not the presence of gay people that makes me think of my family as queer. It's the way we live and make room for people: new lovers, old lovers, new friends, old friends. As I said earlier in this essay, queer people have a history of creating family in ways that go against the grain of the nuclear family model. It is, as far as I'm concerned, my family's willingness to remain open and fluid, its absolute rejection of the preeminence of the nuclear family, that makes it queer.

Brave New Families

So what does queer parenting look like? I believe it begins in a family that rejects singular notions of what it means to be family. It includes a willingness to share the burden and joy of child-rearing and to create and live in fluid families and family structures. It also means taking seriously our relationship as queer people to other, often more seriously marginalized people.

It means, for example, for a middle-class person, not fleeing urban areas for the possibly too-easy comforts of the suburbs, not taking your kids out of inner city schools, but instead becoming involved in those schools. It means, for a white person, not buying a house in an all-white neighborhood no matter how perfect the house or how nice the neighborhood. I know that these are hard decisions. I have the dubious good fortune of not being faced with having to make some of these decisions because I lack the financial resources that would push me to do so. With my education and training, though, that may not always be true.

No matter how hard we queer people work to erase our differences, we'll never fit into the nuclear family model prevailing in the suburbs of North America. That may be an unpleasant truth, but it's real nonetheless. The suburbs are the architectural manifestation of an ideology that defines family as the biological product of a legally bound man and woman. At best, we'll be tolerated in places like the outlying areas around Minneapolis, where people are too well-bred—or too repressed—to express their distaste. Which doesn't mean we can't choose to live in these places or that our presence in these middle-class enclaves does no good. Outspoken lgbt parents, for example, are effecting changes in curriculum in some suburban communities.

Queer the family and everything changes. That's why the religious Right is so terrified of gay people, so bent on reasserting a family model that has long been archaic. We're already doing this work, we already have an established history of treating as family the people we love instead of relying solely on bloodlines or legal documents for family definition. As more lgbt people decide to have children, we need to resist the temptation to make ourselves over in the image of the nuclear family.

Ironically, as queer people gain a grudging acceptance in certain urban areas, the temptation to conform becomes stronger, but we're not doing our children any favors when we reject our differences or pretend they don't exist. Our kids won't be fooled, nor will their friends. For twenty-five years, a basic tenet of the gay liberation movement in this country has been that we should feel pride in who we are, and pride is something the children of gay people need as surely as their parents. As my youngest daughter Alix says, it doesn't matter "what" she is when she grows up—lesbian or straight, bisexual or transgendered, tall or short, fat or thin, partnered or single—her whole family will love her anyway. A simple definition of queer families could be this: your queer family is the one that accepts you for who you are.

Thanks to Kim Surkan, Capper Nichols, and Betsy Handlson for ideas and feedback on this essay.

Jenifer Fennell (pictured here with her daughter Alix) is a graduate student in English literature at the University of Minnesota where she is working on a dissertation about the inhumanity of the criminal justice system. She is also a teacher of literature, women's studies, and writing; the mother of two daughters; and editor of A&E, the university's arts and entertainment weekly.

Writers

and activists Jewelle Gomez and Minnie Bruce Pratt posed the questions in this piece to each other in a keynote address on November 11, 1991 at Creating Change, the annual lesbian and gay leadership conference organized by the National Gay and Lesbian Task Force. The administration in Washington may have changed since then, but the struggles that these poets talk about are still with us. Congress annually renews its attack on culture through de-funding of the National Endowment for the Arts. With each right-wing volley, the work of lesbian artists and writers—from the ones Minnie Bruce mentions here, including herself, to Sapphire and Holly Hughes—is held up to the vilest form of ridicule. As a result, the keepers of our culture, the tellers of our truths, have become even more precious. We can only guess at the lesbian voices silenced by the ripple effects of these attacks on the arts and the general climate of homophobia.

In this elegant conversation, Minnie Bruce and Jewelle explore what brought them to think of themselves as activists as well as poets, what keeps them going in the face of such assaults. They inspire us to dare to imagine, to "cling to the beauty and truth of our own lives."

Poets Live the Questions
Jewelle Gomez and Minnie Bruce Pratt

WHERE DO WE BEGIN TO QUESTION OUR OWN CLASSISM, RACISM, ANTI-SEMITISM? WHEN DO WE NOTICE "WE" ARE ALSO "THEM"? WHEN DO WE DEMAND AS MUCH OF OURSELVES AS WE DO OF THE OTHER?

Minnie Bruce: We've been inhabiting the dreary terrain of the Reagan-Bush years for a long time now, a landscape in which acts of injustice and oppression are presented as inevitable, part of the natural order, or part of a well-ordered government. In this land, men in power steal and call that "deregulation," men in power lie and call that "mis-speaking," men in power subvert the Constitution and call that "national defense." When we who long for a more just world object to injustice, we are trivialized by the label "politically correct," we are accused of limiting others with "censorship." When we testify to another reality, our reality, we are called "fantasizers" and "liars." When we attempt to depict our reality in art, or have it reflected in public policy, we are called "indecent" and "disgusting."

How do we cling to the beauty and truth of our own lives, our own reality, in this land? How do we stay connected to the passion of creating change, which is the art of creating out of our lives a future that is not inevitable, like a poem whose ending we don't know, can't know because we are in the middle of writing it, in the middle of the joy of creation?

Jewelle: At a time when we feel attacked politically, economically, sometimes from within as well as from the outside, asking questions may seem irrelevant. Yet over the years it is really those who dare ask the questions who are the touchstones for change.

On her deathbed, Gertrude Stein said to her beloved Alice, "What's the answer?" When Alice admitted she did not know the answer to the meaning of life, Gertrude said, "More importantly, what is the question?"

These questions were posed and answered as the keynote address at the 4th annual NGLTF Creating Change conference in 1991 and subsequently published in *OUT/LOOK* magazine (Spring 1992).

In looking for a means of changing our own inner lives and thus promoting change in the world around us, it is often the torturous journey that leads us to articulate the question that is the most profound and empowering.

Minnie Bruce: To a younger poet, the poet Rilke once said: "...be patient toward all that is unsolved in your heart and try to love the *questions themselves* like locked rooms....the point is, to live everything. *Live* the questions now. Perhaps you will then gradually, without noticing it, live along some distant day into the answer."* As a way of clinging to our own truths, here are some questions we ask of ourselves, of you, as part of "liv[ing] along...into the answer."*

WHAT IN OUR EARLY LIVES GAVE US A SENSE OF POLITICS? THAT LARGER CHANGE WAS POSSIBLE? WHAT WAS OUR FIRST POLITICAL ACT?

Jewelle: Early in the sixties it was clear that my life had been outlined for me simply as a projection of someone else's fantasy-Hollywood myth, TV news, educational propaganda and the expectations of the black community. But several events opened up the possibility that there was reality beyond the lies, beyond the stereotype. The narrow place of schism between society's myth and my reality was a deeply powerful place. A political place.

In 1963 Black Day was declared by local civil rights organizations in Boston. All black people were asked to stay home from school and from work as a way of letting the rest of the city see us, simply see us. I didn't stay home. I was fourteen years old and believed the newspaper when it said that those who called for this action were simply troublemakers. My great-grandmother, who'd grown up poor, black, and Native American, felt the decision should be mine. I seemed to know more of this world than she did; it wasn't until the following year, when I was fifteen, that I realized the newspapers were lying. Sitting at my school desk in a predominantly black school, with only a handful of white and Chinese students and even fewer black students present on that first Black Day, brought home to me the singularity of my position as a black person in white society.

Rainer Maria Rilke, *Letters to a Young Poet*, trans. M.D.H. Norton (New York: W.W. Norton, 1934), p. 35.

The isolation I felt looking at the other black girls who also had been afraid to be labeled as troublemakers made me understand the power of unity with others and the fear such a unity inspired in those who are in charge. Other incidents broadened the light that shone on the schism between myth and reality. The time I saw a woman riding the trolley car with me and noticed the numbers tattooed on her arm. I realized that even though the schools told us nothing of the Holocaust, it had really happened, and not just in the movies. Watching my great-grandmother make the decision to not buy stockings so she could send me to those movies. These were the moments when I saw myself unexpectedly in a political sea. Not observing Black Day was a first political act. The nature of it still stings me and shapes the urgency of my political life.

Minnie Bruce: My first political act was not about change at all but about keeping things they way they were. As a teenager in the early sixties, I had a German pen pal, a matter of great excitement for a young, curious girl isolated in a tiny town in the deep South. His name was Horst Werner—I can remember it easily, thirty years later. As the civil rights movement in Alabama began to receive international attention, he wrote inquiring what I thought of it. I replied with a justification of segregation in which I used many stupid lies about black inferiority. My mother read and praised the letter. It was the first—the only time—I wrote down a defense of the political and social views I had been raised with. Proud of myself, I thought I had answered all the questions. Yet why did he never write again? I had no way of standing outside of myself and asking questions as if my life were the locked-room mystery.

But the civil rights movement kept on, and the people in it were asking questions, the ones marching, the ones being beaten, the ones dying. All of this was at the edge of my attention, at the periphery of my vision; I did not want to look too closely. Yet their questions changed me, nevertheless.

In 1967, when I turned twenty-one, I committed my second political act. In the courthouse named after my grandfather, I went to vote for the first time, in a big room with no voting booths, no curtained privacy, just a table and the paper ballot handed to me. Some of the candidates were running as members of what was Alabama's equivalent of the Mississippi Freedom Democratic Party—their symbol the black panther instead of the coxcombed rooster of Southern Democratic white supremacy. I sat at the table and my father leaned over my shoulder; he began telling me how to vote, and though I had given no thought to this election, when I saw the black panther I began to make my X by those candidates. My father said, "NO. Don't vote for them." But in me, deep down, was my mother's voice telling me, as she always had, "You have to do what you think is right, no matter what others say."

WHAT DID WE LEARN ABOUT LIVING FROM OUR FIRST LESBIAN AND GAY GATHERING, EVENT, DANCE, NIGHT AT THE BAR?

Jewelle: If we don't include the Saturdays of my teenage years devoted to best girlfriends, my first lesbian gathering was outside of the "lesbian community." In the mid-seventies I went to a salon in Brooklyn designed to share the work of black women. For a number of years, Alexis DeVeaux invited women to read their writing, dance, perform their music for each other. It wasn't specifically lesbian but the ethos was lesbian. I first heard Edwina Lee Tyler there, first heard Evelyn Harris of Sweet Honey sing there, June Jordan read her poetry. I first read my vampire stories there.

My entire world opened up. I could actually imagine myself creating, living, thriving as a lesbian with the women I met at these events. They were erudite, politically savvy, and stylish. They were independent women in the U.S. without having lost their sense of Africa, the Americas, Japan, Puerto Rico or the many other places that their ancestors may have come from. Those moments gave me the sense of myself as a lesbian connected to other women, loyal to other women in the world. That sense of connection and loyalty has been at the heart of what I expect, what I demand from others when working politically.

Today, when many intellectual streams of thought aim to deconstruct our historical experience rather than acknowledge its impact, and which seem to devalue the idea of community rather than try to mine the elements that are nurturing, this part of my life becomes even more treasured. I realize that this group of women was quite insulated from the lesbian/feminist movement and the academic interpretations of who lesbians were. We were outsiders because we were not white. No one thought about us in 1975 out there in Brooklyn creating a world, and many of us maintained that isolation deliberately, trying not to think about them/you.

It frightens me to be reminded how many other lesbians—small-town lesbians, working-class or poor lesbians—remain outside the realm of lesbian politics because we don't remember them or because they don't think they have anything to teach us. When I feel comfortable living a relatively safe lesbian life, I try to keep in mind that most lesbians in the U.S. and certainly in the world take their lives in their hands when they take their lovers in their arms. There are still more of us living on those margins than we'll ever know if we only read the glossy girl magazines. And that's still where the elemental energy comes from.

Minnie Bruce: With my lover and some friends, I sat at a table in my first gay bar, The Other Side, in Fayetteville, North Carolina. It was 1975. I knew no one else in the room. A woman walked over, leaned over me, tough, butch, asked me to dance. Confused, I said no-thank-you and whispered to my lover, "What do I do? I don't know the rules." She said, "There are no rules." Later, she danced with me alone on the tiny spotlit stage, backed me up against the wall, and kissed me there, everyone watching. Of course there were rules, but she wasn't telling. I learned as I went along how we've made up our own rules, hurtful, joyful, and sometimes we don't tell each other because of power, because of shame, or maybe we're just in a hurry, but sometimes we do tell, sometimes we ask our questions again, and then make up new answers together, make a new place to dance.

I can't remember if I went to the bar before or after I went to the Great Southeast Lesbian Conference in Atlanta, spring of 1975, but I remember, as one of the happiest nights of my life, sitting in a little auditorium with my lover and several hundred other dykes, singing our question: *I've been cheated/been mistreated/when will I be loved?* The Red Dyke Theater was about to perform, and my political education was beginning with a troupe of revolutionary socialist lesbians, one dressed in male drag, doing a hot number to "Steam Heat," another doing a wicked femme routine complete with whip. During the day, we had trotted around to workshops held in different lesbian homes in the Little Five Points area, sessions on lesbian mothers, armed revolution, women in nontraditional jobs, lesbian culture. Later at the ALFA (Atlanta Lesbian Feminist Alliance) house, in the middle of a lot of drinking, I began thinking about how I had to go home and figure out what to do about my husband and my children. I had seen that there was no one answer given by these women, that I had to make up my own answers to my questions of how to have a family, a community, and a political coalition that included me and my boys and my lover, and the people at the bar, the drag queens, the military women and men, the closeted teachers, and the political lesbians at the conference. I know now that there are more of us than I ever suspected, but still we are not the majority. As I suspected then, change will take every one of us, asking still, When will we be loved? And how can we be family, community, allies to each other?

WHAT SPECIFIC PERSONAL CHANGE CAME ABOUT FOR US BECAUSE OF POLITICAL CONSCIOUSNESS? HOW HAS POLITICAL CHANGE CREATED CHANGE IN US?

Jewelle: There was that smug satisfaction that I got from not buying grapes in the sixties in support of Cesar Chavez and the Farmworkers Union and the same with not buying Polaroid products then because of their development of the passbook system implemented against black South Africans. But where did real personal change come? Still hard to say. In 1968 when I was working for public television in Boston, our show regularly explored the issues raised by the Black Arts Movement, and one day I decided to stop straightening my hair and have a natural, or Afro, as it was called then. It seems trivial now, but after years of having the world describe my hair as "bad," "unmanageable," "undesirable," it was the most liberating thing for me to realize I didn't need to be tortured by hot combs and chemicals in order to try and look like I had "good" hair. Once I made that decision, and faced my great-grandmother with it, anything seemed possible. And I never looked in the mirror with that type of dissatisfaction again. I actually saw myself for the first time. That changed my reaction to others. Because I felt less inadequate I was able to insist on more respect from others, and I expected more from myself. That elemental, supposedly cosmetic change shifted my entire perspective.

Minnie Bruce: Before I came out as a lesbian, when I was still married but becoming familiar with the ideas of women's liberation and with some of the women who had those ideas, I was shopping for groceries at the A&P and saw, hustling by with her cart, a tall, strong woman whom I recognized from the university and realized to be a neighbor. Inspired by the politics of my women's liberation friends, I said to myself, for the first time ever making a conscious choice of this, I want to be friends with that woman; I'm going to try to have that woman as a friend. That began my knowing that I did not have to be alone as a woman, nor did I have to accept values or community chosen for me by others. That began my understanding that political consciousness could mean a way to end the fragmentation and isolation imposed on people by inequality and prejudice, a way to work at being friends with people I had been told should not be, would never be my friends—other women, women and men of color, Jewish women, gay men, lesbians. I could create the life I wanted to live, not in some theoretical future, but in the very moment. I learned then what I had to relearn in the future, that I didn't have to wait for someone else to do something about the question: *When will I be loved?*

WHAT IS STILL OUR GREATEST OBSTACLE TO CHANGE, PERSONALLY AND IN OUR COMMUNITY? WHAT CUTS US OFF FROM WHAT WE MOST WANT TO DO AND BE?

Jewelle: For me the greatest obstacle to personal change is succumbing to the desire to be liked and accepted. In grade school I didn't want to be known as a troublemaker; that's why I didn't stay out of school for the first Black Day. I was desperate for society to accept this fat black girl as one of its own. Thirty years later it's not much different. There's a part of me that wants to be accepted by the larger society and by lesbians and gays and by bisexuals and trans people and by the Afro-American community. I want everybody's mother to like me. That desire for acceptance is the complete antithesis of the desire to change. I fight every day not to give in to that desire to be accepted into the familiar order of things. It is difficult to maintain the balance between good manners, which I think are crucial to communication, and simply giving way to others' demands and needs.

As the position of our community shifts in the changing political winds, the obstacles shift too. I see the same danger for our community that I recognize in myself: that desire to assimilate. The instinct to say, "See, we're just like you," is frightening. It means we accept the lie that the world is okay if only we can get in on the goodies. If they'll give us insurance, let us have babies, and wear red ribbons at the Academy Awards all is right with the world. That instinct to meld into the mainstream has to be consciously fought in order for social change to really be profound.

The other obstacle is our self-righteousness. We know a lot about the world by virtue of our experience as outsiders. But increasingly, that experience is codified into an insular world. We often want more of the same rather than to challenge the actual shape of the world we've created. We rarely take enough of a global perspective to see that our struggle is one part of a larger circle of struggle.

And as I go into my middle years I have to work harder to stay active and conscious of all the issues, to not be impatient with the younger activists. We have Phyllis Lyon and Del Martin, we had Mabel Hampton, but there are so few examples of how to age as lesbians and keep the heart it takes to be an activist. I sometimes worry that my health and disappointment might come between me and the ongoing work.

Minnie Bruce: Last year when Jesse Helms renewed his attack on lesbians, gay men, and feminists in the arts, and I was one of the people he targeted, along with Audre Lorde and Chrystos, I was seized by a terrible fear, like that I'd lived with for years in North Carolina when I was coming out as a lesbian. I was struck back into the isolation and helplessness I felt as a lesbian mother, my knowledge that the social and judicial system was designed to punish me, was based on values that held me to be despicable. For months after Helms pointed his accusing finger at me and my work, I was surrounded by fear and unable to write, my belief in my own reality shaken, my personal life constricted, under siege.

I was trapped in the past, the immediate threat calling up the pain I still carried from that time, amplified out of proportion. Though I was no longer isolated, though now I was part of a lesbian and gay movement, thousands of people organizing, lending support, I shivered, frozen in the past, unable to imagine myself strong in the present.

And how many other, different times have we seen ourselves immobilized when the pain of the present calls up the pain of the past? During the Gulf War, over and over I heard friends speak in numbed depression about how the invasion evoked memories of brutal fighting within their family, or their sexual abuse as a child, or their rape as a grown woman. I have listened to students in my classroom: the gay man, beaten as a sissy as a child, now death threats on his answering machine; the lesbian whose female roommate moved her boyfriend into their dorm room, would never be alone with her, forced the lesbian out to stay with friends, sleep on their couch, trying to stay in school through all this. I have watched this man, this woman, try to articulate their reality to a circle of uncomprehending listeners. I have watched them, weighted by the past, heroically moving on in the present.

We need rituals of memory among us. We need ways of listening carefully to each other about what has really happened to us in the past, the distant past, the past that was just yesterday. We need this because a political movement, the public policy and tactics of our movement, does not come from our ideas, but from the bloody and joyful substance of our lives. We need to be conscious about what our lives have been, to grieve and to honor our strength, in order to break out of the past into the future.

And we need rituals honoring each other, not banquets acknowledging one or two already well-known people, but small, frequent affirmations of how we are strong in the present, of what we are learning from each other. It is not enough to be creating a new reality for ourselves through political action and personal change; we must reflect that reality back to each other, consciously, constantly, and question that reality. We can challenge the *Washington Post* and NBC news to more accurately reflect our reality. We can support our artists, our alternative newspapers and cable TV programs. But we know these efforts will reflect only a fragment of our amazingly complex lives: the rest of it is up to us, in the small circles of our daily lives.

WHO DO WE SPEAK TO, WHO DO WE QUESTION, AS WE ATTEMPT TO CREATE CHANGE, AS WRITERS, AS ORGANIZERS?

Jewelle: I want the people I admire for going to the barricades to also feel a deep sense of full political involvement when they return to their regular gigs, or just walking down the street, or deciding what house to buy. I want the people I work with, read poetry with, to feel the connection to "community" in a concrete, feminist way. I am also trying to talk to the people I grew up with. When I spoke at the twenty-fifth anniversary reunion of my high school class in October 1991 I realized how strong a part of each other's pasts we still are, and the kind of power that represents. Rather than distance myself from them and condescend to them about their lifestyle or beliefs, I recognized that I was still a part of what made them who they were and they a part of me. It felt good to be able to say I'd written a book that I knew they'd like. And if they picked up feminism and socialism on the way, then great! I'm sure they can get to it since I really learned it alongside them. I just interpreted it for a different future.

Minnie Bruce: To me my writing is sometimes: A shout to someone to do something. A reminder to myself of what I need to remember, words to center me in a hostile and chaotic universe. A prayer, a justification of need. A repetition to keep my sanity, a stubborn clinging to what I need in order to go on with my life on the edge, on the margin of power. Sometimes I feel like I'm writing a letter, the page covered with scrawled words, the same letter over and over, without knowing who will read or answer it.

And organizing has often been like that for me, the difficulty in believing that anyone is listening. I've seen this insularity of oppression in the demonstrations that I've organized, been part of, when none of us bothered to talk to people on the street, when we didn't have flyers that clearly explained why we were doing what we were doing, when we didn't make signs big and plain enough to be read by those watching. But people are watching, are listening, and we have been answered. Sometimes the listener raises his hand, his voice, to stop our life, like the man who publicly questioned me: "How can you justify the fact that your selfish sexual desires cost your children their mother?" (And a woman says to me: "You answered him?" Yes, of course I answered him, with an analysis of male domination of women's lives, of compulsory heterosexuality; I answered him for all the others who were thinking his question.) Sometimes we speak and the listener's voice sends her life back to us, like the acquaintance in Michigan who phoned after the 1987 lesbian and gay mass civil disobedience action. She had been listening to National Public Radio and had heard my affinity group preparing to be arrested, singing, *When the dykes go marching in;* she told me that she'd burst into tears, listening, she was so happy.

WHAT ASPECTS OF GAY AND LESBIAN LIFE ARE WE STILL NOT LOOKING AT? WHEN DO WE AVERT OUR EYES?

Jewelle: Power. The fear of it, the use of it. We have power. White gay men have power they use over each other, and over women. They use it to the benefit of each other and the few lesbians they find accept-able. Lesbians use their power of acceptance in their various social cir-cles for each other and against others they don't think are cool enough or well-dressed enough. White gay men use the power of the press to promote each other, and ignore women. Or harass lesbians for not let-ting them into women's clubs or lesbian conferences. Black gays use our power to 'dis' to keep ourselves isolated from the movement, to jus-tify not participating. Lesbians as well as gay men use their power to buy property in economically disadvantaged communities and don't think about what they might do to help that community to stay whole. Some lesbians curse the power of sexual imagery without ever exam-ining what the power really means to lesbians. We, as victims of the power and bigotry of others, are terrified of the power we possess. Even when we are using it for and against each other. Some of us want to use our position as preeminent lesbian author or preeminent gay editor to cre-ate a little fiefdom of opinion. Others want to be the ultimate voice lis-tened to about AIDS, rather than acknowledge that there are many valuable approaches. We don't want to examine how we buy into power and author-ity, sacrificing our political movement. We will not look at our own power and how we misuse it.

Minnie Bruce: We avert our eyes from the one who is different from ourselves, from the other; but the other shifts endlessly, depending on who we are. For at least one white gay man, "the other" this weekend was me and Jewelle and Mario Solis-Marich, women and people of color; he objected that there were no white gay male plenary speakers this year or last year either; he charged "overt discrimination."* But he is certainly not the only person within our movement to feel threatened by "the other" raising questions about how power, prestige, money, and privilege are distributed among us. When do those kinds of questions make us uncomfortable? When do we wish someone would just shut up? Here is a voice I've heard lately, a voice that made me uncomfort-able; I'd like to read you some of the words of Lee Evans, who writes in an article titled "Dykes of Poverty: Coming Home":

Rex Wochner, "Readers Forum," *Washington Blade* (October 11, 1991), 27.

As a poor dyke, I think about my teeth a lot. I have a memory of a day spent swimming at a lesbian-owned retreat when the subject of dentists came up. One dyke, a dental student, asked, "What kind of parents wouldn't provide their children with something as important as dental care?" shaking her head in what I think must be disapproval. No one says anything. My friends, a group of ten dykes from upper-middle-class, middle-class, and working-class backgrounds, change the subject. I grow quiet as I think of my childhood, of not having gone to the dentist until I was in my mid-teens (and only then because I was visiting relatives who felt obligated to take me), of having teeth pulled because they were too decayed to fill, of knowing that what stood between the pain of an infected tooth and the relief of Novocain was something as simple and elusive as a couple of twenty-dollar bills.... I have the urge to stop this playful group...and tell them, "The answer to that question is my kind of parents, my parents couldn't provide their kids with dental care." But as I watch my friends...gossiping on a sunny summer afternoon, there is no context to talk about poverty, about scarcity. So I keep my mouth shut, for my mouth is one of the places I carry evidence of my poverty.*

WHAT HOPES DO WE STILL HOLD? WHAT DOES OUR IMAGINATION HAVE TO DO WITH OUR POLITICAL WORK? WHAT MIGHT BE POSSIBLE THAT WE HAVEN'T YET IMAGINED?

Jewelle: As a fiction writer I'm always trying to find a way to push myself to imagine the best that we might be, and it ain't the army! I feel that my imagination is what makes me able to be expansive, to not give up. To feel the urgency of an election in Nicaragua or the U.S. invasion of Iraq or the high death rate of newborns in Spanish-speaking communities and know my immediate stake in it. It is imagination that has made lesbian publishers struggle along each year to keep putting out the magazines and books that it has become so fashionable to disparage now that commercial publishers have found out they can make money off of us.

Lesbian Ethics 4, no. 2 (Spring 1991), 7-18.

It's imagination that makes it possible for me to think there might be friendship and coalition with Minnie Bruce. It is imagination which allowed women to work in coalition with gay men to fight AIDS although we have received little but rude dismissal or cleverly cruel jokes for the previous fifty years. It's imagination that gets us the sex we want. If you return to your adolescence and try to remember how desperate it all seemed back then—friendships, desire—and compare it to what's going on for you now, you'll know just how much is possible. We may never in our lifetimes know the end of the exploitation of capitalism, or the dissolution of patriarchy and other oppressive philosophies, but if we fail to imagine that end is possible, life isn't really worth living.

Minnie Bruce: I grew up in a place which was literally an authoritarian state, where the violence done to black people by white people laid on all of us a paralyzing fear, a silence, a deadly conformity of thought and of feeling. The violence set strict taboos against any voicing of dissident opinions, against any kind of loving that might challenge the belief that some people should not talk to others, and some could not lie down with those others except in degradation, and someone had to be on top in love and someone underneath. We lived in a fear that was meant to kill the imagination, any yearning in us toward what was different from ourselves. Yet enough of my imagination survived so that, offered the possibility, I eventually imagined myself living as a lesbian, and then writing as a poet, my voice raised against the voice of the demagogue. But I was only able to do this because others were imagining this possibility at the same time, were working politically to make lesbian and gay life a reality.

That we have all imagined ourselves into living today as lesbian and gay people, that we have done this over and over, in a country, in a world, that says over and over that we do not exist—the incredible power of our imagination gives me so much hope. We know that the love between us crosses all lines and boundaries, all divisions of class, gender, ethnicity, race, physical ability, language, religion, culture. With the power of our collective imagination we can create a future that contains us all, where those old divisions do not reappear to perpetuate inequality among us. We are already doing this in many ways—the call for national healthcare, for instance, as a radical alternative to healthcare benefits that might go only to those in coupled relationships. And because our community crosses every boundary, if we can imagine ourselves into the future all together, true to our selves, true to our love for each other, we will offer to the world the practical details and the vision of a community creating change that is rooted in the liberation of all people.

Jewelle Gomez, *writer and activist, is the author of three collections of poetry, a collection of essays, and a novel,* The Gilda Stories *(Firebrand), winner of two Lambda Literary awards. Her new collection of short stories is entitled* Don't Explain *(Firebrand). She is on the national advisory board of the National Center for Lesbian Rights.*

Diane Sabin

Minnie Bruce Pratt's *second book of poetry,* Crime Against Nature, *was chosen as the 1989 Lamont Poetry Selection by the Academy of American Poets, was nominated for a Pulitzer Prize, and received the American Library Association's Gay and Lesbian Book Award. She co-authored* Yours in Struggle: Three Feminist Perspectives on Anti-Semitism and Racism, *with Elly Bulkin and Barbara Smith. Her other books include* We Say We Love Each Other, Rebellion: Essays 1980-1991, *and* S/HE, *stories about gender boundary crossing (all from Firebrand). Her most recent book,* Walking Back Up Depot Street *(Pitt Poetry Series), is a collection of narrative poems about growing up in, and leaving, the segregated South. She lives with author-activist Leslie Feinberg in Jersey City, New Jersey.*

Doug Lawson

Some

years ago, my lover and I were forced to put her ninety-year-old grandmother into a nursing home. It was, as it happened, considered one of the best in the area, and we thought at first we were lucky they had a Medicaid bed available. As we got to know the community of mostly elderly women in this home, we realized that two of them had developed a "special friendship," holding hands, taking walks together, taking naps in one or the other's room. It was very sweet to watch and gave me hope that there would be a way for Gram to have a life in this place that otherwise felt like it was run by prison rules. But it didn't last: one day the two women were separated and one of them was sent to live in a different part of the home. The nursing home, we were told, couldn't have the families of these or any of the other women getting offended by this behavior. What behavior? Love? Friendship? Lesbian romance?

As a founder of Older Lesbians Organizing for Change, Shevy Healey, born in 1922, has added ageism to the numerous social justice struggles in which she has become involved over the seventy-seven-plus years of her life. In this essay, adapted from speeches given at the National Gay and Lesbian Task Force Creating Change conference and before the American Society on Aging, she calls upon us to do the same. Ageism is not confined to the society "out there"; it is daily expressed in the lgbt community and its organizations as well. While Suzanne Pharr exhorts us in "Thoughts on Youth" to pay attention to how our movement incorporates the leadership and voices of youth, Shevy Healey makes a persuasive case that the elders in our movement are also being given short shrift.

One Old Lesbian's Perspective
Shevy Healey

I was considered different growing up, and frequently viewed with suspicion because I was foreign-born, a Jew, half-orphaned, on welfare (definitely a source of shame in the 1930s), and worst of all stigmas, my mother was a communist. As an adult I continued to be treated as "other": as a communist myself, as a woman in a patriarchal society, as a feminist, as a lesbian, and, now, as an "old" woman.

Perhaps my life-long activism was established when, at age five, I attended my first picket line and experienced my first taste of police brutality. Philadelphia's finest, mounted on horses, charged and broke through the garment workers' picket line at precisely the spots where women strikers and their children had been strategically placed. I remember clearly the steaming flanks of the advancing horses, the shrieking and screaming, as my mother and I ran down an alley to escape the pandemonium.

I must surely have been given another jolt when, foreign birth certificate in hand, my mother tried to register me for school and was told, "We don't have names like Seviera/Shevy in this country. We'll just call her Evelyn." So the day I entered kindergarten, I also lost my own name!

I certainly received an additional jolt toward activism during the Depression when my mother, exhausted from trying to support the two of us on four dollars a week, got sick. We eventually became eligible for welfare, which meant periodic visits by the county welfare worker, who, each time she came, would carefully spread a paper napkin on the wooden chair before she sat down to ask questions.

It helped that my International Workers' Order Kinder Schule (a secular Jewish children's school) taught me not only Jewish literature, history, and culture, but political economy as well. I learned the Jewish term *mervert* long before I heard its English equivalent—*surplus value*.

With such beginnings, it was almost inevitable that I became and have remained an activist all my life.

I survived the terrible witch hunts of the McCarthy era, which first decimated the Left in Hollywood and then spread to every sector of life in the United States. It was the "Time of the Toad," as Ring Lardner so aptly characterized it. Countless personal tragedies resulted from the so-called loyalty oaths, wholesale blacklisting and firings, vilification and jailing. It was a time when informers and spies were glorified as patriots and the Bill of Rights was considered seditious. I can remember making arrangements for who would care for our daughter if both her parents were arrested, and being reminded by Dorothy Healey, already in jail as a Smith Act (anti-sedition law subsequently ruled unconstitutional) victim, that if things got that bad, who did I suppose would be left?

I think the backlash of the religious Right today comes as close to scaring me as did the frenzy of the McCarthy days.

It was in those days that I learned to confront my fear of telling who I was. Even though it was always frightening to let people know that I was a communist, it was more frightening NOT to tell. For that meant living in dread of someone finding out. I learned in those terrible times that, oddly enough, I feel the safest when I am most open about who I am.

That means a never-ending coming out process: telling an all-Christian group that I am Jewish, even though my name is Healey; or telling a group of conservatives that I am a political radical, even though I am no longer a communist; or telling the nice heterosexual couples in the RV park that I am a lesbian; or calling myself an old woman when I'm supposed to hide my age and say thank you to someone who says I act younger.

I had my mid-life crisis in my forties, when I decided first, to start college, then, to get divorced, and finally at age fifty, to fall head over heels in love with a woman. This took me back to memories of my tomboy years, my longing to be a boy—not because of penis envy but so I could run and climb and do "boy" things rather than "girl" things. I remembered the tremendous crushes I had on other girls in my all-girls high school when I never even knew the word *lesbian*.

I felt I had come full circle. True, it took a while for me to get it that falling in love with a woman meant that I was a lesbian, but when I finally did, I avidly pursued "the life," wanting to learn and know and be part of the community. Along the way there were some knocks, some eye-openers. I certainly won't forget the first time I got dumped by a woman—somehow that seemed to me to be a male prerogative. I expected a woman to be gentler and kinder. She was not.

Given this kind of political and activist history, I thought growing old would be simple and natural. Not so. As with the rest of ageist society, I equated old only with weakened physicality and undesirable traits. Old meant sick and feeble, unattractive, unimportant, and uninteresting. That was not for me. No way!

In the typical fashion of white culture in this country, I denied the whole business. After all, "old is just a state of mind," isn't it? I had started a whole new life. I was "only as old as I felt" and I felt great! But as I went from my fifties to my sixties, the rest of the world—doctors, clerks, service people of all kinds, young and mid-life women—seemed to be treating me differently. I felt increasingly either patronized or ignored. My own mirror reflected back that I was growing not just older but old. I didn't feel different, but the older I grew the more invisible I became, and invisibility, with its implied meekness, did not suit me at all.

I got angry. My rage over the rampant ageism and sexism in the medical establishment, with which I had an almost fatal encounter, provided me with the impetus to once more want to do something to change not only the medical system, but all the other systems with ageism and sexism at their core. I also wanted to assuage the hunger I began to experience for the companionship of other old lesbians, whom I had previously shunned in my desire to pass for young.

My activism really kicked in, and before I knew it I was totally involved in organizing the first West Coast Conference By and For Old Lesbians held in 1987. At the second West Coast Conference in San Francisco in 1989, I helped found Old Lesbians Organizing for Change (OLOC).

OLOC, although barely ten years in existence, by its very presence as an organization by and for old lesbians sixty and older, has become a force to make old lesbians visible. Our first priority has always been to confront ageism wherever we see it, including the internalized ageism in our own old lesbian community. As we share our lives and the ageism we face, we sharpen our thinking and our determination to make old lesbians visible.

In this process I learned that it is, of course, impossible to talk with old lesbians only about ageism.

The "O" word is often more frightening than the "L" word to them.

Although steeped in the legacy of secrecy they bring with them from the past, they are frequently ready to take steps out of the closet with more bravery than when they were fearful of losing their jobs. Nonetheless, we still have to talk about homophobia and the presumption of heterosexuality, first among ourselves, and then wherever we face that crunch, particularly with healthcare providers.

And when old lesbians talk about hating their looks, then we have to talk about patriarchal ideals about beauty—young, white, slim, heterosexual—ideals which denigrate our old bodies and our wrinkles, and label us ugly and disgusting.

And when old lesbians talk about feeling betrayed by their own bodies and repeatedly say that what they fear most is being disabled, we have to talk about the oppression of ableism, which is the denigration of those with disabilities and the crass worship of a fantasy perfect body. This leads us to consider making common cause with the growing disability rights movement, for both groups work to be considered fully human.

When old lesbians are terrified of losing their sturdy independence—the cornerstone of much of lesbian culture—we have to talk about the higher goal of interdependence, about our need and desire to be part of our larger community (with all due respect to those who want to set us up in special old age homes).

When old lesbians suffer the indignities of poverty in their old age, we have to talk about sexism, classism, and racism, these institutionalized oppressions which result in first paying women, particularly women of color, less throughout all their working lives, then compounding the indignity by cutting welfare and rationing healthcare for the old.

The complexities of these oppressions for old lesbians are sharp reminders to me of my first organizational lesson—that all issues are intertwined and interconnected. It is simply not realistic to expect to build and maintain an organization with a narrow focus only.

Another dilemma we faced in OLOC was how to organize old lesbians, our first priority, while at the same time insisting on being part of the larger lesbian and gay community. It is cozier and certainly feels safer to be with our own group, whatever group that may be. Being with old lesbians is not only a nurturing experience; it is a relief to be away from those who do ignore, patronize, or blame us. For, of course, we experience the same ageism in the lesbian and gay community as in the rest of society.

It has been an ongoing and sometimes depressing struggle to find effective ways to broaden the consciousness of our community so that we old lesbians and gays can be visible and included. OLOC has tried many different approaches to build bridges between old lesbians and the established lesbian and gay organizations, particularly the National Gay and Lesbian Task Force (NGLTF) and the Lesbian and Gay Aging Issues Network (LGAIN) of the American Society on Aging (ASA). In the beginning of our struggle we often found ourselves in an adversarial position, much to our distress, with those who were supposed to be our friends. For example, in 1994, after none of the points of a memorandum of agreement between OLOC and NGLTF had been honored, OLOC leafleted the next Creating Change conference (instead of attending it), saying, "...we are more visible by our absence than our presence...."

Similarly, OLOC's experience with LGAIN was that at its inception, although primarily an organization of professionals working in the field of aging, it appeared indifferent to including the voice of nonprofessional old lesbians as more than mere tokens. This was compounded by the financial policies of ASA which made it impossible for old lesbians and gays to attend and participate in its yearly deliberations. This has been a particular source of concern to OLOC since the primary agenda of LGAIN is to improve the work of all in the helping professions to provide sensitive and welcoming services to old lesbians and gays who may need them.

Both of these organizations have made improvements in their consideration of the place of old lesbians and gays in their deliberations. NGLTF, through its Policy Institute, has prepared a draft for discussion of policy issues facing "GLBT seniors." LGAIN has been publishing articles written by old lesbians in its newsletter and pledged to do an ageism training for its leadership, as well as to raise money to help old lesbians and gays attend the yearly ASA conferences and participate in LGAIN's leadership.

But why has it taken so long? We are dealing here with people in leadership, lesbians and gays who work very hard, who are neither callous, boorish, nor unfeeling. There is clearly a problem.

Foremost, of course, is the problem of ageism itself. When old lesbians and gays are invisible in our own organizations, either as leaders or as members, then the issue of ageism becomes invisible as well.

With LGAIN, there is the additional problem of the institutionalized ageism existing in the helping profession itself, resulting in the reluctance, conscious or unconscious, of professional helpers to deal with old people as equals. The social service model is still mainly based on the constricting roles of helper and helped, benefactor and supplicant, provider and victim. This is an attitude promulgated by a system that becomes self-perpetuating and is steeped in ageist stereotypes.

Secondly, there is our own community's response, or lack thereof, to both its own institutionalized ageism as well as that of the larger society. None of us, as individuals or as a community, are exempt from this particular Socially Transmitted Disease (STD), so aptly named by my friend Dr. Ellyn Kaschak.

How then to get beyond the simple stating of the problem that ageism is an organized institutionalized oppression existing both in our society and in our community?

With no undue modesty, I consider myself somewhat of an expert in the field of ageism. And this is certainly not only because I am an old lesbian. My first qualification for expertise began with the recognition of my own virulent internalized ageism. My STD broke out in full bloom in my mid-fifties when, in a most unconscious manner, I really acted out my fears about growing old. It was then that I investigated a face-lift (I fortunately gave that up), refused to attend a yoga class in a senior center (me, a senior?), really believed that diet and exercise would keep me "young" forever, and in general felt myself to be an exception to whatever rule it was that made people grow OLD.

It cannot be simply serendipitous that at that time I found and devoured *Look Me in the Eye: Old Women, Aging, and Ageism* by Barbara MacDonald with Cynthia Rich (Spinsters), a book that profoundly changed my life. It forced me to an intense and honest introspection about my own aging and a realization that I had no possibility of living a good old age if I continued to deny my own aging, or if I did not challenge the stereotypes and oppressions that accompany aging in this country.

My next step toward expertise was my actual daily experience of ageism. As I reached my sixties and now my seventies, it appears that my contacts with all manner of institutions (banks, HMOs, medical personnel, markets, service agencies) are all heavily tainted by the worst stereotypes about both queers and old people. I fill out forms, get greeted and mistreated not only by society's presumption of my heterosexuality, but ageist presumptions about my helplessness, powerlessness, and incompetence. A whole array of organizations and providers stand ready to interpret me and other old women. They all want to speak for us, to explain us and define us, as we ourselves continue to remain voiceless. It is for this reason that OLOC has adopted the disability rights slogan: "NOTHING about us WITHOUT US." If *old* is the subject, then we old lesbians and gays must be able to speak for ourselves in order to avoid becoming the object.

This principle seems so self-evident that very few self-respecting persons will deny it. But here's the rub: If there really is agreement on this basic principle of self-determination and autonomy, why are old lesbians and gays so seldom seen or heard, so seldom a part of leading bodies and think tanks, even when invitations are extended to us? Surely there is no discrimination on this block!

In reality, of course, there is. Not only ageism, but classism, racism, and ableism stop us from coming in. In other words, we don't have enough money, we sometimes don't have enough energy if no special provisions are made for us, and if we are people of color, we are tired of feeling alien in a white world. So we stay away and will probably continue to stay away, unless the equivalent of a strong affirmative action policy is practiced. Yes, in this time of general attack upon affirmative action, I call upon all of us to examine what NGLTF and LGAIN and other lgbt organizations can do to make it increasingly possible for the old lgbt's to become more active participants. The critical issue of ageism must be tackled first, and then there is the very difficult task of coming up with subsidies, and maybe hospitality rooms for resting, and special welcomes and appreciation of our words—not as tokens, but as ideas and information from people worth listening to. None of this is easy. The real payoff is that tackling ageism helps every individual involved in this process to live a better old age.

Of course, OLOC bears some of the responsibility for making this happen. The squeaky wheel does get the attention, and we haven't been squeaking much. But OLOC is small and very poor, and it *is* tiresome to always be pushing for acknowledgment, especially from our friends. We do not question their good will. But it is still unacceptable that ageism, for whatever reason, has been so far down on the list of our own organizations' priorities, organizations empowered to give voice to us all. I know that it takes lots of effort on everyone's part to form a working alliance, to close the gap between the language and the practice of inclusivity.

A young man in one of my trainings pinpointed another difficult problem when he said: "Not I, of course, but others of my generation, the MTV generation, are saying about old people, 'You are in our way. You've had your turn. It's our turn now. Move over.'"

The college lecture circuit is full of speakers peddling this frightful scapegoating of the old. Make no mistake. This pitting of one generation against another, as well as whites against people of color, middle class against the poor, able-bodied against the disabled, serves only to keep us distracted from looking hard at who and what is the real enemy.

As long as young people can be diverted to believe that old people are the ones who have it all, they will not notice that 72 percent of this country's wealth is controlled by 10 percent of its population, and of that number, the top 1 percent owns 37 percent of the resources! The disparity between the rich and the poor is greater than it has ever been, with the class in the middle becoming increasingly impoverished.

So one of the big lessons I've relearned in my late-life organizing is that since our issues are connected, and we are connected, the old union songs *are* true: our greatest strength lies in unity. None of us can achieve our common agenda, unless we find ways of working together, unless we refuse to let ourselves be divided.

What to do? The challenge for us is how to maintain that tricky balance of focusing on our own special oppression while also making common cause with others who are oppressed. We need to work in a collaborative, respectful manner, even when the agencies and organizations where we work remain patriarchal; do our own personal internal work on ageism while continuing to engage in public political work; insist on naming old gays and lesbians as part of the constituency of old people addressed in the White House Conference on Aging; fight for domestic partnership discounts in long term care and medigap— and everywhere else; come out and speak up; take on the religious Right.

In short, change the world to make it a better place for all of us of whatever generation.

As my own life circle comes to closure, I am proud that I and others of my generation continue to struggle for change, for social justice, continue to learn lessons, and continue to want to share our learning. For me, the greatest revelation and joy is that our old lives continue to be in process.

The final sentence of a baby dyke manifesto that I found on the internet directed, I presume, to older generations of lesbians and gays, states: "In return for changing the world, we agree to continue the struggle for queer rights and visibility in every aspect of our lives, and to take care of you when you get old." I respond by saying thanks for the thought, but we don't really want payback for the past. We want partnership and equality now in the present and in the future, in our common struggle for queer rights and visibility.

I was reminded by an eighteen-year-old lesbian that young people are being tokenized because they are the "wave of the future," just as we, old people, are tokenized because we are the "keepers of the past." Neither of us, young nor old, is being listened to very seriously in the present. Only in unity with each other and in coalition with our allies can we move ahead to achieve our common agenda: nothing less than to change the world—to make it safer, better, more just, and more joyous for all of us.

Shevy Healey, Ph.D., born in 1922, is a proud old lesbian. She is a retired clinical psychologist, having worked primarily with women, lesbians, and people with disabilities; a founding organizer of Old Lesbians Organizing for Change (OLOC); activist, teacher, speaker on feminism, ageism, and ableism.

The

question of identity is complex and sometimes filled with seemingly inherent contradictions. Class, race, sex, nationality, sexual orientation—the individual specificities of these aspects of identity can be at once both painfully oppressive and powerfully liberating. Surina Khan is an activist whose primary work is monitoring the religious Right in the U.S., work that brings her into close daily contact not only with that movement's tactics and strategies, but often with its grassroots targets as well. She does not explore that work here, but rather steps back to share how the layers of multiple identities in her own life—Pakistani American, upper-middle class, immigrant, woman of color, formerly assimilated conservative, now committed leftist, nonobservant child of an Islamic culture, and lesbian—have informed her activism. Though her multiple identities may be uniquely her own, her willingness to mine the criss-crossed veins of those identities for resources and insights valuable to her work as an activist proves an inspiring example. She shows us that by examining and claiming all the parts of oneself rather than downplaying, belittling, or even denying any of those parts, makes one a more effective activist.

Color Me White
Surina Khan

I grew up thinking I was a rich white girl. This is problematic for many reasons, not the least of which is that I am not white. I was born in Pakistan. I am brown-skinned, though I was regularly complimented by my mother and others in my extended family for my "fair" skin color. In Pakistan, lighter skin is coveted, and I picked up on the privileges of lightness from the time that I could understand the spoken word. My mother tried to entice me into drinking milk by telling me my skin would become even lighter the more milk I drank.

My family left Pakistan abruptly on a cold night in November 1972. At the time, my father's brother was running for prime minister against the incumbent, Zulfikar Ali Bhutto. Although my parents were not politically involved, our relation to my uncle put our family in danger, given the often violent nature of Pakistani politics. Without even packing up our home, we drove through the Black Mountains of the Khyber Pass into Afghanistan, where my parents, two brothers, and three sisters stayed for five days. We then traveled to Iran, which ironically, under the rule of the Shah, was my first exposure to a westernized country. After two months in Teheran we went on to Spain, England, and finally Connecticut. I was five years old.

I immediately set out trying to assimilate myself into the dominant U.S. culture. Although I didn't speak any English when we first arrived here, I became fluent in two months. I spent those early childhood years perfecting my American accent, my adolescence affirming my American identity to others, and my late teens rejecting my Pakistani heritage. I wanted desperately to fit in. I wanted to be an American. And sadly, I equated American with white.

When I was eleven, my parents felt we were losing touch with our Pakistani heritage, so they temporarily moved us back to Pakistan. They kept their house in Connecticut in order for the older children to continue going to school here. I was miserable in Pakistan; I hated it. It made me feel stifled. Constrained. Women are often limited to traditional gender roles in Pakistan, and I picked up on this double standard early. People were always talking about getting married. It was either, "Oh, you're almost old enough to start thinking about finding a husband," or, "When are you getting married?"

I felt like an American on foreign soil and I looked forward to summer vacations when we would return to Connecticut. In Pakistan, my sister and I attended the International School of Islamabad, where most of the kids were the children of diplomats. There was a fairly large American population at this school although the majority of these students had never spent more than a few months at a time in the U.S. Nonetheless, they were *real* Americans. Even though I had lived most of my life in the States, and felt like an American, the kids at ISI identified me as a Pakistani. This was very troubling to me. I had spent years distancing myself from my Pakistani identity and embracing my American identity. In Pakistan, no matter how light, or even white, I felt, I was still a Pakistani. But in the U.S., assimilating into the dominant white culture made me feel like an all-American girl. And so I was relieved when my parents moved us back to the States so I could attend high school.

As a girl, my internalized racism was intermingled with my class privilege. I picked up on the advantages of light skin color and this led me to abandon my identity as a Pakistani. My emerging identity as a white girl living in the U.S. had everything to do with my class privilege. I had the advantage of being in a family that was upper-middle class. My parents had money, which meant we lived in a nice (white) neighborhood and we went to good (white) schools. I attended an all-girls boarding school in Simsbury, Connecticut, where I had no trouble fitting in. Sadly, after years of assimilating myself into the dominant white culture around me, by the time I reached high school I had succeeded in creating a white upper-middle-class identity for myself.

Although my high school was predominantly white, there was a handful of girls of color. And as often happens in white dominated spaces, the colored folks bonded. At mealtime they would all sit together. It was a glaring image—a room full of white girls with a cluster of colored girls off to the side. I, however, didn't sit with the other colored girls. Although I was friendly, I didn't bond with them, because in my mind I had nothing in common with them. I didn't see myself as a person of color. I sat with my white friends.

My desire as a girl to construct an American identity for myself came at the cost of my culture. As an adult I'm feeling the void I created for myself. Although I can still speak Urdu, my first language, my vocabulary is only equivalent to that of a five-year-old. I have cousins I would never recognize if I walked past them on the street. I've never read the Koran, and I don't have faith in Islam.

After I came out as a lesbian I refused to visit Pakistan. My family had a very difficult time accepting my lesbian identity and their reaction distanced me even further from Pakistan. For years after I came out, my mother would ask me to return to Pakistan every time I spoke with her. And I would reply, "I'm too busy. I can't get away." But the truth was that I didn't feel comfortable visiting a country that is publicly hostile to lesbians and gay men. Where there aren't even any words to describe homosexuality. And also, my years of assimilating into the dominant culture in the U.S. left me with little interest in being in my homeland.

Pakistan has always been my parents' answer to everything. When they found out my sisters were smoking pot in the late seventies, they shipped all of us back. "You need to get in touch with the Pakistani culture," my mother would say. When my oldest sister got hooked on Transcendental Meditation and started walking around the house in a trance, my father packed her up and put her on a plane. She's been in Pakistan ever since. Being the youngest of six, I wised up quickly. I waited to share my sexual identity until after I moved out of my parents' house and was financially independent. If I had come out while I was still living at home, I would have been on the next flight to Islamabad.

When I told my mother I was a lesbian, she suggested I go to Pakistan for a few months. "Just get away from it all. You need some time. Clear your head," she begged. But I insisted I was a lesbian and told her I was moving to Washington, D.C. to live with my then-girlfriend. My mother grasped at straws. "You and your lover better watch out. There's a large Pakistani community in D.C., and they'll find out about you. They'll break your legs, mutilate your face." I was stunned. Did these words come out of my mother's mouth? In that moment, my mother validated my fears associated with Pakistan, and I cut off all ties with the community, including my family. For me, Pakistan became synonymous with homophobia.

My mother disowned me when I left for D.C. A year later, when my girlfriend and I broke up, she came back into my life, however, motivated in part, I'm sure, by wishful thinking. I do give her a lot of credit, though, not only for nurturing the strength in me to live by my convictions with integrity and dignity, but also for eventually trying to understand me. I'll never forget the day I took my mother to see a lawyer friend of mine. She was unhappy with her lawyer and I reminded her that she didn't need to retain him if she didn't agree with him. So I took her to see my friend. "I presume this lawyer is a lesbian," my mother said on the way to the law office. "Yes, she is," I replied, thinking, Oh no, we're about to get into another argument over the gay stuff. But my mother completely took me by surprise. "Well, the men aren't helping me," she said. "I might as well go to the dykes." I didn't think she even knew the word *dyke*.

Her changing attitude about my lesbian identity was instilling a desire in me to reclaim my Pakistani identity. The best way to do this, I decided, was to seek out other Pakistani lesbians. I barely knew any Pakistani people aside from my family, and I certainly didn't know any, or even know of any, Pakistani lesbians. Having rejected my culture from a young age, when I came out I identified only as a lesbian. It didn't occur to me to identify as a Pakistani lesbian. I may not have been ready to go back to Pakistan at this point, but I was ready to start examining the hostility I felt toward my culture.

This has been a painful process of realization for me. Looking at my own internalized racism as a young person of color has not been easy, and discussing it and writing about it has been even more challenging. And ironically, it has been my involvement in the queer rights movement that has lead me to this important point of self-reflection. Finally, nine years after coming out to my family, I made the trip home.

It was June 1998, shortly after Pakistan joined the ranks of the nuclear nations by detonating its first atomic bombs. I arrived to find the prime minister, Nawaz Sharif, urging my homeland's masses to join him in an austerity drive. A catastrophe loomed on the horizon, rising up in the mushroom cloud of an arms race: playing nuclear catch-up with neighboring India had cost billions of dollars, throwing the national economy into chaos. Worse, the specter of atomic warfare between India and Pakistan, countries which have warred three times since 1947 and still skirmish over Kashmir, wrought a devastating series of international sanctions. By the middle of a sweltering hot summer, both the rupee and the stock market had plunged to record lows.

Among some, there was much cheering when the nuclear tests went forward despite international pressures. If India had the bomb, the rallying cry insisted, then surely Pakistan should have equal ability to blow up the subcontinent. But among the great masses of impoverished Pakistanis there were more important things to worry about. To them, the splitting of atoms was not as much a symbol of newfound might as another drain on an already struggling nation. A woman selling fruits and vegetables in a small, rural village told me she'd heard about the bomb, but she was more concerned with feeding her three young children than fighting with India. The average wage in Pakistan is sixty-five rupees a day, or about one dollar, depending on the unsteady exchange rate.

Sharif took to pleading with the masses. Most dramatically, he invoked Allah in calling for a sort of collective fast. "We will take in food once a day," he declared. "The children of Nawaz Sharif will have one meal a day. We are not scared of sanctions. We have true faith in the God almighty who gives food to his creation." For those who couldn't afford even that one daily meal? "Eat grass," Prime Minister Sharif said. For many, eating grass is not unthinkable.

Such is the price of progress.

The poverty in Pakistan is staggering, almost overwhelming. Healthcare, sanitation, and education are not yet on the screen of Pakistani public policy. The water is untreated, which means you risk horrific stomach cramps and diarrhea if you don't boil it before drinking. There is no educational infrastructure. The literacy rate hovers between 38 to 50 percent for men, and 28 percent for women. And *literate* in Pakistan includes people who can only sign their names.

I am one of the lucky ones. When I was a little girl I lived in a house called Rocky Ridge, built of sturdy black rocks on a hill just outside the small town of Abbottabad in northern Pakistan near China's border. My oldest brother lives there now with his wife and three sons. The last time I was in Abbottabad, for a brief two-week visit, was for my father's funeral in July 1989. My father, Commander M. Afzal Khan, is buried in Abbottabad next to his mother, his father, his half brother, and his sister-in-law in our family burial ground. My father's family moved from Kashmir to Abbottabad in 1947 after England relinquished colonial India and partitioned Pakistan as a separate, mostly Muslim, nation.

I was brought up in a family that not only had money but a promi-
nent position on the social register, a class status that shielded me from
the indignities and poverty most Pakistanis suffer. I was taught that we
didn't have to give money to beggars on the street or worry about servants—ubiquitous in middle- and upper-class families—who were
paid the equivalent of eighty dollars a month. "They're used to it," I was
told. "They don't know any better."

In Pakistan it's difficult not to notice my class privilege, let alone my
skin privilege. It has taken years for me to come to terms with the racism
of my youth. From an early age I felt the pressure to assimilate into a
white culture because, even at five years old, I could see that people
were rewarded for being white, and if you couldn't be white, you could
behave like a white person and still receive some of the same benefits.
And now I feel duped. I gave in to the dominant culture rather than taking pride in my ethnic heritage. I have lost too many years trying to assimilate into the dominant culture, not realizing the importance of my Pakistani
heritage. I have been critical of Pakistan for being a fundamentalist culture but, in fact, many of the injustices in Pakistan are not unlike those
I see every day in the U.S.

In Pakistan, as in other countries, there are elements of racism based
on different ethnic backgrounds and skin color, with many Pakistanis
revering light skin. While most people, particularly in the U.S., see racism
as a form of white supremacy, I see it as a global problem that even people of color must confront. It is not entirely a white construct, but rather
a complicated issue that grows increasingly complex as some sectors
of the U.S. political Right seem to reach out to people of color.

As a self-identified Pakistani lesbian activist who researches the U.S.
political Right, I can see that there are important similarities between
the white supremacist ideologies of the Right and conservative people of color who have assimilated into a dominant white culture and
work within a racist paradigm.

People of color get drawn into the Right because the Right has become effective in encoding their racist, misogynist, and antigay language. For example, the U.S. Christian Right, aware that it needs to
continually broaden its base, cultivates people of color by calling for
"racial reconciliation." Yet the Christian Right does not have a commitment
to racial justice. In fact, it continues to attack racial justice organiza-

tions and people of color through its opposition to affirmative action and bilingual education. Some leaders of the Christian Right have become expert in choosing the words they use to attack us with great care, so that they are racist without appearing to employ overtly racist language.

The same can be said for their views on homosexuality. There are Christian Right leaders who have increasingly adopted "tolerant" language when referring to lesbians and gay men, at the same time they are proponents of "conversion" therapy and the "exgay" movement. They are antigay while carefully choosing language that does not sound obviously homophobic.

Others promote an accepting, welcoming, and loving approach toward people of color, even toward lesbian and gay people. This represents a strategic shift meant to recruit people into their theocratic movement. Love homosexuals, the line goes, welcome them and then lead them to an exgay ministry where they are told they can change. Love them, welcome them, and tell them it is okay to be a person of color as long as they behave a certain way. A certain white way, that is. And then let these whitified people of color speak for your organization to show that yours is not a racist organization or a racist ideology.

Love the Muslim Pakistani woman and minister the Word of God to her. Love the lesbians and gay men and lead them to Christ. Love the prochoice feminists and change their minds. Unfortunately, the Right has made inroads into communities of color, working-class communities, and lesbian and gay communities. We've seen this with the rise of both gay and black conservatism. And I have seen it in my own life, where the conservative forces around me appealed to my desperate desire to fit into the dominant white straight culture. I very easily could have walked down a different road.

I'm thirty-one years old now, and I identify as a left, progressive, Pakistani lesbian. But I was not born with this identity; it has developed as part of an evolving process. When I came out almost ten years ago, I was a very different person than I am today. In fact, when I turned eighteen, I registered as a Republican and voted for George Bush. I was one of those conservative people of color.

Voting Republican felt right to me at that time in my life. I grew up in a conservative family, and conservatism was what I understood to be true. My conservatism stayed with me for a while after I came out. I didn't see myself as a political person, and that was okay. I knew in the back of my mind that being an out lesbian meant something huge, but I wasn't willing to look at the larger picture then. Being out was all I was could do.

Gradually, I began to understand the connections between my sexual identity, my ethnic identity, and my class privilege. Through my lesbian identity I found a progressive movement that was nurturing, stimulating, and filled with an integrity and sense of purpose that I had not known in the conservative world of my youth. Along the way I had the good fortune of meeting progressive people who affected me deeply. One such person is my friend, Victor D'Lugin, who died in 1996.

I remember telling Victor that I considered myself radical because I had come out as a lesbian, going against everything my family had hoped for me. But, I confided, I still felt that my family upbringing had stayed with me in many ways, especially the way that I viewed relationships. I told him that even though I was an out lesbian, I still wanted all the conventional things I was brought up with—a monogamous relationship, kids, a house, a white-picket fence, the American Dream. Victor listened to me, and even though he was a deeply committed sex radical, a communist, a fag, he tried to understand me. He listened to me and didn't write me off for having these traditional ideas. He was patient and kind while he challenged my thinking by suggesting that I might feel differently one day. And now I do.

I believe that I have a responsibility to similarly listen to other people in my life. My main challenge lately is to articulate my beliefs, my values, and my commitment in language that is accessible. I'm interested in reaching people around me who may not necessarily be political, or even interested in the kind of work that I do. They may not have given the welfare system a second thought, for example, because they have never had to encounter it in their lives. Some of my friends don't understand why affirmative action is worth fighting for. Or why it's not okay to call an immigrant an illegal alien.

How do I explain it in language that doesn't sound like a lot of rhetoric? This is an ongoing process, one I am still trying to figure out. But I take great strength from Victor. Like him, I try to understand that people are at different places on the political spectrum. It's not okay for me to dismiss them or be judgmental because I disagree with them. It's my challenge to appeal to their sense of fairness and justice. I find that when I frame things within a human rights paradigm, I can appeal to people's commitment to fairness for all people. It helps me to personalize my work and remind those around me how it is that I became involved in actively working to make this world a better place.

I am hopeful that we, as progressives, can continue to build relationships, not only with each other but with people who, like me, may be taken in by the dominant rhetoric that claims to know what is good and what is bad; a rhetoric that seeks to oppress those of us who don't fit into the rigid definitions of conservatism; a rhetoric of punitive intolerance cloaked in a language of love and compassion; a rhetoric that minimizes our different ethnic experiences and identities. By continuing to reach out to people in a respectful and meaningful way, perhaps we can appeal to the integrity and dignity inherent in all of us and work together for a world in which justice and democracy prevails.

I'm not interested in fitting in anymore. But the sad thing is that after years of trying, I mostly do. The prep school training, the fancy neighborhoods, and being constantly surrounded by white privilege has shaped my existence. Challenging the assumptions I grew up with is a lifelong task. And no easy one at that. Undoing a self-constructed identity takes years of self-reflection and self-criticism. And throughtout all of this, my life's work to oppose the narrow dominant vision remains informed by all of my identities—Pakistani, American, leftist, dyke, feminist.

Surina Khan *is an associate analyst at Political Research Associates, a progressive think tank that monitors and researches the right wing. Her writing has appeared in a number of lgbt periodicals. She is a former member of the board of directors of the OUT Fund for Lesbian and Gay Liberation, a project of the Funding Exchange.*

John Groo

While

each of the essays in this book is, in its own way, an attempt to visualize the many meanings of "lesbian," Deke Law's particular contribution takes us back to the seventies, where, s/he explains, the conflict between lesbian-feminism and masculine, bisexual, or transwomen was already present. Deke then fast-forwards us to the present-day struggles around gender expression, gender identity, and who decides who "gets to be" a lesbian. Through the example of hir own life, Deke shows how it is possible to grow in the context of a political or personally challenging issue, and more importantly, why we need to. Women are good, men are bad, *s/he argues, was an understandable but ill-conceived lesbian-feminist construction that helped to create the parallel tracks upon which our community travels today. Not unlike the dominant culture, lesbian-feminism has remained entrenched in a rigid system of fixed sexual polarities. And this, says Deke, will not lead to revolution.*

Evolution
Deke Law

To a drag queen and an old stone butch

I remember sitting in the car on my way to the Red Bull, a gay bar on
St. Louis' east side. I was nineteen. I don't remember who was driving
or whose idea it was to sneak me in. I do remember being indignant
that I was going to see drag queens. "How dare they presume to be women?"
I said in my early feminist righteousness. "Who do they think they are?"
I got into the bar. I think I even got a drink and I watched in wonder as
the first queen came onto the stage. She was white, with long red hair,
dressed in a green gown and wearing stiletto heels. She was beautiful.
And as she danced and sang on the stage to a sad, my-man-done-me-
wrong kind of tune, I got turned on and fell in love.

I am a forty-seven-year-old queer, transgender butch. I was born in
1951 to working-class parents, their first child, my mother's second. Before
I was three, my mother revealed to me that I was supposed to have been
a boy; that the doctor told her my heartbeat was strong, like a boy's;
and that she and my father had originally named me Danny. I have spent
most of my life in some sort of reaction to or relationship with that information.

I am not certain my folks know what a gift my mother gave me with
her set of declarations. I was a tomboy, playing baseball and football,
trying to kiss my elbow. I had been told the folk belief that if I could kiss
my elbow, I would be able to change into a boy, the boy I really was. I
had my name—Danny, my games, and my buddies. I watched other
boys and men all the time for tips on how to dress and act. I knew if
only I could become the boy I should have been, everything would be
all right. Of course, the rest of life kept getting in the way. I had to wear
dresses/skirts to school, my period started when I was eleven years old,
and I couldn't play organized sports as a girl because I wasn't allowed
in the boys' leagues.

A few years after my first drag show, in 1972, I was living in California, working to develop the Feminist Women's Health Centers and doing
self-help clinic presentations. I liked doing this work. It was good organizing, bringing all kinds of women together to talk about their health-

care experiences. We used a popular education format which assumed that the answers were in the room. This was still a time when Western medicine viewed women with health concerns as hysterical. One day, at a halfway house self-help presentation in Orange County, an old butch came to the session but did not participate. She said she did not have a "hole down there." I was stumped, not because I didn't understand what this butch was saying but because I didn't know how to deal with it. The fundamental philosophy of the self-help clinic assumed that any woman would want to look at her vagina if she had speculum, a light and a mirror. This stone butch, who, I recognized in my bones, rejected the speculum, the light, and the vagina as irrelevant.

I was torn between my commitment to the self-help clinic and my intense connection to this butch. I continued with the presentation, but s/he haunted me for twenty years because I felt I let hir (and myself) down. S/he was a connection to something I knew about myself. If I had meet hir at the bar, it would have been different. We would have had a drink and talked about sports or pretty women. We would-n't have even pretended we could talk about our bodies and our most intimate struggles with them.

Over twenty-five years later, in 1998, I was at a weekend event for women to revitalize and re-energize. I was feeling neither revitalzed nor re-energized. I wasn't feeling like a woman, either. The planners of the event had instituted a "no penis" policy. This prevented some members of and volunteers within the sponsoring organization from attending, specifically male-to-female transsexuals who had not been able or had chosen not to have genital surgery. It did not matter that they lived as, worked as, and identified as lesbians. As women. A friend of mine who could not yet afford surgery said to me, "It put a fourteen thousand dollar surcharge on my attending." (Unfortunately, a policy such as this is not unique to this event. Perhaps the best known exam-ple is the woman-born-woman policy at the Michigan Women's Music Festival.) Since this event had a "no penis" policy and not a "woman-born-woman" policy, I thought there was room for conversation. I dis-agreed with the policy and joined with others in asking the organizers to reconsider it.

One of those in the inner circle came up to me. She was close to my age, a bit older if anything, and said something to the effect that she didn't know who I thought I was but she did not want to see a penis; that she wanted only lesbians there; that her generation worked for space like this; that if *they* want space, *they* can work for it themselves. I responded that *they* were women/lesbians who were being kept out and that there were self-identified heterosexual and bisexual women in attendance. She said she knew this, and it was also a problem for her. I wanted to say, "I don't know a transwoman who would want to display her penis. I don't know a transwoman who doesn't feel greater distress about her penis than any lesbian separatist I know." But I held my tongue because that was not really the point. I didn't want any one's distress about his or her body to have to be the point. I agreed to disagree with her, but she continued to talk at me for another five minutes: she did not feel safe; she did not feel respected; she was very concerned about the women who were doing healing work around sexual abuse. "How would they respond to a penis, or to someone they thought was a man?" she asked.

I thought my generation had fought for and was still fighting for an end to sexist oppression and for the right of every woman to control her own body. While I'm not trying to say that in the early seventies I understood that work to include transsexuals (I didn't know of transsexuality) or drag queens, it has increasingly made sense to me that it should. My own life tells me I am much more complex than my genitals may indicate. I have been verbally abused, had rocks and bottles thrown at me, and have been in physical fights with people who disapproved of the complex expression of my gender and sex—all of which is sexist oppression.

From my point of view there is no reason to prevent any transsexual lesbian from attending a women's retreat. No, these women are comrades and allies. It is both irresponsible and disingenuous to use the red herring of women needing healing in order to keep other women from attending a women's weekend that was advertised as such. It is both irresponsible and disingenuous to talk about safe space as if translesbians make space unsafe. Who is in danger? This, too, is an expression of sexism.

Perhaps Bernice Johnson Reagon said it best in her essay "Coalition Politics: Turning the Century," based on a presentation she made at the West Coast Women's Music Festival in 1981:

> …We have pretty much come to the end of a time when
> you can have a space that is "yours truly"—just for the
> people you want to be there. Even when we have our
> "women-only" festivals, there is no such thing. The fault
> is not necessarily with the organizers of the gathering.
> To a large extent it's because we have just finished with
> that kind of isolating. There is no hiding place. There is
> nowhere you can go and only be with people who are like
> you. It's over. Give it up.*

"The" lesbian community has always been defined by those who have access to language, resources, and a sense of self. Yet there is no single lesbian community nor only one way of defining what/who a lesbian is. Because of the convolutions of my own life, and because of my social justice work, it is not surprising for me to be in the middle of the struggle over lesbian identity: who gets to decide who is a lesbian, who is a woman, and who is part of lesbian community. It doesn't really matter if the world is increasingly complex, or if, instead, more communities are developing the language to better understand and communicate the complexities of their/our lives. What does matter is that we become aware of having a rich and varied community to organize within and support.

If activists are doing what we have set out to do, if we are working to change the world and are being effective, the world around us begins to look/be different. Then our work changes. Then the world changes. Then our work changes. If a piece of what we labored for in the seventies was the right to love whom we choose, to be whom we choose, to challenge conventional wisdom and dogma about how a woman could look, act, and feel, doesn't it make sense that our success would mean the world would look different now? No one could control who would be affected by the message or how the changes would manifest. We are, in fact, experiencing some of the exciting and challenging results of being taken seriously. And shouldn't that be cause for celebration?

I struggle for a just and equitable world. Sexual liberation is part of that struggle. For me, this is about the right to be sexual, the concur-

Home Girls: A Black Feminist Anthology, ed. Barbara Smith (New York: Kitchen Table: Women of Color Press, 1983), p. 357.

rent right to not be sexual, and the right to be public about my sexuality. Sex and sexuality are central to our existence, to our spirit and our soul. I am talking here about love, compassion, connection, intimacy, sex.

Sex has been used to intimidate and control women. As a result, the goals of sexual liberation and of women's liberation haven't always been the same. This is one of the reasons lesbian-feminism derailed in its journey to social justice. The early construction of lesbian-feminism in the seventies was based on several assumptions, one of which was that women are good and men are bad. Another was that if you had a penis, you were a man, and that having a penis brought all kinds of privileges. These were certainly not crazy assumptions; there is much in the experiences of women in this culture lending these views credibility.

But just as we used to do in those self-help clinics, we have to question our assumptions with every new piece of information we are given. We used to say that if you have a uterus, you will want to do a self-exam. When a woman meekly raised her hand and said that she had had a hysterectomy, we were forced to change what we said and thought. After a few more corrections by women attending presentations, we began to understand that we could make no assumptions, no grand statements. We realized we were doing so daily, informed by our class, race, religion, sexual identity, etc. So we learned to listen to what women were saying to us and to continuously revise our work. We had the basic philosophy of each woman controlling her own body by knowing her own body; of receiving good healthcare by advocating for change in the company of others; of caring for each other in sickness and in health. To live up to that philosophy, we had to be ready to incorporate every woman's reality.

Lesbian-feminism challenged compulsory heterosexuality as an undeniable truth. In much the same way, the thinking around transgender and transsexual liberation challenges some of the underpinnings of dominant lesbian-feminist thought. The very understanding of the relationship of the body to privilege gets called into question and our grounding in gender is discarded. *Women are good and men are bad,* which underlies a "no penis" policy, is built on the assumption of a rigid binary system where everyone's experiences and identities are fixed by biology. We know this is not true. Where does the well-credentialed lesbian who transitions to a man fit into this? How does a male-to-female transsexual who has been abused and assaulted because she was too effeminate as a boy fit into this? What does this mean to the intersexed adult who was hormonally and surgically transformed into a girl because at birth his penis was not thought large enough by the surgeons? Acknowleding the complexities forces us to challenge the basic tenets of our belief systems.

It is not good political thinking to confuse men with patriarchy, male energy with male privilege, transsexual women with a predetermined biological destiny. I could say *Women are good and men are bad* years ago and believe it. Over time, I had to qualify the statement as I was confronted around race and developed a better understanding of class. Today, I can no longer say it. I used to justify the behavior of any woman until, in 1973, my father married a woman who stole all of my dead mother's things. I won't use faulty analysis to justify bad behavior any more. I find it helpful to borrow from the early work around HIV and AIDS, just as those activists borrowed from the work of women's health activists: *It is not who you are but what you do that matters.* To live by that tenet requires a different kind of relationship building and a generosity of spirit. Many of the standard markers we have long been told are true, such as the view that a person's appearance can reveal his or her sex, no longer serve us. While questioning familiar assumptions is often disorienting and uncomfortable, it can also be incredibly liberating.

I understand what male privilege is. I see it around me all of the time. I even experience a bit of it, both as an aging butch and when I pass: men do not display a sense of sexual entitlement around me. I do not feel past my prime at forty-seven, while many of the femmes in my life worry about being "old" in their forties. At a distance, I am safer on the streets. The privilege is transitory. I cannot hold onto it since it is both attracted and repelled by my transgression. As a result, I know that the experience of having a penis when one is not male, as is the case with pre- or nonoperative transsexual women, does not automatically confer male privilege. It most certainly does not confer privilege when a transwoman is living as the woman she is. The argument that all male-to-female transsexuals have male privilege before and after transitioning is still used to prevent transwomen from working for their liberation within the lesbian community.

What is the essence of masculinity? What is male energy? Is it real? How culturally specific is it? How do race and class effect it? What makes either or both a negative? Whose purpose does it serve to demonize masculinity and male energy instead of working to dismantle patriarchy? Why is bad behavior viewed by lesbian-feminism as male? I have had people say to me that male-to-female transsexuals take up too much space. I really do not understand what they are saying. I actually do not know what "too much space" is. If we have not learned how to deal with people who may take up too much space, then we need to develop the skills to do so rather than negatively labeling a group of people. We will have a very difficult time working with other communities for libera-tion if we do not come to grips with male energy, masculinity, complexity, and difference.

I have something I call male energy. I have only named it as such, claimed it as such, in the last five years. The truth is that I am happy to have it because I would feel very lost and spiritless without it. I have been attracted to the cultural expression of masculinity for as long as I can remember, and even before that, given the stories told in my fam-ily. It is, in part, an expression of sexual energy and, in part, an expres-sion of the boy, the guy in me. I did not have the expectation put on me at birth that I would fulfill some working-class white boy destiny. Yet my upbringing, painful though it was at times, has provided me some insight to the workings of a world that are not uniquely *woman* or *man* as either has been constructed in this culture.

The misunderstanding of male energy and male privilege has hin-dered the involvement of butches, bisexual women, drag kings, work-ing-class dykes, transwomen, masculine women, and he/shes in a broad movement for sexual liberation and social change—to the detriment of the movement. This work is hard and we need everybody who is will-ing to struggle. We shouldn't run the movement with the same criteria that we might use to plan a party.

Another assumption contributing to lesbian-feminism's misfiring is the view that bisexuality is suspect. I remember when lesbian com-munities would question the authenticity of a lesbian's credentials if she had been married, or if she came out later in life, or if she chose to spend most of her time in the company of men. The argument that hanging out with men makes one an untrustworthy comrade is still used today to discredit bisexual women, among others, and keep them outside the community. What is this fear of bisexuality? Does it seem more sexual than *gay* or *lesbian?* It does put *sexual* on the marquee and makes it harder to de-sex our movement with assimilationist claims that we are just like everyone else. It reminds us that we are struggling for sexual liberation, not just civil rights. I think that is a good thing. Bisexual women have always been a part of this struggle. We cannot fight for the right of women to love whom they choose and then dismiss some of them because of whom they sleep with. I believe our very survival depends upon dealing with the full complexities of our lives and the realities of our relationships rather than in maintaining a gate-keeping system that shuts many of us out.

I used to argue that *lesbian* was about who you did in bed, about sex and desire. I have come to understand that *lesbian* really is a political, social, and cultural construct, built around a sexual orientation. The dominant construction was developed by white women in response to sexism in the U.S. Left and in the gay men's movement, with an apparently rigid definition for membership. Whether expressed through clothes, politics, or space, there is an implicit understanding that all lesbians are alike in fundamental ways.

How can this be true? The expression of my sexual self has been and continues to be informed by my class, my gender, my politics, my location, and my relationships with other sexual beings. It is constructed, as best I can tell. This does not lend itself to a single definition. Anyway, who gets to decide?

My lesbian community includes many who choose to live their lives in very different ways. Some have sex with men. Some spend much of their time with men. Some are attracted to straight women. Some have a penis and some have a cock they may take off. Some look like men. Some look like hookers. Some are 6'5" tall with stilettos on. Some walk with a swagger and some with a swish. Some have children and some have husbands. I don't want a community or a revolution without all of them.

What I want, what I need, what I work for is to step outside of my own comfort zone, to make certain that no one of us has to leave a part of ourselves behind in the struggle for true liberation. Why do we feel that our very selves, our very identities are being challenged simply because a trans lesbian, a masculine-identified female, a young queer, an old dyke, or a bi woman becomes a part of what has been "our" comfort zone? Certainly, things that challenge us make us uncomfortable for a while and can be confusing. I do find that when I am challenged to the point of discomfort, I have the possibility of real growth if I choose to stay with the it.

It was only seven years ago that I was finally able to talk about the pain of my experience with that old stone butch at the self-help clinic some twenty years before. I talked because I was beginning to hear a language that recognized the complexity of hir life and mine. It was the early language of transgender liberation. I could use that new language because I had always known, in my heart, that it was as much about who that stone butch was as it was about how s/he was oppressed. S/he was the one of the first people to pop up in the middle of my early organizing work and remind me that I had not made the circle big enough, that I had left a part of myself at home. I never had the chance to say thanks and I love you. I say it now.

Deke Law, *until recently, was the staff organizer with the Lesbian Community Project in Portland, Oregon. Deke has worked in the antiwar movement, the women's health movement, and as a community-based AIDS activist. S/he served on the board of the OUT Fund of the Funding Exchange from 1993-97. Deke continues to work as a white, antiracist activist, identifying as queer, butch, trans, and midwestern.*

Linda Kliewer

At *seventy-four, Vera Martin has a lot of years on most of the people who will read this book. In this talk, presented at a workshop at the 1997 Creating Change conference, she distills those decades of experience into an almost deceptively simple message: deal with your racism as individuals and within your organizations, she tells white lgbt activists. You have nothing to lose and everything to gain. She's in a position to speak to this issue: she has lived long enough to have seen most of the manifestations of racism this country has to offer. I am reminded of the number of times I have heard a queer person say, "I'm not doing any organizing work anymore, I'm too burned out," or, "I'm getting too old (at thirty or forty-something) to be doing this"—leafletting, going to meetings, protesting, fill in the blank. Vera Martin takes the time to address queer activists one-third her age; she bothers to be involved in Older Lesbians Organizing for Change (OLOC) and work with them on their racism. She seems to know that she can't take the easy way out because it's not easy—it's giving in to injustice. It's a message anyone can take to heart.*

Being a Woman of Color and Surviving Racism
Vera Martin

I am Vera Martin, seventy-four years old, and I live in the state of Arizona. When I was born in Natchez, Mississippi, in 1923, I was categorized as "colored female." I was taken to Louisiana when I was one month old by a couple in their late fifties and grew up there. I was a multiracial person being reared in a state with Jim Crow laws. We had white water, white toilets, white schools, white churches, and white sidewalks. Disobey the rules and anything could happen—ANYTHING.

I saw a lynching, a fatal beating, a shooting of a black male on more than one occasion, and many other horrible abuses. White males had access to all women, black and white. And so much more. I learned to tap dance around a lot of danger involving racism. These memories are not forgettable.

At sixteen, when I left Louisiana and arrived in California, I really believed that place to be a place of freedom for equal education, employment, housing, and worship. Not so. Same behavior as the South, only unwritten laws. I experienced bigotry in every area of my life, and saw worse happening to many other people, especially males of African descent. I lived, went to school, married, raised my children, and worked in Los Angeles over a period of fifty years.

During the sixties I was very active in the civil rights movement. I really thought and hoped we had done a successful job of educating the white power structure that all people are human, bright, creative, and definitely survivors. We need, are entitled to, and want a good life, too. The polarization between the races, as I speak, is really frightening and discouraging. This is not what I dreamed of and worked for, so I'm still educating and trying to keep hope alive.

The lesbian and gay community is not exempt from such mean behavior. We write about inclusivity in our pamphlets, brochures, etc., but we are not a living example of tolerance and respect. Those of us who have been labeled "minority" and "people of color" would like to belong to and be a part of a community where racism doesn't exist, at least not so much of it. Many believe that a community of people who face discrimination because of their sexual orientation would be the last group to perpetuate racial antagonisms. That gives me pause to smile. Didn't we bring all that stuff with us from our growing up, from our heterosexual parents?

There are numerous humiliating experiences of racism that I have encountered in my journey through life. I am not a racially supersensitive person looking for danger behind every rock, and I feel I can handle myself pretty well; however, I am very much aware of what goes on around me. Being a person of color, my antennae are supertuned. I see a lot of terribly ugly and insensitive behavior much too often. For about eight years I have been a member of Old Lesbians Organizing for Change (OLOC). Following a consciousness-raising session on racism at an OLOC Steering Committee meeting a while back, a committee member suggested that the entire committee go home and "think black" until the next time we met. This exercise would let us know what racism felt like. I could hardly restrain myself. You really have to be awfully naive, ignorant, or insensitive to think of anything so ineffective and believe it would increase your awareness. If you are white, deep inside you know you are privileged and have endless access. You can sidestep the issue of being a person of color and any rejection it brings at will.

In another instance, a woman stated at a meeting that she had new neighbors who happened to be people of color and would like very much to meet them and get to know them. She just didn't know how to accomplish this. My question to her was, "Why not just say hello, good morning, or good afternoon?" Are people of color really so different, difficult, out of your experience that you need a special plan to get acquainted? *Give me a break.*

I am very much aware of how part of the problem is the result of the systematic fostering of ignorance. Our educational system teaches "American" history totally excluding the teaching of any positive facts about *any* people of color. People who are not of color were never and are not now encouraged to learn anything about people of color. So both groups are robbed of the true American history. As adults we have to get past that deprivation on our own and make the effort to learn about each other and our respective cultures.

More and more these days, we "minorities" must hear whites, "the majority," and grant them benefit of the doubt when they swear that they bear no real animus, that they are offended by discrimination, that they would welcome a level of diversity and equality in their lives that previous generations could not have imagined.

If whites, "the majority," are to join the hard work of closing the last racial gaps, they must accept that the racist past has left current social deficits. But we, "the minority," must also let them off the hook of guilt for a past they neither created nor admired except for a nasty few.

Other minorities in the U.S.—Hispanic, Asian, and Caribbean, to name a few—are increasing in numbers rapidly. It is no longer a simple black and white issue. America's racial calculus, already confounding, is becoming more complex. However, it is the black/white seam that our social tectonics grind most dangerously. I hope we are listening.

My dear sisters and brothers, I need you to know that as persons of color we have had to have the strength to fight the oppression and to survive. In my age group, we all came through the Depression when even white persons assumed they would not be able to go to college. We had to pay our way by hard work, doing maintenance, washing floors, toilets, and dishes on campus and anywhere else we could. Doing that kind of work was just understood. We did it and got the degrees, and then we got jobs as garbage collectors, janitors, and some few social workers, teachers, and postal workers. The post offices had really well-educated employees!

As a young woman looking for employment, I used every tool that I had been taught in my business courses: wear navy blue or black; make it simple; wear a hat and white gloves; appear for the interview armed with the expertise to perform the duties. Even with this positive presentation, all too often I still didn't get the job. Most times when I did, my identity was mistaken for something other than an African American. I prefer not to recall how many white persons I have trained who were rapidly promoted over me.

I can only speak to black women in this instance. One of our strengths has been that we have not absorbed so many programs and statements put out by the white male power structure. For instance, they put enormous fear out there that to lose your youth and beauty would really be terrible. Since white males set the standards and they never included us, we have been free to set our own standards and know that we will never be thought of as beautiful. How many times have you heard the expression, "She is black, BUT she is really attractive"?

Sadly, racism is as alive and well in our lgbt community as it is in the larger society. Although our community is itself a minority, it has all the same baggage as the larger society on race. Look around the room and notice how few people of color are present. Why is that? The reason is simple. In the younger generations there is not the same willingness to accept rejection, slights, and innuendoes that let us know we are not really accepted. We will be here in greater numbers when we feel more assured that we're welcome. I have serious questions about those who enhance their self-esteem by feeling they have unlimited access and privileges because of blue eyes, silky hair, and white skin. Shouldn't you want to have more to bring to the table?

People of color have many skills to offer to our common struggle. African American people, especially, have noteworthy skills in survival. The gay and lesbian community has paid great attention to our civil rights struggle and used whatever skills and strategies were suited to the needs of the community. We are happy to help: we know how to go over, under, and around many kinds of obstacles.

We must not allow our gains to be lost bit by bit by letting our guard down. We must be forever vigilant. Even with all of our efforts and as much unity as we can muster, racism will be with us for a long time.

Because misinformation about people of color functions as the justification for our continued mistreatment, it becomes socially empowered or sanctioned misinformation. It is recycled through the society as a form of conditioning that affects everyone. In this way, misinformation about people of color becomes part of everyone's *ordinary* assumptions.

The term *reverse racism* is sometimes used to characterize the mistreatment that individual whites may have experienced at the hands of individuals of color. This is inaccurate. While it is wrong any time humans harm other humans, we should not confuse the occasional mistreatment experienced by whites at the hands of people of color with the systematic and institutionalized mistreatment experienced by people of color at the hands of whites that has gone on for centuries and is ongoing to this day.

I hope some of the information I have shared here will cause you to think and reflect. Find a way to be committed to ridding our community and our total society of the dreadful disease of racism. If we really apply ourselves we can make major and meaningful changes, even during my lifetime.

Vera Martin was born in Natchez, Mississippi, in 1923 and lived most of her life in the Los Angeles area. She has been National Coordinator for Older Lesbians Organizing for Change (OLOC) since the founding of the organization and co-coordinator since 1997. She is a lifelong civil rights activist involved in numerous organizations including NAACP, Urban League, and NGLTF.

Pam

McMichael and Carla Wallace, friends and long-time activists in Louisville, Kentucky, are white women active in antiracist work. They have helped launch three organizations which are becoming models for doing queer work in the context of race, class, and gender: the Fairness Campaign, the Kentucky Fairness Alliance, and Southerners on New Ground (SONG). The Fairness Campaign is an attempt in Louisville to end antigay discrimination, particularly to get sexual orientation and gender identity added to the city's current civil rights statutes, and to do that in the context of a larger progressive vision. SONG is an alliance-building project undertaken by black and white Southern lesbians to develop models of organizing that connect race, class, gender, and sexual orientation, as well as build lasting relationships between people and their organizations. In the conversation that follows, they talk not only about what moves them to do this work, but share stories of what that work actually looks like.

Who Is the "We"?

Pam McMichael and Carla Wallace

Carla: How do the experiences of your childhood influence your political work?

Pam: Sometimes people say, "Wow, here you are from the farm, and you're doing this work." What's the surprise? That farm shaped my values: working-class parents, awareness of the have's and have not's, looking to each other to solve problems. When we had extra tobacco plants, my folks called around the county to see who wasn't done setting so they could have our extra plants. All the farmers did that. These are the values that shaped me. This experience gave me the sense that individual problems are community problems. It taught me that people are connected and interdependent. It showed me that when people work collectively, two plus two adds up to so much more than four.

Believe it or not, my church also politicized me. We had a great youth choir. The director put out a call to other youth in the county to come join us for a summer tour, and a couple of black kids came. We were First Baptist church and they were from, get this, Second Baptist church. Then the minister and deacons said we could no longer be a mixed church choir because we would be accused of proselytizing. But they didn't say that when white kids came from Sand Spring or Alton Baptist. They only got worried about proselytizing when the black kids came to sing. The church's hypocrisy politicized me.

Another politicizing factor was being a girl who wanted to do all the things boys got to do, who had no patience for the stupid reasons why I couldn't do those things. When I was in high school, our church had an annual tradition where one Sunday, young people took over all the jobs of the church. My peers chose me to be the preacher, but church leadership said, "You can't be the preacher, you're a girl." Then they couldn't find a male student to preach so they crafted a compromise. They let me preach; they just called me a devotional leader. Some boy in my class was the preacher and all he did was get up and read a scripture.

The other big thing is that Mom and Dad crossed the color line because of class. For economic survival, my parents started working in factories in addition to farming and made friends with black co-workers. It gave me an interracial experience most white farm kids in Anderson County did not have.

My mom and dad really did treat people like they wanted to be treated and taught that to my sisters and me. I could see there were many examples on a societal level of people just not being treated well.

Carla: After Fairness participated in an antiracist action, I got a note from a white gay man asking, "Why aren't you working for gay people instead of being out there on race?" I remember this happening to you. When you became involved with broader justice work, you were accused of not working for lesbians anymore.

Pam: When I started to call myself a lesbian, it was a political, spiritual, and cultural birth that completely absorbed my attention. But I eventually started to feel that my world was really white and that I was missing something by that, not just personally but politically. I was searching for more and started going to meetings of the Kentucky Alliance Against Racist and Political Repression. My first meeting I heard a black male activist say something about empowerment as a black man, and it knocked me over. I had thought lesbians owned that word. So when I started working on Nicaraguan solidarity issues, or against South African apartheid, or doing local antiracist work, I was still working for lesbians, at home and abroad, but I was no longer working for lesbians only.

Pam: Talk about how you became political. You were kind of destined to be an organizer.

Carla: I was born into a family that had much, much more than enough to meet its material needs, and then some. But I was also taught that it was not fair that a few, including us, were rich and others were poor. And this went beyond a liberal do-gooder philosophy. My childhood heroes were Rosa Luxemburg, Ho Chi Minh, and Patrice Lumumba, folks who were not out to "fix" an imperfect system, but were about creating a new one.

Pam: I'm sure I had never heard of them at that age.

Carla: In her childhood, my mother was part of the Communist-led Dutch resistance to the Nazi occupation of Holland. My father kept getting arrested at civil rights marches while I was in grade school. At seven, during the war in Vietnam, my sister and I got in trouble at school for not standing up for the flag. My mother is an internationalist and taught me that our struggle for justice cannot be limited by national borders. I grew up knowing that this system of a few exploiting the many was not necessarily the natural order or some will of God. In the eighth grade when others turned in assignments on the wines of France, London's Big Ben, and the grandeur of the Grand Canyon, I wrote about healthcare and literacy achievements in Cuba.

Pam: Not your typical childhood experience.

Carla: Sometimes my siblings and I talked about whether or not when things changed and everyone was equal, would we get to keep one pony? And who else would be living on the farm? That was not scary to me. The scary part was realizing that the world wasn't going to change all by itself, and that the people who worked to change it often got hurt. I knew that activists got imprisoned, tortured, napalmed, shot in the back, or run down in big, empty underground parking garages. I knew this not from TV murder dramas, but from my mother's work to free political prisoners in Franco's Spain, picket lines to end the war in Vietnam, and desegregation battles in Louisville.

When I was very young, my Dutch grandmother, Oma, told me about hiding people fleeing the Nazis under the floorboards in her living room. I remember feeling this chill come across me and saying, "Oma, they could have killed you!" She pulled me to her, smiled, and said, "That's just what you did." And then it seemed to me like it was the most natural thing to do, too.

Later, during Louisville's desegregation struggles and the growing movement against the war in Vietnam, bombs exploded our farm mailbox, my father got hate mail, and people stopped our peace sign-plastered car in traffic to scream threats at us. At demonstrations people heckled us and threw rotten eggs. It was very clear to me that speaking up and taking action against war and racism was not popular.

Pam: No kidding.

Carla: I wondered a lot about why people were so mean to people different from them—be they black or yellow, or poor, or from another land. I could not understand why my country was sending soldiers all the way around the world to kill people we had never met. It didn't make sense that blacks couldn't live in certain places or black kids I played with had to come to our pool because they couldn't swim anywhere else. I decided very early on that I needed to figure this out.

Discovering class analysis and the concept of maximization of profit for a few was huge for me. Suddenly there was a method to the madness of inequality. I was sixteen or seventeen and I remember thinking, Wow, they have a scheme! And where there was a method and a purpose, there was the possibility of its undoing. That was the hope.

Pam: Yes. If it's constructed, it can be dismantled.

Carla: The great challenge to our fight for justice, I was already learning, was the divisions among the targets of exploitation. My mission became how to get everyone to join together. I have been obsessed with that ever since.

Pam: We come from very different places, but we have ended up in the same place of working to bring people together across lines of difference to make change for everybody. How do you integrate that in the queer work that you do now?

Carla: A movement friend asked me the other day, "You've been doing this queer work for the past seven years. When are we going to get you back to the broader justice movement?" My answer to her was, "It is out of my commitment to the broader work that I'm doing queer organizing." The two are inseparable for me. If the barrier to equality is the way the oppressor keeps us divided, then the challenge is how to help the queer movement see itself as connected to, and an ally in, the broader justice movement. This is critical not only for queer people, but for all of us, to achieve justice.

As a white person birthed to class privilege, I know that the perspectives that challenge class and race privilege are not automatic. Those who run the show sell everyone the American Dream. Most get the illusion without the goodies. Only a very few get it all. So part of our work as queer organizers with a commitment to justice for all is to do our work for queer rights in ways that challenge racism, economic exploitation, and sexism.

Pam: Which is what Southerners on New Ground is about, too. Tell the Fairness story first.

Carla: When we started the Fairness Campaign (Louisville 1991), there was a very conscious vision and plan about tying the struggle for queer equality to struggles against racism and for workers' rights and women's equality. The work we do continues to be cradled in that foundation of an inclusive vision. If queer leadership does not have a broader vision, the definition of "we" remains narrow and sectors of our movement go to the "big money" and the politics of privilege to fund our liberation. If that's where you lay your foundation, bets are you stay there, and no one ends up winning much of anything—not the queers and not our allies. We keep forgetting that they don't really want to give any of us anything.

Take the Fairness Campaign's focus on winning antidiscrimination protection. You have those who say, "That's a reform struggle and it's not radical enough," or, "How is a legislative battle addressing race or class issues?" In Louisville, this "reform" battle is raising questions about the rights of workers to justice in the workplace, the need to build black/white relationships, and the danger of the growing power of the fanatical Right. The struggle for antidiscrimination legislation has done that here in Louisville, not because it is inherently that kind of battle, but because of the way we are consciously choosing to fight it.

For me, that is what is key about our organizing. Whether we are organizing around civil rights legislation, marriage rights, for a living wage, affordable healthcare, or against the Klan, the question is: What vision of justice guides us? What definition of "community" do we act out of? A justice vision cannot be a "just us" vision. It's noninclusive and, from my experience, bad strategy as well.

Pam: What is your validation that you've made the right choice about where you do the work?

Carla: When key antiracist struggles come up in this community, the Fairness Campaign is viewed by other groups as a natural ally in the broader organizing. Fairness sees itself as a natural ally and responds to a call for action as part of our mission, as integral to our queer work.

The early groundwork we laid establishing the interrelationship of justice struggles means we do not have an internal battle when we help organize the anti-Klan rally, or walk the picket line in a Jobs With Justice action protesting low pay and part-time work expansion. That is not to say there are not differences within the Campaign about particular issues, or our focus at a given moment, but the justice vision is codified in the Fairness mission statement and there is a commitment to that vision in the daily work.

When activists get together we usually spend much too much time arguing with one another about what issue we are organizing around. It's not what we organize around but rather what vision guides us that's important. For example, I find that many progressives shut down and tune out when it comes to electoral work. I see that as a cop-out. For me, electoral work is an organizing opportunity to bring people together across lines of difference. It's not that electing this or that candidate is going to fix the world for us. What matters to me about the electoral work is that when it is done with an inclusive, broad-based justice vision, its potential for mobilizing, training, and empowering large numbers of the disenfranchised is incredible.

My electoral classrooms were the Jesse Jackson presidential campaigns of 1984 and 1988. The relationships built in those electoral mobilizations have been the foundation of my movement relationships in Louisville ever since. Clearly, having a progressive person of color to mobilize around was key. It puts class and race issues smack in everyone's face.

When Jackson spoke at the high school gym in Hazard, Kentucky, he was the first presidential candidate to do so. But that was not the big deal. The real story was that a black man, and the movement he energized, was mobilizing thousands of eastern Kentucky people, many of them young, most of them white, and all of them poor. The unity in that Hazard gym was electrifying.

Fast-forward a decade later to the Kentucky primary elections of 1998 —that rainbow spirit is alive and well in the Fairness electoral strategy. The Fairness Campaign helped facilitate the participation of queers and our allies in the election of black and white progressive women and men to the Board of Aldermen (Louisville's city council) and continues to emerge as a reliable and powerful ally in the struggle for progressive leadership in Louisville.

Pam: Does this framework get tested?

Carla: There are those sleepless nights when a particular challenge faces us and I know that the the definition of the "we" and the broader justice vision are being tested. It happened in this primary election. In a predominantly African American ward there was an electorally viable, pro-Fairness African American man running. However, few of our Fairness leaders knew him, and he's not gay. There was an openly gay man, who is white, in the race. While the gay man was actually weak on Fairness issues, never mind race and economic issues, it was still seen as a sensitive point for some of us to argue that even if the candidates were equally supportive of queer issues, being an ally on the race issue meant endorsing the black candidate. With the Fairness endorsement for the African American candidate, a black/white, gay/straight alliance was built.

Another "who is the we" moment came when Fairness joined forces with the Justice Resource Center to protest racism and homophobia at Kentucky Fried Chicken headquarters, one of Kentucky's sacred cows. KFC management quickly produced documentation of the company's personnel policy covering sexual orientation, at the same time launching an attack on the credibility of the leader of the Justice Resource Center, a black activist minister. KFC hadn't bargained on the Fairness commitment to the antiracist piece of the protest and their divisive tactics failed. Two years later, Fairness helped to elect the lead plaintiff in the race discrimination suit against KFC, community activist Denise Bentley, to the Board of Aldermen.

Pam: It's not common for queer work to be shaped with such a broad vision.

Carla: No, and that vision translates to who feels part of the movement, who feels part of the "we." I went to a board meeting of a lesbigaytrans group in another part of the country recently, and it looked like a corporate meeting. At Fairness, we are a wonderfully motley crew.

I remember speaking at Nashville Pride a few years ago and these two lesbian factory workers approached me. They felt that because of class there was no place for them to be visible but wanted to know what else they could do. I was heartbroken that this is the message they were getting.

Pam: I hate that too, and the sad thing is that queer leaders would often agree and want to send in the "suits."

Carla: Talk about SONG.

Pam: We formed on the heels of right-wing videos, particularly *Gay Rights, Special Rights,* that pitted queers and black people against each other. We were deeply concerned about the fragmentation that happens when people are asked to choose only one of several issues that affect them, as if we could actually split and leave part(s) of ourselves at the door. Pat Hussain (SONG co-founder) puts it this way: "I am no longer willing to choose between my skin, my ovaries, my wallet, and my partner Cherry."

We felt an urgent need for the lesbigaytrans work to move beyond "me-mine" single-issue identity politics to doing queer work in a multi-issue, multicultural way. Our purpose is to help connect race, class, gender, and sexual orientation to build a more just and humane society, to integrate work against racism, sexism, and economic injustice into lesbigaytrans organizing, and to integrate work against homophobia into freedom struggles in the South. Organizing that cuts across those lines is powerful and our biggest hope for change.

We were intentional about setting SONG up with an interracial staff and board. Our policy is that people of color will always outnumber whites on the board and women will outnumber men.

Carla: How does SONG find the people with whom you work?

Pam: The face of the queer movement has too often been white, middle/upper class, urban, and male. We work to connect and project those other lesbigaytrans voices—people of color, rural/small town, poor and working class, women, Appalachians. We find people who move, or want to move, within the broader framework and focus on that. There are those who are interested in "gay" only and will tell us that. They are not our focus. But many others are realizing that lesbigaytrans oppression is one of many things not right with this world. While they want to do their work in a way that connects issues, they sometimes don't know where to start, or how. We try to help folks find those action steps.

SONG organizes an annual lesbigaytrans people of color retreat. This retreat provides a rare opportunity for southern queer people of African, Asian/Pacific Islander, Latin, Native, and Middle Eastern descent to come together to meet and share stories of survival and celebration and their work in order to bring their communities together.

On the flip side of the need for the queer movement to shift, the justice movement still has some ways to go to fully "get it" about homophobia and how that homophobia weakens their own efforts. It's not okay for progressive social change groups to drag their feet on this. We've bumped into Robert's Rules of Order being thrown around when it's time for something to do with queers. We're told we're selfish to bring queer stuff up. The biggest obstacle we run into is people who believe that supporting queers will hurt their own cause. To tell you the truth, I think leaders in organizations lag way behind their constituencies on that one.

We've heard some horror stories from queer organizers about employment discrimination: stories full of denial, being silenced, suddenly being disbelieved by people who trusted you for years. These are stories about employment in social change groups, not corporate America. *Don't ask, don't tell* is not just in the military.

Carla: How do you know SONG is fulfilling its purpose to connect people and issues?

Pam: We were surprised by the level of isolation and pain we were finding among progressive lesbigaytrans people and the knocks people felt they were taking from the queer community as well as straight groups. At a men's retreat early in the work of SONG, a black gay man from Arkansas said, "I can't tell you how much I needed to know that other gay people were thinking and talking about things in this way. For so long I have felt like I was standing in a pile of manure motioning to people to join me. Now I don't feel so alone."

I also want to answer that question with a couple of stories connected to the MountainTop Festival: Celebrating the Many Faces of Appalachian Lesbian and Gay Cultures. The festival came out of conversations at a retreat SONG facilitated with lesbigaytrans organizers and cultural workers from eastern Kentucky, east Tennessee, western North Carolina and southwest Virginia. People said, "Look I'm Appalachian and I'm gay. I don't want to leave the mountains to have a gay culture." We came up with the festival as a way to celebrate visibility right where folks live and to break down isolation. We also tied the festival to organizing. The festival itself gave people something to organize around that could spur further organizing.

Picture this. There was a woman—black, older, straight, urban, in a wheelchair—playing her accordion with a man—white, younger, radical fairy, rural, in a dress—playing his mandolin, and the only thing on their minds was who was taking the lead on "Whiskey Before Breakfast."

Also attending the MountainTop Festival was a group of southeastern Kentuckians from the Echoes of the Foothills chapter of the Kentucky Fairness Alliance (KFA) in the Richmond/Berea area. Seven members of their new chapter, six white and one Cuban Appalachian named Marta, rode to Tennessee together and participated in the festival. Later in the summer a black church about forty miles north of their community was spray-painted with racist epithets. Members of the KFA group contacted the church, bought paint, and at the invitation of the pastors, a husband and wife team, attended a Sunday morning worship service.

Early in the service there was an introduction of the delegation which included KFA members and straight allies mainly from the Inter-Faith Task Force. The service was three hours of good Pentecostal preaching and dancing and sharing, and at the end the pastor did a three-minute condemnation of homosexuality. Then he looked directly at the Cuban Appalachian woman and said, "Sister, what did you learn here today?"

She responded, "I learned we have an incredibly long way to go, and my heart is broken."

After the service she went up to the minister and said, "Here is the money we collected for your repairs on the church. We would like you to use that money to rebuild your church because hatred is wrong regardless. And we do want you to know that the money is from gays and lesbians as well as Catholics and Quakers. If you cannot accept that, then please send the money back to us so we can put it to good elsewhere."

The group left, went to a sandwich shop, and processed what had just happened. People were angry and some felt they had been naive. They were clear that being at the MountainTop Festival helped them process their experience with a broader vision, a political maturity that kept the lines of communication open and their commitment to multicultural organizing intact. Two weeks later they got a thank you for the money and the check was cashed.

That fall, Marta organized a community panel on violence and invited the woman pastor from the church to be on the panel. She agreed, and the panel also included a gay man who shared his story of being beaten. At the end of the program, the pastor said, "I don't agree with you about being gay, but I don't believe in discrimination and I don't think you should be beaten." Marta replied, "I don't agree with everything you say in your church, but I agree with your right to say it without your church being attacked."

Carla: Sometimes we want to measure how we are doing by whether our groups are integrated. We hear a lot in the queer movement about outreach.

Pam: This concept of outreach is one of my biggest concerns. Outreach means keeping your butt in the same chair where it has always been and asking people to come to you. In SONG we are trying to shift the question. Instead of outreach, instead of wondering how to get people to come to you, we encourage people to think how to change where they are, what organizations they can become involved with. Instead of asking how do we get black queers to join our group, we encourage people to ask themselves how they can do antiracist organizing.

I think it's important for white people in general and white lgbt's in particular to get involved in black-led organizations fighting racism. They at least need to turn out for antiracist actions. There's an understanding, a perspective from action, that you don't get in workshops, you don't get in trainings. You get it in the trenches. Protesting a professional golf tournament for exclusion of contracts to African Americans, for example, is the kind of action where you put your body where it counts.

Carla: Yes, being in the trenches is key. That's my problem with most study groups—they aren't tied to action. Talk about SONG's workshops.

Pam: Most frequently we get two kinds of requests: queer groups want an antiracism training and straight groups want something on homophobia and how to counter it. We also have a workshop on the economy and lesbigaytrans liberation because we are trying to make the link between a conservative social agenda and a conservative economic one. In all our trainings we connect the dots to other issues, the interlocking nature of oppressions, and bring the conversation to concrete action steps people can take in their home communities.

We try to model the "we" by having an interracial team of trainers facilitate workshops. That physical reality is critical, plus an interracial team of trainers changes the content of what gets said.

We use stories a lot in our trainings. People don't think of themselves as economists, for instance, but most people are quite knowledgeable about what's going in the economy. They know from the stories of their friends, family, and neighbors. They know about economic history by looking at the stories down their family line, what their grandparents and parents did for work and what has happened to those jobs.

Stories have the power to demystify politics. They make the concepts and systems which affect all of us real to people.

Carla: Your retreat model is interesting. Talk about that.

Pam: We bring lesbigaytrans organizers and cultural workers together for a weekend of living and eating and working. We are intentional about bringing together a mix of folks in terms of race, gender, and geography, and cover the costs of the retreats for those who need it so the "we" doesn't become just who can afford to be there.

In a retreat at Loblolly State Park in North Carolina, we got into a big discussion about language and what people wanted to be called. I guess that some of it got started from SONG, since sometimes we joke that we were launched by six women: two black, one African American, and three white; two dykes and four lesbians. People were being specific about their identities at the retreat. "I am a black gay man, period." "I am a white dyke-identified trans." "I am a Japanese bisexual disabled person." "I am an African American dyke."

Then someone said, "You know, the ship is sinking and we're sitting around talking about what we call each other." But we decided that respecting each of our identities, truly knowing each other, would plug up the hole in the boat. If we didn't know how to talk to each other as queers with multiple identities, how were we going to talk to other people and create a broader-based movement? Together we, an inclusive and expanded we, can move that boat forward.

Pam McMichael has lived in Kentucky all her life and is Co-Director of Southerners on New Ground, an alliance-building project she helped found with Mandy Carter, Joan Garner, Pat Hussain, Suzanne Pharr, and Mab Segrest. Her activism for the last fifteen years has included antiracism work, Central American solidarity, lesbigaytrans equality, and economic justice. She is a founder of the Fairness Campaign, the Kentucky Fairness Alliance, and on the board of the Kentucky Alliance Against Racist and Political Repression. She has particular interest and experience in art and social change and is a playwright and poet.

Carla Wallace grew up in Kentucky and the Netherlands and has been a community organizer for over fifteen years. As a grade schooler, she began her activism in opposition to the war in Vietnam and went on to involve herself in South Africa and El Salvador solidarity work, the battle for affordable housing, anti-Klan organizing, and, more recently, the struggle for lesbigaytrans equality. She is a founder of the Fairness Campaign in Louisville and a member of the Board of the National Gay and Lesbian Task Force. She has particular interest and experience in training activists in the trenches.

During

the halcyon late-fifties Dick-and-Jane years of my white, middle-class suburban public education, the idea that this education was both universally available and the "best" for educating citizens in a democracy was deeply instilled in me. As any advocate of social justice knows, this sad mythology has taken some even more frightening turns today: religious Right stealth candidates on public school boards, a school voucher system increasingly draining funds and good students from beleaguered public schools, a private university education prohibitively expensive, and a public one less and less available to those for whom it was intended. Underneath all of this, the student's mind itself has become a contested site. Who has access to an education? What is the value and purpose of that education? Who decides what sorts of things students, even university students, will learn? Where are radical, edgy, experimental, and iconoclastic ideas being tested today? Who stands to benefit?

In this elegant essay, Joan Nestle departs from the sexual explorations for which she is better known to pay tribute to her own university education, to the ideas and thinkers who gave her the resources to take her working-class destiny and shape it to her own ends. She peels away the mythologies surrounding a university education today to reveal that a little learning can still be a dangerous thing.

The Politics of Thinking
Joan Nestle

Ideas have been both the prison and the hope of queer people, and I have known them both. In the mid-fifties, my mother took me to a doctor because she thought something was not right with me. Perhaps it was the never-ending late-night telephone calls to Sheila, my fifteen-year-old co-worker in the five-and-dime. "Yes," said the doctor, his bookcase full of popular psychology books, "your daughter suffers from excess facial hair, definitely a sign of hormonal imbalance." I thought it was because I was Jewish. Later in the decade, after having found me in bed with a young woman, my mother ran to another doctor, this time a psychiatrist. "My daughter is a lesbian," my mother cried. "Don't say that," hushed the well-educated doctor. "That is like saying she has cancer."

For so long, we existed in their ideas about us and that translated into judgment, enforced treatments, and often terror, shame, and despair. Now, gloriously, we have been given an understanding of ourselves by ourselves. We can trace our movement through time and economic systems, through systems of power and desire, through shifting definitions and connected communities. We now have sex and discourse, and often one is as exciting as the other. Our thinkers have given us room to breathe, creating a new paradigm for questioning the "natural." With all their play and all our seriousness, the vision of our own humanity, and therefore of all, only grows wider and deeper.

I am stunned when I think of the road I have traveled in the last forty years: from pervert, policed and contained, to a queer lesbian fem woman who writes of sex and history. Decade by decade we suffered and fought our way to sense. This journey was made possible by lovers—lovers of the body and the mind. I have often thanked those who touched my breasts and spread my thighs, but now at the end of this century, I am honored by the touch of another kind of lover—the thinkers who tell me that perhaps it didn't have to be that way at all, perhaps we can understand things differently. These words, at this time of my life, are as exciting and as necessary as a kiss.

One of the greatest joys of going to college for me in the 1950s was

From *A Fragile Union* (San Francisco: Cleis Press, 1998).

the discovery that ideas did not have to wear the same gray hopelessness that so much else of my working-class childhood did. In my classes at Queens College, part of the then-free university known as the City University of New York (CUNY), I sat in worn classrooms and ate at a rich man's table.

There I was introduced to ideas that seemed in their own time large enough and complex enough to carry truth forever, and there I learned that every generation had to let go of certainty as economics changed people and people changed their society and technology changed people's lives and poets changed their dreams. Here in this cauldron of youth, politics, and ideas, I left behind my Bronx and Bayside territories of loss, and peered into the minds of other centuries to see where I could live.

I was most drawn to the intellectual drama of the Victorians, under the guidance of Dr. Viljoen, an elderly frazzled woman whose lips were blurred with shaky red and whose cigarette never stopped glowing. I read the essays of Darwin and Huxley, of Arnold and Ruskin. Here I heard for the first time the cries of anguish that signal the most dire challenge to intellectual certainty. The Bible or Darwin, the past or the future, total commitment to what we know to be truth or the despair of waiting on a moonlit beach listening to the ceaseless pull of the tides that promise nothing we can be sure of—these were dramas of the mind that moved my heart. I know a little better now why I, as a Jew from the Bronx, a young fem woman opening up to lesbian love for the first time in her life, was drawn into these mid-nineteenth century conflicts of faith and science, of the tension between grueling work and the need for daily beauty. Here was a time when power, and all the ideas that carried it, could be seen to be fallible, and in the cracks of certainty, I saw a place for myself. I also saw integrity and despair, not about money or love, but issuing from a concern about our fragility in the face of knowledge so huge we were afraid we would disappear.

Through my education, I began to understand that even though I was not of the ruling class, I could carry away ideas and make them mine. And so I did. Existentialism with its resounding right to say no, with its brave loneliness, found a home in me. Marxism, with its call to pay attention to who eats and who does not, found a home in me. The ideas of Frantz Fanon and Albert Memmi, their understanding of colonized selves, of how much is lost in the psychological turmoil of cultural displacement, became like flesh to me. I still remember that late-fifties afternoon when my Shakespeare professor drew the interlocking circles of the Great Chain of Being on the sun-drenched blackboard. I was charmed by this Elizabethan diagram of thought that suggested people, at their best, could partake of the godhead, and that animals, in the full complexity of their development, could reach for the human sphere. Forty years later these ideas still live in me, a gift given to me by teachers who could have no clue about what I would do with them in my life, a gift of ideas that allowed me to be an autonomous being no matter what social role others may have planned for young women like me.

Having ideas that differed from what the country was supposed to be thinking was not a popular stance in the late 1950s. I learned soon enough that the word *subversive* stood for the policing of thinking, whether that thinking led to action or not. I saw both the power of ideas to ruin lives and their power to inspire courage of the highest kind. I listened carefully to the statements read against the banging of McCarthy's gavel as the House Un-American Activities Committee made victims out of defiant thinkers. "You will be held in contempt, sir," a committee man would say, as people like Paul Robeson struggled to explain their beliefs.

I was no longer a formal student by the time the black and women's studies movements poured their passions into the intellectual insurrections of the 1960s. But I was a teacher of students who needed these ideas, and I, too, was changed by them. Soon it became clear to me that rethinking American history the way Frederick Douglass had suggested in 1845, from the bottom up, was essential not just for those who lived the history of marginality but for all world thinkers. How could we have ever turned away from the ideas that lead us to listen to those who create the wealth of nations? How could we ever have pretended that entrenched gender and racial power does not shape nations? We did for hundreds of years, until people rose up with their thinking and, unfazed by scorn and trivialization, changed once again the mix of ideas, changed once again the nature of hope.

Now I am fifty-eight years old and I have retired from teaching, but because of my wonderful, international world of smart women friends, and my work with the Lesbian Herstory Archives, I stand once again engaged with ideas, and my blood runs as hot. Now I sit with comrades and read Michel Foucault and Judith Butler, just as I read T.S. Eliot and James Joyce in Queens College so many years ago. Now as then—when I struggled to learn Eliot's world of high Protestant symbolism, translating some of his images into the walking dead of my mother's garment industry world, and just as I traveled with Stephen through a Catholic boyhood, until I found the moans of Molly in the closing pages of *Ulysses*— I experience the generosity of ideas, how they make me a citizen of the world.

And now I add the hope of postmodern thinking to my intellectual geology. What follows is my eclectic understanding of what is important in this current offer of ideas. I have not sat in a classroom speaking postmodernism; I have not read the French poststructuralist thinkers, male or female, and I do not have a job dependent on how well I manipulate the markers of its language in my latest book or article. But I have read *Queer Theory: An Introduction* by Annamarie Jagose (NYU Press), and to her I owe the outline of my thinking.

First there is the question of subjectivity—the process of becoming a self which is always re-forming in response to the forces of the world around it. Yes, I know this. To be working class is to experience the need to re-create one's self almost continuously if one wants to move about in the world of places and ideas, so the concept of "contested sites," or the idea of a mythical self that we use as if it is real, is old hat in some ways. But I also know when to give respect to speakers who need to be all themselves in one self, those whose struggle to live is too severe to be undercut by theories of the nonexistent subject. Then there is the deconstruction of what have passed for centuries as theories of knowledge, of philosophical regimes, of forced totalities, the myths of cohesion, the faith in foundationalism. I find nothing hopeless in this worldview of continuous disunities, in this belief that identities are created over and over again under the pressure of shifting social, historical, and linguistic terrain, in this questioning of the efficacy of one story for all. The commitment to engagement now exists not under a banner of absolutes—perhaps it exists under no banner at all (except when conservative forces say we cannot carry one)—but in the name of the complexity of the human experience.

I find no nihilism here or a cynical disavowal of the preciousness of human life. In my postmodern soul, I see a chance for a multiplicity of heard histories. I see the hope of power revealed and beauties created every day. My Marxism, my understanding that people must have enough to eat and a place to live and cures for their physical suffering and roses for the soaring of their dreams, becomes a more inclusive demand when it is coupled with the understandings of postmodern humility.

I do find some other problems, however, with the present debates over this new presentation of very old certainties.

Postmodern thinking, with its richness of shifting perspectives, must never be just the plaything of academics; political struggle, in the face of economic injustice and social exclusion, must never be dismissed as meaningless behavior. All economic classes of students must have access to both the play and the power of these ideas. Two public events that I recently attended made me realize that there is a growing politics of thinking in the country, a politics and an economics of who will have the ability to explore unsettling ideas, new world images, the way I did as that unsophisticated student so many years ago.

The first site of disturbance was at a publicly funded college in New Paltz, New York, in November 1997. When women gathered to discuss sex in a conference sponsored by the Women's Studies Department, conservative forces called for the dismissal of the college's president and for the protection of "children" from such disturbing ideas. "It is an outrage that public money is used to fund such gatherings," said the governor of New York. SUNY/New Paltz, is home to a predominantly working- and lower-middle-class community of students. Representatives of the governor's office and members of the board of trustees met for long hours behind closed doors to determine what these students had a right to hear.

Two months later, I attended a discussion at Columbia University entitled "Intolerance and Sexuality." I expected a lively debate. Set in one of Columbia's on-campus theaters, the discussion was quiet and unfocused. The audience of mostly older people filed in quietly; the novelist Mary Gordon introduced the speakers after they entered, one behind the other, and sat themselves down in a theatrically relaxed way. "I don't know why I am here," said one author, a gay man. "I haven't found anything to complain about." Except for the older straight literary figure who wanted to bring back the concept of sin, which would include abortion, promiscuity, and sodomy, no one in the semicircle felt they had anything pressing to say about the topic. And then the gay author remembered that Maine had that very day voted to repeal its gay rights protection bill, but this did not arouse him or the others out of their lethargy. Boredom predominated, and each speaker was greeted with polite applause from the audience.

All this decorum broke apart when it was time for questions from the audience. One woman, a visitor to the campus who had been to the SUNY conference, spoke in anger. "How can you all sit there in the comfort of this well-appointed space and act as if speaking about sexuality on a college campus is just the norm?" She informed them about what had happened at New Paltz, an event that had made all the city's newspapers, and students' voices rang out through the theater. "They tried to fire the president," one shouted. "The students organized and petitioned for their right to hear discussions about all kinds of sexual communities—why don't you address this?" another demanded. The few students in the audience began to walk out.

Then Mary Gordon came to life. "Yes, my husband teaches at New Paltz and he says the campus is still traumatized by what happened." She spoke, half-turned in her chair, finally looking at the audience, like a person slowly waking up. But the evening was over. I left, bewildered like the others at the contrast between these two events.

Now I know what I was seeing: the politics of thinking. Privately funded schools can put on all the "literary" events they want; the accusation of the misuse of taxpayers' money is not going to be used like a club to stamp out discussions there. It is working-class schools that are going to be "protected" from the new ideas, the very ideas that these students need the most, the ideas for which I hope they will create a language not bogged down in impenetrable self-conscious prose. Postmodern discussion can be all the rage at Harvard and Yale, Brown and Duke, but at public colleges, conservative forces are using the same techniques that have won them control of community school boards to police the campuses of higher learning.

When we add to this agenda the assault on affirmative action, the campaign to keep remedial help from working-class students in four-year public colleges, and the general downsizing of quality public college education, the picture becomes even clearer. Give postmodernism back to the young people: they have already found a suitable language to discuss it in—body piercing, music, performance, genderbending, their visions of the future.

But we who have been part of history longer have work to do to honor their explorations. In the newspaper on the day I was drafting this essay, an article appeared about a leader of a Christian family values organization who is leaving his not-for-profit organization to put his efforts into "jump-starting" a religious Right third party whose agenda will be the elimination of abortion, homosexuality, and promiscuity. Fundamentalism has made queer people the enemy once again. While we delight in discussions of the performance of sex and gender, philosophers like John M. Finnis use the ancient decree of natural law and gay people's exclusion from it to carry us back into a time when we were Satan's spawn.

Here is a fragile union of crucial importance whose challenge is to keep alive the generous textual insights of Eve Sedgwick; the dialectical and humane understandings of John D'Emilio, Liz Kennedy, and Jonathan Katz; to take pleasure in the clarity and power of Gayle Rubin as she dissects this society's (including our own) fear of sexual minorities; to keep dancing on the edge of definitions and questioned reality with Judith Butler; to learn from the hot and wise narratives of Pat Califia while we struggle to stop the advance of an iron-bound war machine with a fixed morality and a growing political army that has made us the people chosen for annihilation. Playing my part in this struggle to keep the intellectual roads open is the best way I know to honor that young woman who worked as a sales clerk by night and traveled through the world's thoughts by day.

Joan Nestle co-founded the Lesbian Herstory Archives in 1973. She is the author of two collections of writings: A Restricted Country (Firebrand) and A Fragile Union (Cleis), and co-editor of three volumes of lesbian fiction. The most recent, a collection of international lesbian fiction co-edited with Naomi Holoch, was released earlier this year. Her own life has shown her that grassroots social change, when it is rooted in a marginalized community's reality, can change the course of history.

Kathryn Kirk

As

first-wave gay liberation activists age into their forties, fifties, and sixties, our liberation movement faces challenges of continuity and leadership. Even focus. Who are in positions of leadership in our organizations? How are they defining the agenda? Who is being left behind? Rather than speak as an elder about ageism as it increasingly affects her peers, Suzanne Pharr takes a look at the responsibility of older activists to examine their own ageism with respect to youth. How do we hold our movement back with the language we use? How is the youth agenda different from the dominant queer agenda? In what ways do they intersect? Does age automatically confer power? Should older activists necessarily be role models for younger activists? When should we be talking about leadership development and when should older leaders simply step aside? How does the homophobic stereotype that older queers prey on young people hinder our organizing efforts? From her position of relative seniority, Suzanne Pharr discusses some of the unique ways these challenges, most common to any movement, play out in the lgbt movement.

Thoughts on Youth
Suzanne Pharr

I have always had a lot of empathy for teenagers, especially queer and questioning youth. Maybe it is because I remember my own youth so well. My teenage years were in the 1950s, when I played basketball with utter devotion, identified with James Dean in *Rebel Without a Cause*, drove fast cars, went to church too many times each week, worked in the fields of our Georgia dirt farm, was sexual with both girls and boys, slouched rebelliously through school, read library books at home by the dozens, and did not even know the words *homosexual, queer, lesbian,* or *dyke.*

I had survived childhood battles with my family who tried desperately to tame me and somehow make me into a gender-appropriate girl—with a ticket to acceptance and conformity. I, however, was the butch kid who wanted most of all to have a horse and a holster, to wear the neighbor boy's hand-me-down clothes, to communicate with animals, and to travel. By the time I was a teenager with raging sexuality, I was in love with basketball, danger, a boy *and* a girl. I was a leader of sorts and was constantly organizing gangs of youth to commit acts of rebellion. I was as ignorant as sin about many things and had more courage than good sense. My survival came from a combination of luck, happenstance, and the miracle that my huge family and small community somehow did not cast me out.

Surviving bad schools and my own often bad behavior, I was then saved by living in a time when young people were offered great opportunity: low-cost education with loans and scholarships available, the new Peace Corps, unionized jobs, a stable economy with rising salaries, and a great wave of social change led by young people.

As I face the millennium and my seventh decade (that is, my sixties), I find myself increasingly concerned for young people. While I feel privileged to have lived through and participated in some of the major movements of this country (civil rights, anti-Vietnam War, women's, queer), and to have been taken seriously at each stage of my life and work, I see young people today as lacking both the context of a movement and respect from society. And when I look at our social change organizations, for the most part I see people with graying hair, particularly those in leadership roles.

Why is it that we in the progressive queer community (and progressives in general)—we who have been so capable in our analysis of the oppression of queers, women, people of color, and, sometimes, poor people—have been so slow in developing a power analysis of youth (people thirteen to twenty-one) in this culture? And in acknowledging them as an oppressed group?

This country's major progressive movements have been fueled by youth and direct action. One need look no further than the civil rights movement and the thousands of young people who took part in sit-ins, boycotts, and were at the front of the police barricades. The same is true for the antiwar movement. Young people and adults worked both in separate, autonomous organizations and side by side. Yet, in today's graying queer movement, young people are in large part unacknowledged, disrespected, and locked out of leadership roles. We not only mirror society's contradictory attitudes toward young people, but we are also limited by our fear of association with them. We are held in terror that words such as *predator, recruiter, abuser* will be aimed at us simply for associating. Our hope for a major movement is hamstrung by our attitudes and held hostage by our fear.

Contradictory Attitudes

First, let's take a look at society's contradictory attitudes toward youth. There is now a greater separation between youth and adults than has occurred over the past twenty years or so. Youth are considered a separate group—either to be protected and mentored to insure the future, or vilified and criminalized as enemies of society today.

Here are some examples of the contradictions:

1. Americans romanticize the young. Youth is considered the time of innocence, of simplicity, of good bodies and easy fun. As baby boomers grow older, many long to be associated with youth, to be young themselves.

2. Romanticizing youth and longing to be young supports a commodified youth culture. The idea of innocence, good bodies, and rebelliousness is used to sell goods, targeted both to youth and to older people. Though char-

acterized as innocent, youth are constantly eroticized and
sexualized by consumerism.

    3. While extolling the innocence of youth that needs
protection, our society has taken away the services and
entitlements that support families. The majority of people on welfare are children and youth. Physical and sexual violence against young people within families of all
classes are rampant. An observer could easily assume that
our culture hates the young.

    4. Youth are also seen as predators, members of gangs,
mass murderers, thieves, out of control—as enemies of
society who should be restrained, controlled, tried as adults
in criminal courts, and locked up.

Though there has always been adult control of the lives of youth and
along with it, oppression, there is now a dramatic change in the attitudes of adults toward young people. This change centers around the
idea of young people as sexualized marketing targets and simultaneously—for poor youth especially—as violent predators who are expendable. Youth are now faced with prejudice against them as a group.

Youth Oppression

If one defines oppression (such as racism or sexism) as institutional
power plus prejudice, one would have to argue that today, youth are
oppressed. They have no institutional power, and prejudice against them
as a group permeates the culture. If one looks at the common elements
of oppression, they all apply to the treatment of youth: they lack social
and economic equality; they are stereotyped, demonized, and dehumanized; they experience isolation and tokenization, self-blame, societal
blame, and internalized oppression; and their sense of powerlessness
leads to horizontal hostility, as evidenced by youth killing other youth.
Overall, they are controlled by violence (often from birth onward) and
by lack of economic access and independence.

In a power analysis, we usually examine the idea of "power over,"
looking at how one group of people has power over another and attempts
to control them. Adults maintain consistent power over youth, limiting their access to money, mobility, association, information, and the
uses of their bodies for sexual pleasure or medical treatment or repro-

ductive choice. Information in the classroom, on the Internet, or in libraries is restricted, and youth are left to gain from hearsay some of the most important information they need. And, as we all know, people without power seek power and survival where they can. The one place where youth can seek personal power is through sexual expression, whether or not condoned by adults, safe, positive, or destructive. It is not surprising that youth sometimes find themselves in sexual trouble, e.g., unwanted pregnancies, STDs, since they are not allowed access to the complete information they need.

Youth and Progressive Organizations

How does all this translate into the work of progressive organizations? While many people would assert a belief in children's rights, our incorporating youth into programmatic work either as employees or board members rarely happens. While we would stand strong on a belief that we should not be violent toward youth and that they should have access to good schools and healthcare, we generally do not see them as part of the immediate social change we are trying to bring about. If there are youth programs, they are service provision, educational, or recreational, and in most cases, led by people over twenty-one years old. Youth are generally not in positions of institutional leadership.

Our attitudes and politics tend to fall into two positions:

> 1. Youth are our future. From this position, we believe that they must be protected, mentored, taught, and "brought along" to take our places someday. It probably comes as no surprise that youth find this point of view patronizing. For the most part, they are left out of leadership opportunities. Sometimes adults say, "We can't hire you because you haven't paid your dues yet." It's a version of the old, *You can't get a job until you have experience/you can't get experience until you get a job.* As adult activists, we have to ask ourselves: In what currency are these dues? To whom does one pay them? Who assesses their value and hands over a card saying they have finally been paid?
>
> 2. Youth are the present. From this position, we believe that they are leaders today, that what they have to con-

tribute is important to the work we do this moment for people of all ages, not just youth. It requires that organizations find ways to hire youth and place them on boards in groups of two or more (i.e., not tokenized) with power and authority to act on behalf of the organization. And it requires that we do not offer leadership only to the culture's most accepted youth: white or college educated or middle class. Believing and acting upon the idea that youth are the present requires struggle and change and growth.

I believe the only truly progressive position is the second. However, I do think it is possible to combine elements of the two. For example, what is *mentoring* other than what we customarily call *leadership development* for other people? We all need political education, consciousness raising, and more exerience in different kinds of organizing. We should provide these opportunities to everyone, regardless of age.

Without the presence of young people in progressive organizations, our efforts for social change are always incomplete. Not only do we lose major sources of inspiration, energy, and fresh ideas for social change—just as we do when we exclude any group—but we fail to understand and respond to the lived experiences of a large segment of the population. Those experiences make up a portion of the political realities of our time. To exclude youth means that we work always with partial truths and incomplete answers.

The Queer Movement

Queers have another impediment to our work with youth that goes beyond the general societal attitudes we hold. Because right-wingers, conservatives, and homophobes cleverly link queer sexuality with the abuse of children—and because many people do not have enough knowledge of queer life to reject this argument—much of the queer response has been to avoid employment, volunteerism, or settings that require contact with children.

This core argument against the rights of queers to live peacefully in the world with equality and justice suggests we are not fit to be in decent society because we are predators and we recruit and sexually use and/ or abuse children. Of all the arguments that comprise homophobic attitudes and policies, this one is the most emotionally charged and damaging.

Because the general population tends to accept this argument to be true, and because there are some among us (as among the nonqueer population) who do have cross-generational sex, a wedge has been driven between queers and youth and children. Many queers live in terror of association with queer youth or with heterosexual youth because they are afraid they will be accused of sexual misconduct. Consequently, we are one of the few oppressed groups that is separated across all other divisions from the young, both queer and heterosexual. Not only does this keep us from being able to combat homophobia among the young who are surrounded daily by homophobic messages, or to provide by our presence examples of queer life, or to support queer youth—this separation keeps us from involving queer youth in the work of queer liberation.

To overcome this separation we have to dismantle the homophobic construction of our sexuality, both for ourselves and for nonqueer people. To do this we will have to know more about ourselves and about each other. It will require telling the truth of our experiences as youth, and with youth. But most importantly, we must listen to the stories youth tell about their experiences and what they have learned from them. Sexual stereotyping will not be stopped simply by presenting a positive stereotype to replace the negative one. For example, it is not helpful to assert that queers do not have sexual relationships with youth, when some do in the present, and when some of us have had youth/adult relationships when we were young. Instead, we will have to hear the many stories that represent the realities of our queer lives, both those from people who were harmed through their relationships with older queers and those from people who relished them as healthy ways to live sexually.

There are many points of view to be heard about adult/youth relationships, but the most critical discussions to be held are those which analyze power, its use and misuse. An analysis of power is the core of all political meaning, all political work, and our coming to understand the uses of power and developing ways that power can be justly and fairly shared is the political gift we can offer each other and the progressive movement. It is also the work that will lead us to be able to include youth fully in the struggle for queer liberation and to support the leadership they provide.

Finally...

As someone who came into my twenties during a time when many of us believed that no one over thirty could be trusted, I always thought that after I reached thirty there would be masses of younger people rising up to take my place in the leadership of whatever movement I was active in. This has not happened in my experience. I have recently begun to witness, however, what seems to be the bubbling up of a youth-driven movement. Increasingly, I have met queer youth (and particularly youth of color) who have taught me new analyses of race and gender and different ways of approaching organizing. I feel privileged to have been offered their leadership.

In general, this activity of youth has not been recognized, but I suspect that is because too many adults are either standing in the wrong place or looking in the wrong direction to be able to see it. We are out of touch with what is happening with youth, especially those who are not attached to our organizations in some way.

It seems to me that there is great possibility contained within youth leadership and this emerging movement, often underground and without resources. There is new possibility for change, not as the people of the 1960s or 1970s or even 1980s may have envisioned it, but with the vision and strategies called for today. The question for older leaders such as myself is whether to join in this new day, embracing change, or to move out of the way.

Suzanne Pharr is a longtime Southern organizer and writer on the issues of race, class, and gender. She founded the Women's Project in Arkansas in 1981. She is the author of Homophobia: A Weapon of Sexism *and* In the Time of the Right: Reflections on Liberation *(both from Chardon Press).*

A
reexamination of the causes and costs of the sex wars that so profoundly split the lesbian community is long overdue. What is at the root of this conflict? Did feminist theory create it? Can we situate "lesbian" in today's newer generation of sex radicals and vice versa? Where does "feminist" fit in? Carol Queen has an enviable ability to make even the most painfully complex issues, such as sex, seem disarmingly simple. In this essay, she deconstructs the sex wars conflict using her considerable skills as a queer/bi/pansexual cultural sexologist to shed insight into how we got ourselves into this mess in the first place, unpacking phobias one by one. As someone who says she more or less missed the sex wars, she is in an advantageous position to articulate a vision locating "lesbian" within a broad pantheon of queer passions and identities.

Lesbian/Sex: About What We Do and Desire, and Its Relation to Community and Identity (or, How I Learned to Love the Sex Wars)

Carol Queen

Before I had sex with anyone I thought about it, about what it would be like, who I would want to do it with, what "it" might consist of. Raised in a world in which heterosexuality dominates, at first I thought only about sex with boys. But that, as they say, was just a phase. I did not wonder, Does this mean I'm a heterosexual? In those not-so-distant days, heterosexuality did not "mean" anything. Except, I guess, "normal," although that was fortunately a word I never cared much about.

But before I had so much as kissed another girl, I already had begun to grapple with who I was for wanting to do so. Girl-kissing led to questions boy-kissing didn't. At least it did in the early 1970s, when this kissing began. By the time I turned seventeen I had already begun to wonder what and who I "was." Was I a bisexual? Was I a lesbian?

I did not kiss first and wonder afterward. I desired first, and to do so marked me, from the inside out. But this was in the 1970s, as I said, when a certain discourse already waited to mark me from the outside, and to ensure that as I came out, I would ask myself some very particular questions. Among them:

What did it mean that I desired women?

What did desire itself mean? What exactly did I want to do? What acts exactly did I want to perform on/with other women's bodies, theirs on and with me?

With women, what did sex consist of?

How would I find other women who wanted to do these things?

How would I know when I found these women whether any of them wanted to have sex specifically with me?

How would I signal my interest to them?

How would I learn to do the sexual things I wanted to do? Specifically, how would I learn prowess (though that was a word, then, I never heard used to describe women's sexual acts)? How in particular would I learn to please women sexually?

At seventeen, I didn't know anyone who might know the answers to these questions. One reason I set out to find the lesbian community, though, was to search for someone who did.

To me, lesbian existence, as well as the specific touches, motions, and responses that made up "lesbian sex," implied action, activity, agency, the opposite of the passivity which seemed encoded in heterosexual femininity. (I should add here that it was many years before I challenged my own assumptions about what heterosexual femininity "was.")

I am writing here about lesbian sex, although for many women, love comes first or comes to predominate. Indeed, my first desires wove in and out of fascinations, crushes, and falling in love—and mostly they still do. But women are raised to love (whether or not, as sociobiologists assert, we are also hard-wired to do it), and many women, absolutely including lesbians, problematize sex in a way they do not problematize love; define sex as existing within love; or feel cut off from other women when they want to prioritize sex and pleasure over (even sometimes within) relationship.

Lesbianism, in fact, can be (and is) defined in two separate ways: as the sexual desire and behavior of women for/with women; and as women's emotional/relational focus on women. The latter definition implies eroticism but does not specify or require it, and casts a wide enough net (think Adrienne Rich's lesbian continuum) to allow the lesbian community to adopt as fellow travelers women who do not in any way define themselves sexually as lesbians.

The very word *lesbian* may be a strategy to distance women-loving-women from the word *homosexual,* which women left behind partly to distinguish themselves from an orientation that carries the word *sex* right in the middle. Men, too, went from *homophile* to *gay* to escape the clinical sexuality of the word. One wonders if the "political lesbians" of the 1970s would ever have elected to affiliate with a movement/identity that left them with the moniker "political female homosexuals."

This brings me to a third way of understanding lesbianism, which is women's rejection of sexual and emotional partnerships with men.

Sexuality may be implicit here, too, but heterosexuality (and its renunciation) is implied more strongly than lesbian eroticism.

Why the opposition (or, at the very least, differentiation) of sexuality and relationship in these definitions? I don't want to make this sound absolutely either/or; certainly it isn't in the lives of most women. At the same time, there has been an explicit thread in cultural lesbian thought which states that sex is not the most important thing, even that an overfocus on sexuality is suspect. Then there were the "sex wars," the years of bitter argument in the women's community about what constitutes appropriate sexual expression for women, especially lesbians. (More about this below.)

Ours is still a homophobic, hetero-hegemonic society in which women's sexuality is presumed to be male-focused, relational, and passive. (Actually, calling this a presumption is rather naive, given the stigma any woman must face for stepping outside this paradigm, whether she's focusing erotically on other women or not. It's more like a cultural law.) In such a context any manifestation of lesbian eroticism may have enormous implications, potentially destabilizing sex-role assumptions, heterosexual identity, gendered relations of power.

This, of course, is why lesbianism was lionized in the 1970s as the logical outcome of feminist theory. But the cultural rewriting of lesbianism required an erasure of its previous definition, as a deviant sexual practice or orientation. This underlying definition destabilizes cultural lesbian feminism, the new dawn for women, and so to greater and lesser degrees the old sexualized definition of lesbianism was overtaken by the new definitions developed by the Lesbian Nation.

Let me return to the questions I posed above, questions which occupied—no, obsessed—me when I was seventeen years old (and whose aftertaste lingers in my sense of myself even now). I knew no adult lesbians who could talk to and advise me. And even as I began to meet some, most were fearful of our age difference or hesitant to talk openly about sex; plus I was too shy to ask direct questions. I didn't find Pat Califia's *Sapphistry* (Naiad), the lesbian sex manual, until I had been out for five years. What little erotica I discovered featuring lesbian sex was not contemporary and so was hard to relate to (though I thank Anais Nin anyway, and even her anonymous patron to whom she sold her erotic stories). I read voraciously, and was deeply influenced by both the ideas of post-Stonewall gay liberation and also by lesbian-feminist voices intent on defining lesbian identity. A certain amount of this writing focused on the kinds of sex and desire appropriate and, especially, not appropriate for lesbians (bisexuality, butch/femme, S/M, pornography—especially the male-produced kind—and dildos. Whether monogamy was more lesbian-feminist than nonmonogamy was up for grabs.)

That many of these sexual interests intrigued or compelled me caused me substantial guilt and grief, and by the time the sex wars really heated up in the early 1980s I felt so alienated from these personal/political issues that I had ceased (for a while) to read about them. (Reading about them, at that point, was mostly all I did anyway.)

Gayle Rubin has said that feminism serves as "a system of sexual judgment." Its overlap with lesbianism has greatly affected the lesbian community's discourse about sexuality. Specifically, feminism is a system of judgment about men's sexuality, but many practices and interests potential to women together have been coded as male-identified and hence harshly regarded. In this way it has, despite its trenchant gender-based social critique, been fixed on binary gender roles, disallowing women the space to explore traditionally male-coded, female-excluded sexual possibilities. In particular, feminist disapproval (and, I would argue, shame and homophobia) regarding butch/femme, historically a specifically lesbian system of erotic signaling and sexual partnership, cut lesbians off from their own history and erotic sources —especially working-class and of-color lesbians.

In many ways, the latter part of the 1980s and the '90s have been a time of recovery as the lesbian community grapples with sexual issues, producing its own erotic materials, rehabilitating butch/femme and dildos, struggling to accommodate gender variant women and transgendered people, and revisiting the issue of lesbian and bisexual erotic diversity.

This is not to say—at least, not in so many words—that feminism has been a negative influence within the lesbian community. Feminism has had the greatest positive influence where it has been most focused and least monolithic, where it has been in the hands of women building community and not in the mouths of theorists constructing systems of inclusion and exclusion.

(Remember that mainstream feminism itself has never been completely comfortable with lesbians in the first place. Twenty-five years ago, the "lavender menace" within NOW caused a huge stir, and the last NOW national conference I attended was actually held on Gay Pride Day, its organizers clueless that lesbians might want to be somewhere else on that date.) And from mainstream feminism's most spectacular failures to address women's diversity issues have arisen new feminisms created by feminists of color, sex-positive feminists, young feminists, etc.

For, of course, there is extraordinary diversity within lesbianism, including great sexual diversity, a fact that many early theorists of Lesbian Nation didn't completely grasp. None of the stigmatized sexualities of my own lesbian youth went away. What *is* true is that the dialogue and uproar around the sex wars made space for an entire spectrum of lesbians to stand up and be heard.

Increasingly, transsexual and transgendered women and men (including female-to-males), bisexual women and bi-dykes, butch- and femme-identified women, S/M dykes, and others on the gender spectrum can find each other and also some space within the lesbian community—if not always enough space, or easily enough won.

Besides feminist attempts to exclude them on the grounds of "male" sexuality (whatever that is in a woman), open sexuality and diverse sexualities have not always been welcome within the contemporary lesbian community—for reasons that are not uniquely lesbian and not especially feminist. They are deeply traditional and ingrained, in fact, which may be why we have spent the better part of three decades learning to recognize them. They are erotophobia, sexphobia, homophobia, and biphobia, "genderphobia," and bodyphobia.

Erotophobia is the fear and/or hatred of the erotic, and includes the pervasive fear of erotic variation. Sexphobia is related to this; it is the fear or dislike of actually having sex. Homophobia is also a subset of erotophobia and is specifically the fear and/or hatred of same-sex eroticism and coupling. Biphobia is related to homophobia; it is the fear and/or hatred of bisexuality.

"Genderphobia" is the fear and/or hatred of "gender inappropriate" expression or behavior, a rigid reliance on and belief in clearly differentiated and impermeable sex roles. This includes, of course, disapprov-

al of transsexuals and the transgendered, and may also include homophobia.

Bodyphobia is the legacy of the Christian mind-body split (and may
also result from abuse): the fear and/or hatred of the body. It includes
sexphobia and can color issues of self-esteem and self-image.

I must say directly that I am not accusing all lesbians or all feminists of these things, but I do assert that these various phobias under-
lie the theoretical and personal discomfort and opprobrium about sexuality
and sexual variation in our (as in other) communities. We share these
tendencies with our enemies in conservative Christianity and the right
wing, who also tend to be steeped (overtly) in woman-hatred. Our own
woman-hatred tends to be aimed at women who are different from ourselves and so is rarely named as such.

One aspect of sharing these phobias with others underscores and
sheds light on how erotophobia and its kin are supposed to function
socially. When feminists and lesbians reinvent old antipathies and
dress them in fancy theoretical clothing, they are still recapitulating to
female sexual socialization. Under patriarchy, women are supposed to
(and often do) fear sex, focusing on marriage, reproduction, and family. Above all, we are not supposed to pursue our own desires, especially
when those desires arrogate the erotic power of men: to say what we
want, to pursue women as lovers, to voyeurize and look, to penetrate.
We are also not supposed to revel in our own bodies, especially when
those bodies do not look "conventionally attractive": when our bodies
are middle-aged or older, dark-skinned or ethnic-featured, fat or even
simply fleshy, buzzy-haired, butch.

Because most women in America (feminist as well as not, dyke and
bi and trans as well as straight) live uneasily in their bodies by doubt-
ing either their erotic attractiveness or physical "perfection" or both,
and because sex is usually experienced through and within these bodies, it has been easier for many feminists to say, as my mother did while
gratefully aging into asexuality, "Sex just isn't as important to women."

Sex is problematic, the body an unruly site of dangerous desire if a
woman is lucky enough to grow into puberty without sexual desire and
curiosity scared out of her. When I began having sex, girls were still being
institutionalized in mental hospitals or juvenile hall for gender-inappropriate behavior. Usually, for having sex (especially with the wrong

person, like an adult male or another girl). They still are. For females, sex is gender-inappropriate.

The body may also betray as an uncooperative site of no desire, as in the example of the political lesbians who colonized lesbianism as a place to hide out from problematic relations with men, but who then proceeded to attack lesbians for the gender-inappropriate presentation and behavior that made the lesbian community an attractive place to occupy in the first place.

It was in part through the influence of these women, who did not in fact desire deep erotic connections with other women at all, that the lesbian community was introduced to the notion of "politically correct" sex. Feminists used the term essentially as the Maoists had to define appropriate conduct and to attack renegades. Erotic egalitarianism sniffed out "male-identified" behaviors: penetration, butch/femme gender identification, pornographic imagery, sexy dress, bisexual desires, S/M and dominance/submission, work in the sex industry. Anything, it seemed, that women imagined a male doing or enjoying wound up on the cutting-room floor. That women doing and enjoying these things might be looked upon as a radical shift in the cultural power dynamics of sex and gender did not compute. We were to construct a new sexuality, not reshape the old.

Why develop such a notion in the first place? To get a handle on the discussion and analysis of a fraught topic (danger was more problematic than pleasure, or so it seemed, and sexual danger equaled men and their ways); to systematize lesbian identity; to encode specifically feminist, specifically female practices within that identity; to corral an anarchic force.

Did it work? Dispatches from the front lines of the sex wars suggest not. So do the numbers of young women who will not identify as feminist specifically because they see feminism as a system of sexual judgment as surely as do Gayle Rubin and her comrade sex radicals.

I have already suggested that this rigid notion of how a lesbian ought to shape her sexuality denied the fact that many lesbians had been shaping and living their sexuality before lesbian-feminism came along. It also tended to ignore the ways class, race, culture, and generation alter and shape femaleness, gender roles, ideas of lesbianism and feminism, sexual practice, and women's safety to explore sex. As sexuality became more reified, fewer women could relate to the narrowness of possibility left them. Sexual possibility was, after all, narrow enough under patriarchy. Sex-positive feminism arose ultimately because it struck many women as more feminist to honor women's expanded erotic choices.

Sex-positivity is, at bottom, an honoring of our sexual diversity. Sex-positive feminism involves making a space within which sexual exploration (already so difficult for many women to do) can be safe, supported by other women, and respected, not criticized and attacked. It does not privilege one type of sexual choice over another, outside a clearly stated emphasis on consent; it does mandate both that and respect. In fact, it would read something like politically correct sex if the codifiers of politically correct sex hadn't spent so damn much time specifying what it wasn't okay to try or to enjoy.

Rather than fleeing the bad reputation of homosexuality, sex-positive lesbian-feminism asks which other practices have also been stigmatized and named deviant. And especially, whose interests have been served to ban, criminalize, or render despised various whole districts of sexual possibility? Often the answer is the hetero-hegemony's—and the patriarchy's. Put another way, if doing it means you're not a good girl, maybe it's worth a visit.

A thoroughgoing gender critique must also be basis for this reconsideration, especially given how many contested sexualities and gender identities have to do with defining femaleness and maleness—which, last I checked, is at the very root of sexism. How ironic that feminism and lesbian-feminism, themselves frequently subject to gender critique, have usually recapitulated impermeable genderedness (to say nothing of virulent genderphobia) to the degree that these communities have often turned a deaf ear to the plight, analysis, and strategies of the emerging gender community. The possibility that we might not be stuck in an immutable gender (and that there are far more than two of them, anyway) would seem deeply relevant to feminism, but so far the dialogue between these communities is minimal, happening mostly among some lesbians and queer-identified transpeople.

Perhaps the simplest message to be heard from this conversation is the one I want to close this essay with: that our diverse queer sexualities (and genders) are all a rebellion against compulsory heterosexuality and homophobia, and that is, as it has always been, a rebellion against the patriarchy.

Wanting to kiss girls (everywhere) does have meaning, as I instinctively knew when I was seventeen, and so does wanting to love them, lave my face in their juices, open my legs to their fingers or fists, spank their asses, get tied up by them, take their pictures naked, lasciviously stroll through the produce section with them, read dirty stories to them, ache with desire for them. It means rebellion…pleasure…change.

Carol Queen, *Ph.D., is a queer/bi/pansexual activist, widely published erotic writer, and cultural sexologist whose essays on sex and culture have appeared in many anthologies and in her own collection* Real Live Nude Girl *(Cleis). She is also the author of* Exhibitionism for the Shy *(Down There Press) and* The Leather Daddy and the Femme *(Cleis), and the co-editor of* PoMoSexuals *(Cleis),* Switch Hitters: Lesbians Write Gay Male Erotica and Gay Men Write Lesbian Erotica *(Cleis), and* Sex Spoken Here *(Down There Press). She lives in San Francisco with her partner, Robert, and two lesbian cats, and is a worker/owner at* Good Vibrations.

Layne Winklebleck

To
be an activist around any issue,
one must have an analysis of that issue. The sentence is simple, but
the task, if it is to be done well, is endlessly complex: it is nothing less
than a lifelong commitment to being honest with oneself and
humble in the presence of others. To make no assumptions. To
always ask the hard questions. No political analysis can remain static
in the face of new information, even as we strive to be consistent in
our ethic of justice. As Susan Raffo so eloquently points out in her
rich essay, in activist work, behind each success lies another challenge. In combining her personal experience of class with her elas-
tic political analysis she gives us a remarkable model for what it might
look like to accept the challenge of a lasting involvement with
social change.

Moving Between Fool and Freedom: The Ego of Activism
Susan Raffo

After the event in New York, I beamed as yet another person came up to me, shook my hand, and said, "You know so much about class in the gay and lesbian community! When are you going to do another book?" I scanned the room for my partner, wanting her to be right next to me, listening as compliment tumbled along after compliment. "Well," I replied to a young man as he handed me a copy of the book to sign, "I hadn't actually thought about writing another book but, well, I don't know, gosh. I mean, maybe I should." He rapidly shook his head and grabbed my arm, saying, "Susan, you need to. You just know SO much. And *someone* needs to be writing about this stuff. I mean our community *has* to hear these things if we're *ever* going to get anywhere."

On the subway back to Brooklyn after the evening's event, I gently replayed every comment, every encouragement, to my partner, Raquel, and friend, Carmen. Outwardly humble, internally I preened and paraded, imagining myself as a new visionary, a kind of working-class intellectual waiting to take queer politics by storm with my insight and skill. Momentarily forgetting the recent and distant past that had brought me to this point, and without any realistic forward vision, I puffed and swelled as I closed my eyes to watch political queers from coast to coast singing my praises.

I should have read this as foreshadowing. This event was a part of an organizing/book release tour after my anthology *Queerly Classed* came out. I wanted to use the publication of the book as an organizing focus, a time to both encourage discussion around the issues of class and queerness and also a time to give my thinking and analysis another push. During the five weeks of travel paid for by the gift of a grant, I went through every kind of emotion. As much as my ego touched the heavens at one point during the trip, just as far down did it descend at another. As much as I sometimes felt that I really "got" class in all of its complexities, at other times I felt like I knew nothing and had been foolish to think I put together a meaningful book.

Being an activist is not something separate from the rest of who I am. My path as an activist who has, in recent years, focused a great deal of attention on thinking about class is as much about the details of my personal life as it is about the books I have read. It is as much about pride and ignorance, growth and stubborn resistance, power and loss, as it is about committees, coalition, and licking the flaps of gluey envelopes. Being an activist is as much about working through my personal limitations as it is about working through the institutionalized limitations placed in the paths of various individuals and communities.

When I think about being an activist, and in particular about being an activist around issues of class, I think of everything that has brought me to this moment in time: Carlinhos Brown on the CD player, cold water in one of the blue glasses my partner and I bought at Target a few weeks ago, and the early darkness of winter making the light around the computer screen seem friendly and warm. As frustrating as it might sometimes feel, everything really is about everything else. My activist story is a class story, it's the story of having white privilege, it's a coming out story, it's a story about my confusions as an Italian American, and it is definitely a story about a writer who thinks too much. This essay merely takes a specific lens—the lesbian activist and issues of class—and pops it into the spectacles before I turn my gaze to the mirror.

Personal growth and front-line activism are often seen by both political and human potential folks as mutually exclusive categories. Personal growth people, I told myself in the past, are those people spending lots of money on books and tapes and courses that help them deepen their commitment to their bellybuttons. The problem with them is that they're not political, they're not activists. Activists, in comparison to human growth folks, are engaged in setting an unbalanced world to rights. I believed that activists were engaged in important productive work, something political rather than selfishly personal. Here I create a perfect separation: personal growth on one side, political activism on the other. And never the twain shall meet.

So what do I do when, in thinking about class and trying to craft an analysis that relies on a combination of personal experience and gained knowledge, I keep getting stuck at the violence in my family? What do

I do with the fact of that violence, how it felt against my skin, the terror of difference and speaking out that it instilled? How do I talk about the ways in which a lack of power and self-determination can make individuals lash out against both those to whom they are closest and those who they have decided are the most different? Remembering this anger and resentment in my working-class family, in the way it was voiced by my uncles and aunts, goes as much into my thinking about class as does Marxist theory.

I am very clear that my life as an activist, my life as a thinking person, even the nature of my radicalism, is as much about my personal life as it is about the combination of political experiences and gained knowledge that move my thinking forward. And I am even clearer that in order to craft a vision for what happens next, to describe the shimmering horizon ahead, I have to think about all of this.

As an activist, I have to remember when I have been unaware and afraid as often as I remember the times I have felt righteous. I have to remember and know all of the places where my own shit hides inside, lest it leak out unawares and begin to infiltrate the work I am trying to do.

What I Thought Class Looked Like

When I first began to think about class and to apply a class analysis to my own experience, I had a very simple and, I believed, complete picture. Working-class people were white and urban; they tended to have some connection to unions; and they shared a list of characteristics that included either caution about spending money or wild spending followed by bouts of poverty, a distrust of the government, and a focus on community as a means of survival. I held this belief in the early 1980s and did not experience any contradiction when I thought about the people around me, particularly the people of color and the white folks who didn't fit the profile. This list didn't even completely fit my own personal profile. It was a romanticized soft lens view.

I didn't create this narrow understanding of working-class experience out of a desire to limit anything. Initially, it grew out of celebration. It was exhilarating for me to realize that such a thing as class existed. Where before I had felt stupid in comparison to some of the people around me, people with greater resources and educational backgrounds, I now felt connected to something, to a culture and a people. Whereas before my grandmother embarrassed me—her use of *ain't* and *youse* making me want to crawl under a rock—now I didn't care about the way she talked. Instead, I asserted her speech as a sign of something I wanted to claim rather than dismiss. My experiences began to make sense to me and, as a result, I began to feel more powerful.

This new way of interpreting the world gave me perspective. It gave me the ability to stand back and understand why I sometimes felt trapped or out of my league. It was from this powerful place of self-revelation that I began to think about class. It took me awhile to look beyond personal experience. First I had to feel comfortable with this new perspective. I had to know that just because I stopped tending and watering this new understanding, the awareness wasn't going to leave me. I also had to let it get deep enough inside my bones that I didn't feel defensive, like I had to prove to people that this new awareness included me.

Remembering that initial feeling of elation and self-awareness, I also have to remember my initial anger at people of color who protested discussions about class, arguing that race had been left out of the picture. In the beginning, I was frustrated and angry, not wanting to own up to my internal picture of working-class people, not wanting to have to think about being white. I felt "they" should see that class is broader than race, encompassing all of our experiences while, and I don't think I would have been self-aware enough to say this, race was only about racism and primarily about the experiences of people who weren't white. I assumed that the mere definition of class and class systems would be enough to overcome history.

It took me some time to realize the problem was mine. I didn't know about the history of many working-class movements and the legacy of distrust they had left behind. I didn't know that in the 1920s and 1930s, the increasing strength of American labor unions also affirmed a policy of American racial exclusion. While some of the children of the most recent wave of European immigration and some of the white children of Appalachian poverty gained political power, their socialist vision denied the same political rights to African Americans, who were themselves new immigrants to the North from the South by way of the Great Migration. I needed to learn, especially as an Italian American, about the history of my people's radicalism, how we sometimes struggled for the rights of our own, the empowerment of ourselves and other European American peasants, while clearly drawing lines between an *us* and a *them:* lines that were racial. I had to learn that this history and my own beliefs made my conversation about class, one that didn't directly talk about race, into something dangerous, something that merely replicated an old racialized system rather than moved toward profound social change.

It took me a while to move away from understanding working-class experience as being only a mirror of my own. In the beginning, I wasn't just making the entirety of "working class" fit my personal list of characteristics; I was also making my experience fit what I thought was working class. This means I left out as much as I put in. I left out my father, the son of Italian immigrants who came to this country with the American Dream neatly stitched into the seams of their clothes, immigrants who saw my father as the one who would wildly succeed. When I talked about being working class I never mentioned that my father had received a doctorate in metallurgical engineering before he died. I didn't tell people that he was one of the inventors of the heat shield for rocket ships, that before he died weeks shy of my seventh birthday, he had received a professorship at the Illinois Institute of Technology which gave him research and teaching time, his dream job, a job of great prestige. I also didn't talk about my parents' dreams for our future—the dreams that died in the same car accident as my father—the big Tudor house in Chicago that our family would someday convert, the arts events and educational activities we would enjoy together.

No, when I talked about my experience I only described my mother's extended family, the family that raised me and trained me after the death of my father. My mother's extended family fit the stereotype so well: unionists and laborers, factory workers and house cleaners. At parties there was lots of beer. My cousins roared up to our family picnics in urban parks on Harleys and in leather, their girlfriends holding tight to their jean-clad hips, music blaring, people outside the family looking warily in all of our directions. These are the stories I told: warnings from my grandmother about not getting too uppity when I thought about college, the closet in the basement that had cans of food against a possible future of starvation, clothes bought at Kmart and JCPenney. I told stories about the first time I tried to go to college and how it felt to walk on that liberal arts campus along with the children of Guggenheims. I talked about not fitting in, about suddenly realizing how small my world had always been. I didn't talk about the privilege that let me even set foot on that campus.

How many ways do we mold ourselves to fit other people's expectations? How many times do we do this unconsciously, afraid of the feeling of not quite fitting in, tired of being challenged because of something we cannot change? How often do we work to fit in consciously, thinking we will be more effective as leaders, more effective talking to people from this community or that community if we appear more of something that we are not? How often have I done this around my class, my culture, my sexual orientation? Have I stopped yet?

What I Thought Lesbians Looked Like

While I did a good job of keeping it simple and squeezing my life history into a tiny box labeled *working class,* I had a harder time fitting into *lesbian.* I was told by those around me, and I believed it myself, that I was too much of a woman to be a lesbian. I had too much body, too much hair—and I'm not talking pits and legs—too much flow and color. While I couldn't quickly squeeze my body into what I thought a lesbian was, I spent a great deal of time trying. I read a lot of books in the hopes that it would get me there. While I found no pictures or words in those books that looked like me, I kept reading. I didn't read just to find something familiar, I read and prayed for assimilation, that suddenly I would be like the dykes around me, even though no one around me actually fit the lesbian box we were all busily defending.

I can remember sitting with a group of white lesbians in 1984. We were destroying capitalism and the patriarchy with each breath, our power astounding and faultless. At one point our discussion veered toward personal choice. Suddenly, a number of the women in the room turned to a dyke who usually sat in the corner, a mousy, quiet woman who rarely spoke up. "You know," said one, "your job is part of the problem. You're supporting the system you want to fight against." The woman addressed grew frightened and tried to protest, explaining that the seniority she held at her job working in lingerie at a major department store gave her free childcare and a wage she couldn't find if she quit her job to start all over again. This didn't matter. Coldly she was told that if she really wanted to destroy the patriarchy, she needed to be willing to take personal risks in order to work toward the "greater good."

This was one of those moments where I knew that I could never be a lesbian. The conclusion I drew from this conversation was that I had to pick: be a lesbian or care about issues of economics and daily survival. I didn't understand that being a lesbian had nothing to do with whether or not you worked in a lingerie department or with your analysis of the patriarchy. I assumed that being a lesbian meant conforming to what "lesbians" believed.

After years of not fitting in as a separatist, when I finally did figure out a way that I could be lesbian, I still found ways to selectively edit my past and my present. Before I moved to Minneapolis, the city in which I now live, I finally came out, once and for all. After twenty-seven years of long hair and makeup, I came out, cut my hair, and began to wear blue jeans and T-shirts. I was clear about my reasons for this. I wanted to be recognized by other lesbians when I walked down the street. I wanted to start all over again, pare down to something simple in order to build up again.

This paring down was happening while I lived in Minneapolis, a city with very few Italian Americans. Whiteness in Minneapolis is a northern European whiteness—Scandinavian and German—while communities of color are small and segregated. Italianness doesn't fit into the picture. I wasn't white like the white folks were white but I also wasn't a person of color. Suddenly, being Italian felt like a precious thing, something that needed to be protected and asserted lest I disappear into a sea of lutefisk and hot dish, of cultural reserve and assumptions about politeness. At the same time, I started to go to university, finishing my B.A. at the age of thirty-one. And as the final piece, I was involved with an upper-middle-class woman, a professional, a small woman with the bones of a bird. All of these things swirled together to affect the kind of lesbian I understood myself to be: something not upper-middle class, not professional, not small, but Italian and working class, big and busty.

When I talked in Minneapolis it sounded loud in comparison to those around me, so I thought I must be butch. When I gestured with my arms, moved my body more than many of the women around me, I thought this was about butchness of Italian American butchness. I started to understand femme as my partner, small and refined, her clothes always looking neat and pressed, while butch was like me, loud and taking up space.

This belief that I was butch went deeper than that. Getting a college degree terrified me. The more knowledge and experience I gained, the more I felt my extended family slip away from me. Getting a B.A. was as much about loss as about gain, as much about grieving my changing relationship to the community in which I was raised as it was a process of learning. This feeling existed even as I was actually moving along the path of my father. I was frightened that with a college degree I would no longer be recognized for where I came from, the community of my mother. Just as being Italian was something I asserted when I moved to Minneapolis, being from a working-class background was something I asserted as soon as I entered college. The two became tied together.

All of this confusion and assertion formed itself into an identity. Clearly, a working-class urban Italian American dyke would be most recognizable as a butch. Sitting with my legs straddling a chair, my gestures hard and sharp, and my body's curves hidden inside the straightness of my clothes, well, I would instantly be recognizable as something other than middle-class-college-educated-generic-white-girl. It didn't matter that for most of my life I had been an unconscious but "natural" Italian American girly-girl raised in the working class. I had somehow bought into the stereotype that working class is easier to spot as butch rather than femme and, therefore, that to be truly recognized as working class, I needed to be butch like the guys in the movie *Bronx Tales:* dark white guys who wore leather but still had supple hips.

It is painful to admit that this is also about misogyny—the belief that to be recognized as powerful I needed to acquire some kind of masculinity or maleness. In order to be seen, part of me believed I could not be femme. Femme and a college degree got tangled up in my head as being about passing, as making invisible my class and my queerness. This was not a thought-out plan of action. I didn't craft an Italian American butch identity as a logical step by step reaction to my fears. It just happened. Each time I felt invisible, I grew more strident, pushed my body and my gestures into a particular kind of public display. Each time I pushed, I developed new meaning for who I was, new ways of justifying my butchness. Most of the time it worked. It was only when I tried to bond with "bone-butches" that I felt like an imposter, like I needed to apologize. Being butch is not a choice or a form of dress; it is who someone is. Just as being butch is what I am not.

I don't know if I have enough limbs on my body or facial expressions to be able to honestly express all the things I am feeling or being at any given time. But when I explained who I was in words that left out far more than they kept in, I was not helping any discussion of class or gender move forward. And, as I began to remember a history of sexual abuse, my understanding of this desire for butchness started making a whole different kind of sense. The crafting of my identity based on convenient stereotypes of butchness as unemotional and uncommitted, of working classness as loud and physical, and of Italianness as the same allowed me to pick and choose the Susan I wanted others to see, hiding all that felt vulnerable. When long-denied memories began to rumble through the foundations of this identity, I realized how selective I had been and how much I had been hiding. It is not unusual to craft a politics or an identity out of personal grief and fear. Being "butch," however laughable it seems today, served me well.

It was just before I began to write the introduction to my book that I realized I had to talk about my father as well as my mother when I discussed class. I had to let my own class story be more complicated than what I had previously been willing to tell. I had long moved beyond understanding that not all working-class and poor folks looked like or experienced class like me. Now I needed to understand that I didn't look or experience class like the me I had created. It was soon after that, when I began to pay attention to the fantasies that floated behind my eyes and to remember the first twenty-seven years of my life, that I realized there wasn't a butch bone in my body.

This is how I am a lesbian activist around issues of class and a working-class girl who is a lesbian. I fuck up as often as I find clarity.

A Lesbian Thinking About Class

A conversation about class in the United States is vital to any successful social change movement. Yet, we don't currently have a language that will allow us to adequately address issues of class. By language, I don't mean that we need to invent more words but that we need to learn new ways of talking and thinking about class and about things related to class. The language we most often use, the one that draws divisions between lower-class, middle-class, and rich folks, is a language born of the industrial revolution and then, over time, distilled into something overly simplistic. I don't believe it's an encompassing enough language if it is the only way we talk about class. With our country's history of slavery, the attempted genocide of Native Americans, the significance of immigration, and our vast geographic and regional diversity, a conversation that only structures class divisions based on economics and labor can never work.

Much of how we currently understand class originally came from European thinkers, individuals such as Karl Marx and Friedrich Engels who, at the time they wrote, lived in countries with fairly ethnically and racially homogenous populations (at least in comparison with the extent of U.S. diversity), and with linked histories. The theories were crafted in an environment in which the individuals and communities making up the cultures they were exploring shared a different kind of intimacy. This does not invalidate the language of their class analysis, or make it inapplicable to the U.S., if the original theory is being read and evaluated. But in considering any kind of analysis, we have to think about the specifics of when it was develped, wonder what questions might not have been posed, and ask whether there were facts/experiences not included in the inquiry which might have broadened the original analysis. The language of class I am hungry to hear and use in my own thinking is one which grows out of this earlier classic theory but does not pose class and economics on one side of the political spectrum (as some leftists do) and other issues, such as race, gender, sex, and disability, on the other.

While mainstream political discussions in the U.S. do sometimes focus on class they do so indirectly, and most often those conversations are racialized. Look at the recent public discussions around welfare reform and immigration. Although the majority of people receiving some form of social services in this country are white, any conversation about welfare is a conversation that relies upon images of people of color. The faces vary depending on what part of the country you live in, but generally, *welfare mothers* means African American women. This is the picture the collective American mind automatically attaches to the word *welfare*. Even though poverty may disproportionately affect the lives of people of color, it is still misleading to link poverty with any specific race.

Other public policy discussions that are fundamentally about issues of economic access—such as affirmative action, a program that helped thousands of white women as well as men and women of color—have also become discussions about race. These representations of race and poverty, or race and social spending, have been used to tap into white racism, encouraging white voters to vote against social programs that are touted as the reason for everything from urban and rural violence to Bill Clinton's sexual practices. White poverty is often invisible, and people of color with middle-class lives are suspected of having stolen them.

There are so many reasons why race and class are tied together in the U.S. Our history of slavery and the attempted genocide of Native Americans continually shapes class experiences, whether explicitly recognized or not. Race and class in tandem determine who has what kind of access to what kind of power. Racial discrimination and genocide are rooted in the earth of U.S. capitalism; they are the very blood loam of profit. Class directly shapes the experience of immigration, in this nation of immigrants, whether our families arrived here more than three generations ago or during the past decade. To assume that race and class are two separate social categories, to talk about one without the other, is to seriously limit our ability to alter the power of their inequities.

The American Dream, or the belief that anyone can advance up the economic scale if they work hard enough, has been the dream held out for immigrants looking to become Americans and to all U.S. folks seeking to better their standard of living. Not all have equal access to this dream, and it is a myth whose popularity is waning. Nonetheless, both the success stories and the stories of failure have crafted many of the current U.S. race and class dynamics.

For me as an Italian American, the story of how my ethnic community moved into both whiteness and the potential of middle classness falls in the middle of this dynamic. When Southern Italians and Sicilians first came to the United States in large numbers during the mid-nineteenth and early twentieth centuries (Sicily had only recently become part of the Italian state, and Sicilian American culture and language has retained its distinctions), they were not considered white. Generally they were listed as *nonwhite* or *other* on census forms. It has been our light skins (skins which grew mostly lighter with each successive generation born here through intermarriage with "whiter" Americans, as well as lives not lived under the Mediterranean sun) and our connection with Europe that acted as passports toward a potential middle classdom and assimilation into white U.S. life. I say *potential* because many Italian and Sicilian Americans still live in working-class communities, sometimes by choice and sometimes because access out of those communities is limited. But even though there are working-class Italian Americans, they are white working-class people. By now, being *white* and working class gives a different kind of access to economic power, however limited that access might be, than when Italians and Sicilians were not considered white. While this history is far more complex than I am describing here, it is clear that the move toward whiteness and the move toward middle-class life are directly connected. The American Dream is not an equal opportunity employer.

When conversations about class occur directly, rather than indirectly, they happen in one of two ways. Either the word *class* is used to discuss economic injustice and institutional power, or *class* is used to talk about a cultural experience, about the lessons learned being raised in a family that stretches pennies into loaves of bread. Rarely do these two conversations overlap. I firmly believe that in order to have a discussion about class that leaves no one out of the picture, we need to do both these things: practice a critical analysis and examine personal experiences.

Class in the U.S. can be summed up very simply: there is a very small group of people who control a very large percentage of the wealth. Few of us ever meet them. They predominantly socialize only with each other. Lower-class folks are the people who make the things and provide the services that the other folks consume. When I say lower class, I mean working-class *and* poor people because, increasingly, the line between these two categories is blurred. Even before workfare and welfare reform, poor people have worked. Additionally, with the decreasing amount of available industrial work through the exportation of labor outside the country, more "traditional" working-class jobs are few and far between. What was once a "working-class" position, such as farm labor, has turned into an arena for migrant labor, where sometimes, although not always, undocumented and first-generation immigrants work for poverty wages.

The middle class in this picture is the most confusing to define. It used to be said that middle-class people were, at the least, people who owned their own homes. Home ownership does not have the same meaning as it did fifty years ago. With the growth of an economy based on personal debts and a system of "affordable" mortgages and interest rates to increase bank profits as well as an ever-expanding suburban sprawl, the meaning of home ownership and who gets to own a home has changed. While people living in poverty are still probably not going to live in a home they own, it is not as uncommon for working-class or lower-middle-class families to own theirs. I would caution against using home ownership as being a place to clearly draw a line. Home ownership and an investment in the stock market and an IRA, however, is a clear sign of middle classness. Middle-class folks are people with access to some economic and social power but without ownership of the means through which that power is granted. Some middle-class folks really are a paycheck away from losing their homes and other middle-class folks aren't ever going to have to worry. This is one of the reasons that just calling yourself or someone else middle class doesn't define much.

At one level, class in the U.S. is as simple as that. But to rely solely on this analysis of class is dangerous. Someone's race, culture, religious background, ethnicity, ability, gender, English language proficiency, birth and home region of the country, job status, level of education, income, numbers of generations after immigration, health, and sexual orientation complicates her or his relationship to each of these categories. It is both true and false to say that an inner-city Los Angelean Chicano male welder is class-aligned with a small-town Iowa northern European male welder. But in thinking about class, we need to be willing to do both of these things at the same time: see the picture as a simple conversation about power and access, and understand it as more complicated than this structure allows.

Activists and thinkers on the Left are constantly stressed over perfecting their analysis. Unfortunately, there is not the luxury of time for figuring out who will get fed and how kids are going to be cared for while public funding is being legislated out of existence. Creating analysis is about connecting to people's lives. It's about the reason for the huge and disproportionate numbers of people of color, especially African American, Latino, and Native men, spending some part of their lives in prison, and the building of even more prisons to maintain the trend; the reason for the bombing of women's health clinics; the reason that the numbers of individuals needing to use food kitchens and home-less shelters is skyrocketing in the wake of welfare reform. Life and death, death and life.

Just as an analysis is deeply implicated with survival and blood, it is also about time. About the hundreds of years of slavery that led to the entwining of race and class, and about the mere moment of time we have experienced since the civil rights movement. Time is some-thing both slapping at our backside and pulling us forward.

This is another one of those both/and moments. How, as activists, do we live with both the urgency of the moment and the perspective on time that makes each of our lives just a blip in the cosmos? It is this double gaze I want to use when thinking about class and trying to learn a language that will help the Left or Progressive or Radical movement (pick your identifier) to create a broad-based social justice movement that understands and takes into account the full range of social con-ditions. I want to feel the fast heartbeat of needing to make changes now, of knowing this is about individual lives and sorrows, and also al-low that none of this will really change until more time, like the effect of water on a stone, has moved on by. It takes work to get a wide-angle vision, and we need to act now. These two things are not contradictory.

A Lesbian Who Spends a Lot of Time Thinking About Class Thinks About Being an Activist

While working on this essay, I kept remembering Bernice Johnson Reagon's piece on coalition building. Reagon says that as activists committed to working for social justice and, at the same time, work-ing across differences, we need to stop thinking about how we can stay comfortable. She tells us that if we're looking for comfort, we're not com-mitted to coalition building. Actually, she says it better than that: "You don't do no coalition building in a womb....Coalition work is not done in your home. Coalition work has to be done in the streets. And it is some of the most dangerous work you can do."* Reagon says that in

"Coalition Politics: Turning the Century" in *Home Girls: A Black Feminist Anthology*, ed. Barbara Smith (New York: Kitchen Table: Women of Color Press, 1983), p. 359.

order to do things we have to know our wombs, as it were, and then get out of them to do the work.

Oh yes, know your wombs as activists. Do the work. I reread Reagon's essay from time to time for a wake-up call. If I'm going to do the long-term work of fighting for social justice, I better know where I can go to relax, where I can go to put my feet up and not have to explain to everyone who I am and why I am that way. The danger, and truthfully I'm struggling with it right now, is how to not get stuck in that place of comfort. If I'm being surprised by coming across someone's overt racism or other offensive behavior, then I've been off in the womb too long. Something has to change. At the same time, if I expect that every white person is going to be a racist idiot and every straight man or woman is going to see me as Satan's spawn, then I need to try and find a place to rest, a place to feel hopeful and visionary again. But not everyone gets the privilege of resting—that's called oppression. It is essential, though, that everyone figures out how to carve out the space to breathe again, even if the time is too short.

There is no shame in not wanting to do coalition work. No one has to willingly put themselves into situations in which they might have to deal with some of the same shit they face just walking through the world. But for those who do want to do this work, remembering as Reagon said that this is some of the most dangerous work you will do, then it is vital that we are honest about the totality of what brought us to this moment. And that we allow that all the folks we are coalitioning with also have a range of experiences that brought them to this moment. If I don't believe that an upper-middle-class white gay man with a platinum card and assumptions about holidays abroad who sees the Human Rights Campaign as the epitome of radicalism might someday pay attention to my experience and listen when I explain what his world does to mine, then I can't expect the people of color in my world to keep sticking with me even when I have been more fool than friend or the trans folk I speak with to have patience for my gender confusions. For me to totally trash this man is to forget all of the people *I* have been before arriving at this place, and to dangerously assume that I have nothing else to learn.

Doing the work of activism means we all have days of slow ego-slide. Days of feeling like effective political people who "get it" and then being tripped up by internal glitches we didn't anticipate, or by new insights that challenge the analysis we had been working with. None of us ever "gets it" once and for all. Being an activist working around the issues discussed in this essay is a lifetime commitment. I will never be free of living as a white woman in the United States and, therefore, I will never be free of racism. Both the kind inside me and the kind that comes from people around me who, seeing my skin, make comments with the assumption that my whiteness means my agreement. I will never "get" race from anywhere other than being a white woman. I can only decide what kind of white woman I will be by having some control over the meaning of my whiteness. Lord knows there are a lot of ways to be white.

This also means that my "getting" of class will always be connected to my "getting" of everything else. As I spend more and more time in a lifestyle that lets me see movies when I want, buy a bottle of wine, or consider traveling to far-away places, my relationship to my class history and present also changes. My world is much bigger than it used to be, and I have a lot more power within it. My partner and I own this computer on which I am typing. In the past, I couldn't have imagined that this would be true—a big piece of white plastic with fortune cookie slips pasted around the edges sitting always available in the place where I live. Having this machine is power; it changes how I can talk about the places I have been.

One gift I brought home from my five weeks of traveling when *Queerly Classed* was released was becoming far more hopeful about the future of a broad-based social justice movement than I had previously been. I met a lot of queer people representing an amazing array of diverse identities in a lot of different places. What I heard from place to place was a frustration with the focus of national queer organizing. People were fed up with the enormous variety of experiences that had been left out of the picture, with the invisibility of most queer lives. I came away from that time on the road encouraged about the future of a movement beginning to create itself, a movement where we let all of our bodies and desires and hopes and beliefs and warts and failings and times of not getting it right be part of how we do our activism, inching us closer and closer to something we don't even have the language to describe.

I want to thank Emma, Jemel Aguilar, Jenifer Fennell, Beni Matías, Elissa Raffa, and Raquel Volaco Simões for their help with the thinking in this essay.

Susan Raffo *is a writer and community activist.*
She is the editor of Queerly Classed: Gay Men
and Lesbians Write About Class *(South End)*
and editor, with Victoria Brownworth, of
Restricted Access: Lesbians and Disability
(Seal). A former managing editor for the
Evergreen Chronicles, *Susan has worked as a cab*
driver, waitress, park ranger, bookseller, campaign
manager, organic gardener…and the list goes on.
She currently lives in Minneapolis with her
partner, Raquel Volaco Simões.

Mattie

Richardson puts a face on the arguments articulated by Urvashi Vaid, demonstrating that if "what you see" is white and middle or upper class, than what you get will be the same. While Urvashi is concerned with how feminist, women's, and lgbt organizations should be addressing issues, Mattie shows us what it's like to be the one who is not addressed, let alone involved in defining issues and shaping policy. Her point is vividly illustrated by the betrayal her family feels when they encounter their daughter's lgbt concerns interpreted in the media by conservative gay pundits. The connection between the punishment of single mothers in this country and the criminalizing of gay and lesbian sex is not merely theoretical for the author: her own sister has been stigmatized as a single mother, humiliated by caseworkers as they pry into her private life. Mattie's call for viable and visible leadership by people of color in the lgbt movement is compelling even as she takes a leadership role in this essay by putting forth a concrete vision for how to go about doing liberation work.

What You See Is What You Get: Building a Movement Toward Liberation in the Twenty-First Century

Mattie Richardson

I have been invited to speak on separate occasions on the third wave of the feminist movement and the next generation of queer activism. The questions all of us who are concerned about justice are asking as we roll into the twenty-first century are: Where do we go from here? Is the movement alive? It doesn't matter which movement you're concerned about—feminist, racial justice, social justice, disability rights, lesbian/gay/bisexual/transgender—we are all poised at the cusp of this new century wondering whether we will make it. Can we put our best ideas about coalition building and revolution into practice in time? I will not pretend that I have the answers, or know what will happen. However, I do believe that the future looks bright if we act on it. I keep seeing opportunities, possibilities for change and growth for all of our movements. Right now, I'm going to start with my own family because so often liberation begins at home, although it never ends there.

If there is one thing I'd like to say about my mother it is that she has never intentionally tried to hurt me. She has said damaging things without realizing it and she has underestimated me, but she has never meant me real harm. Unfortunately, I can't say the same about many other individual women or women's organizations. Every time a poor woman is not taken seriously or her opinions are ignored by a woman who calls herself a feminist, serious damage is inflicted on the future of feminism.

I called my mother on her birthday. She sounded tired and distracted and said she was reassessing her life and needed to talk to someone. I offered to talk with her about anything she wanted. "Mattie," she said, "you are my daughter and I love you, but you are twenty-six years old and I need to talk to someone who has lived. It's my birthday. I've worked every day of my life, but it seems I can't get a firm hold financially. Look at the conditions that I live in. I need to talk to someone who has lived a Christian life, someone who has been around a while and can tell me something I don't already know."

I said, "Momma, I can only give you my best. I can't say that I've lived a 'Christian life,' or that I've lived long and seen everything. But when I look at you I don't only see a women living in a run-down house with few material comforts. I see a person who teaches children to read. You teach some of the most despised children in this nation—poor black and Latino children labeled as emotionally troubled, or as developmentally disabled. Every day you make them feel like they are human beings worthy of love, respect, and kindness. When they leave your class they know how to read. What greater gifts could you ask for?"

She was stunned for a moment, and then she apologized for ever thinking I didn't have something to teach her about life.

I tell you this story not only to demonstrate an instance in my life when my mother disregarded me because she thought I was too young, but also to make the point that wisdom often comes from unexpected places. My mother decided that I couldn't possibly tell her something that she could use at her age because in her opinion I haven't lived long enough, nor have I lived a life that she necessarily thinks of as being ideal (meaning that I am lesbian). But in doing so, she overlooked me as a potential source of help to her.

The women's movement has made similar mistakes. In the search for leaders for the next generation, the contemporary feminist movement has focused its attention on the collegebound and the college-educated, once again overlooking the voices of non-college-educated young women. Young women who have never been asked their opinions on anything, who are almost never called to be leaders, yet who have a great deal to contribute. Wisdom comes from unexpected sources, but it will go to waste if untapped and unacknowledged. I think the future of feminism is sitting in welfare offices and free clinics all over the country. They are poor women, they have not had the benefits of higher education, and they are scapegoats for the faltering U.S. economy. These are women like my sister.

Shortly after high school, my sister became pregnant with her first child. She married the baby's father and left him three years later, fleeing the terror of domestic violence. By then she had two children, no job experience or vocational training, and no money. My sister tried a series of low-paying jobs, but childcare and transportation consumed most of her weekly paycheck. Destitute and determined to make a life for herself and her children, she applied for public assistance as her only option. Over the years, my sister has gotten off welfare and gone back on whenever she found it absolutely necessary to do so.

The feminist movement should include young women like my sister within its ranks. So far, however, she has gotten nothing but condescension from feminists who regard her as a subject for research or a passive recipient of services.

I stayed with my sister the summer after my graduation from college. She lived in a small Southern city. One of the ideas she had for contributing to the community was to become involved in the women's center in town. We went to the center together with the intention of volunteering. The director, a white middle-class woman, happened to be the only staff person present when we got there. She asked us about ourselves and why we came. My sister spoke first and then I did. As soon as the director heard that I was a recent graduate of an Ivy League school her face brightened. She was immediately interested in what I had to say. She explained everything that they did at the center and took my name and number. My sister said, "I would like to volunteer as soon as possible," but the director hardly looked in my sister's direction and told her to call back later to ask about their volunteer opportunities and other services. There was an implicit understanding that my sister was a client, a person who would receive services. I, on the other hand, was viewed as a possible resource to the organization: I could help with programming. I could eventually help the center establish goals and set priorities. I was seen as able to contribute to the future of the center, and my sister was left out of the plan. It never entered the director's mind that my sister could play an active role in contributing to the center.

Another women's organization in the same city organized a lobby day to pressure the state legislature to veto a bill that would have ended Medicaid funding for abortions. It was the first event that we participated in with this organization. When my sister and I arrived at the capital, there were approximately six prochoice advocates, all middle-class women, all white; they were attorneys, professional lobbyists, women's health providers, and my sister and I (who were the only people of color participating in the prochoice demonstration). The anti-abortion side managed to bring in a busload of people, about a third of whom were people of color and from different class backgrounds. My sister saw the busload of anti-abortion protesters and asked one of the prochoice organizers, "Did you go to the welfare office and tell the women there about the bill and today's protest?" The woman said no, but that she had gathered as many of the women who were committed to this issue as she could given that the university was out of session. Who were they to assume that only university-educated women were committed to reproductive freedom?

I envision a movement where organizing at the welfare office would be the first order of business and where the leadership would come from the women who were the subject of the protest in the first place—women on public assistance.

If this movement does not include women like my sister—my blood sister and my sisters in struggle—in its expectation for leadership, then it doesn't include me. If we can't walk in together and receive the same respect and consideration, then I don't want to walk in at all.

Last year I went to a protest at the United Nations organized by a coalition of welfare rights organizations run by welfare mothers. There was relatively little publicity about the rally and, consequently, not many people attended. There were no reporters, just a handful of welfare rights activists. The women had come up with a plan for each to visit a select group of foreign embassies and apply for political asylum based on the treatment they received in the U.S. One young black woman I talked to said that she wanted to go to the South African embassy and apply for asylum. I thought about how this symbolic act would embarrass the U.S internationally. I began to dream of the streets filled with protesters all going into embassies and demanding that the attack on poor women be considered a violation of the UN universal declaration of human rights and that poor women are in need of political asylum because they are a politically targeted group. What a powerful statement that would send all over the world!

It was an example of an idea that came from young women, from poor women. That is the feminist future I would like to see—a feminist movement that uses everything we *all* learned from previous liberation movements, in the U.S. and around the world, to rock this country at its foundation.

There is another woman whose story weighs on me as I think about the questions that concern the third wave of the feminist movement. I met her about four years ago when she was moving into town just as I was getting ready to leave. We hung out together, talked about sobriety, writing, and our futures. She said she was giving up heroin and trying to live a healthier life while she was battling chronic illness. We didn't keep in touch, and I had soon almost forgotten her.

Forgotten her, that is, until she turned up on a segment of *America's Most Wanted* a while back, a segment called "Lesbian Bank Robbers." She was being led into a courthouse in shackles on my TV, accused of participating in a string of twenty bank robberies. The Feds were looking for her lover/partner in crime. I later learned from people who love her that she started doing dope again soon after I moved away and then she left town. I have no idea whether or not she is guilty of any of the charges brought against her. I think of her now as we are discussing the third wave of the feminist movement. I think of this white woman who is about the same age as I am being led into courtroom in shackles, a heroin addict, a lesbian, and I think: will this new wave speak to her, too? If it doesn't, we are all in trouble.

It reminds me of a saying made popular by black drag performer Flip Wilson: *What you see is what you get.* If what you see is a women's movement that is centered around the academy, what you get is a self-aggrandizing, self-absorbed academic feminism that talks only to itself. If what you see is a movement that cannot organize beyond the colleges and universities, what you get is a movement that lacks imagination and has few constituents.

What about the lesbian and gay movement? Is that a place where an agenda of liberation is being pushed to the forefront? Recently my mother asked me, "Why are you struggling so hard for those white people?" She meant the work that I do as an out, active lesbian. I was startled by her question, to say the least. But I had to consider where her question was coming from. My mother has taught me so much about surviving day to day against the crushing forces of racism and the brutality of poverty, that when she says something about struggle, I have learned to stop and think about it. My mother, like many other straight people of color, sees the lesbian and gay community as consisting of mostly white people. There isn't much to counter her impression except for when she sees me, in person, flanked by a few co-workers and friends. Until there is strong, viable lesbian and gay of color leadership, many people like my mother will be asking that same question. If my mother, my mentor in resistance to oppression, has to ask me why am I spending too much energy on a solely white agenda, I know my work as a lesbian is not done.

How could I respond to my mother? I took a deep breath and tried to explain that, of course, I am not out there busting my butt just so that a few white gay men can gain access to their place among the privileged. If what you see are pro-military, pro-capitalist, conservative queers, you will get the message that militarism and capitalism are what all lesbians and gays stand for. If all you see are conservative rich whites speaking on behalf of all lesbian and gay communities, you will come away thinking that all queers are white and rich and the rest of us are aberrations on the theme. If what you see are white lesbians who proclaim a victory when Ellen DeGeneres comes out despite the resounding absence of people of color on the program, you will get white lesbian chic. No, I told my mother, I am fighting to end injustice and for the liberation of all people through antiracist and anti-imperialist practice as an out lesbian.

My sister pulled me aside and wanted to know, "Does your fight against injustice have anything to with the injustice that I face?" So when my sister has to ask if the movement that I am a part of includes her, and by extension all poor black women whose sexuality is under scrutiny and control, and I cannot answer yes, well, I have to be concerned. If my sister, my sister in struggle, has to ask if she is included in the quest for liberation, then my work as a feminist activist is not done. If my family and my cultural community has to ask these questions, then this lesbian and gay movement does not speak to them and it does not speak to me either.

My sister is part of one of the most scapegoated groups in the U.S. today: she is a black single mother of three boys. She has taught me about surviving despite the dehumanizing effects of sexism, misogyny, and racism through her battles with the welfare system. Her struggle has made me aware of the intense heterosexism that is perpetrated in the war on poor black women. Everywhere she goes—from black community leaders to white politicians—the message is: Get married. Otherwise you are raising your children in an unfit environment. If that is not compulsory heterosexuality put into policy and practice, I don't know what is.

If the main focus of lesbian and gay organizing only concerns the right to join heterosexuals in privileges given through the patriarchal system of marriage, you will get a movement based on securing a "place at the table." If this is all there is to see, what we will get is a civil rights movement that speaks to the few instead of a liberation movement that includes everyone. If what you see is what you get, I want to see the strong leadership of progressive lesbians and gay men of color who put forward an actively antiracist and anti-imperialist agenda. What we will get is a lesbian and gay liberation movement.

Well-heeled white queers are more visible than they ever have been before. They can be seen on national TV waxing poetic about a vision of the future where all the obstacles to taking their seat at the table of white privilege will be removed. Recently, I watched C-SPAN's coverage of the Log Cabin Republicans' annual meeting. I have long gotten used to seeing Andrew Sullivan and his ilk paraded across my television. What caught my attention this time was that except for the presence of anti-affirmative action University of California regent Wardell Connerly, the Log Cabin agenda was virtually indistinguishable from the mainstream queer platform.

Where was the lesbian and gay movement when, in the name of welfare reform, the Clinton administration slashed and burned the few remaining programs that stood between poor people and homelessness and starvation? Where were we when poor women were first forced to submit to fingerprinting in order to continue receiving food stamps, Medicaid, and other social service benefits? Where were we when people on welfare were first forced into the involuntary servitude of workfare programs? We could have said something beyond the cries of individual activists. We could have taken to the streets en masse because these issues are our issues. Every lesbian mother is legally an unwed mother regardless of her partner status. We could have taken to the streets because many lesbians and gay men are on welfare. We could have taken to the streets because policies that demonize women for not being married are a threat to the sexual freedom of every person in this country.

I would like to see a queer movement that has another vision of itself. Queer activists have successfully fought antigay initiatives in several states. How I longed for that expertise in my work with the predominantly straight-identified movement for racial, economic, and educational justice in California! In California we've seen the passage of the "three strikes you're out" law, Proposition 186; the initiative that got rid of social services to all immigrants regardless of legal status, Proposition 187; the "English-only" law that demolished bilingual education, Proposition 227; and the initiative that destroyed affirmative action in California and was recently replicated in the state of Washington, Proposition 209. It has been a litany of numbers, a scorecard tallying our demise. A coalition effort with progressive queers would have the potential to break barriers and mend bridges. It could create a visible link to another part of the movement that my family and colleagues don't have a chance to see because it is eclipsed by the white sheet of conservative queer organizations like the Human Rights Campaign and the Log Cabin Republicans.

Where do we go from here? I look to what first inspired my mother and what still inspires me—the civil rights and black power movements of the 1960s. During that time, there was a small, independent newspaper that the Student Nonviolent Coordinating Committee (SNCC) put out called the *Nitty Gritty*, published in Atlanta. The main purpose for using that name was to reach all levels of the community, including the poorest, most disenfranchised members, with the message of liberation. They wanted the *Nitty Gritty* to be a vehicle for making public their perspective on the pressing issues facing black people because they believed that a sound and relevant political analysis is part of what gives liberation movements vision and momentum.

I think that as feminists/lesbians/gays/bisexual/transgender people we have to get down to the nitty gritty and start acting in a conscious way to deal with the issues that affect the majority of us—those of us who are poor, who are people of color, and who are women. Every movement needs a clear vision of its goals; the outcome depends on what the members of that movement see.

If what you see is that the fate of poor people and the fate of queers are linked, what you get is not a narrow plea for gay rights, but a movement for the liberation of all peoples. If what you see is that the wisdom necessary to build a nationwide liberation movement lies with the most disenfranchised, then, I believe, what you get is a revolution.

Mattie Richardson *is a writer and activist whose work has been anthologized in* Sisterfire: Black Womanist Fiction and Poetry *(Harper Perennial), E*very Woman You've Ever Loved: Lesbian Writers on Their Mothers *(Cleis), and* Does Your Mama Know: An Anthology of Black Lesbian Coming Out Stories *(Redbone). She is a former member of the board of directors of the OUT Fund for Lesbian and Gay Liberation, a project of the Funding Exchange.*

Assimilation

often comes at both a personal and a political price. Marlene Schuman, a working-class, activist Jewish lesbian of immigrant parents acknowledges those costs while she works to "reclaim," as she says, the multiple pieces of her identity, to become a whole person. Much mainstream discussion about assimilation is concerned with how "diversity" is divisive, how respecting autonomous subcultures will fragment society. This thinking infects our movement as well. How many times have white middle-class- (and Christian-) dominated organizations resisted sharing power using the argument that these issues (class, race, sex) were divisive? As Marlene so eloquently demonstrates, it is precisely through these cultural reclamations that she has been able to connect to the experiences of others. She further argues, using herself as the example, that it is only by claiming, rather than denying, both the privileges and the oppressions that are our own that we can be effective agents for social justice.

Reclamations
Marlene Schuman

I am a Jewish working-class lesbian writer. That I am able to identify
so definitively is part miracle and part constant struggle. I did not know
how Jewish I was, nor perhaps how "first generation" I was, until a day
in 1967 when I literally became paralyzed—temporarily but completely immobile—trying to walk off the Washington University campus where I was a second-year student attending on scholarship. I was
unable to move my legs for several minutes. It was only when I recognized that I was over the edge, about to break down, and that I could
get help if I chose to, that I was able to slowly turn around and make
my way to the campus clinic. It took me more than twenty years to develop a consciousness and a social/political analysis that offered a meaningful and complete explanation for this incident. I had long thought
the campus classism and elitism had simply intimidated me, and while
there may be some truth to this interpretation, it seemed inadequate
and left me feeling ashamed that I had failed solely due to personal
weakness.

It required discovering the devaluing effects of assimilation through
the writing of several authors, most specifically the work of Jewish working-class lesbian author Irena Klepfisz, to recognize the shame-based
legacies of too many immigrant and minority experiences. Even as a
student at City College (now the City University of New York), a school
with a predominantly Jewish student body at the time she attended,
Klepfisz noted there had been nothing to encourage the students "to
look to their homes and backgrounds for cultural resources worthy of
preservation. The message was just the opposite: [they] were to erase
all traces of who [they] were and where [they] came from." Like Klepfisz, I had also wondered why I had experienced so many setbacks in
staying remotely loyal or even connected to the Jewish culture/religion
that had filled the first twenty years of my life. "The problem stems from
American society, which does not tolerate cultures outside the mainstream and does everything, materially and psychologically, to weaken
them. [And, to discount them, I could add, thereby triggering the internalized oppression many experience.] Whether to Spanish-speaking

or Chinese-speaking or Yiddish-speaking children [or African American children, or the children of lesbians and gays], the message is monotonously the same: Change your name. Americanize. Forget the past. Forget your people."* The message was and is to deny your individual humanity, to disappear, i.e., assimilate. I would venture to say that to those children, seen not only as culturally different but impoverished as well, the message is even more blunt: the message is not just to assimilate, but to die.

It became clear to me that the trauma of my parents' immigrant experiences, particularly my mother's, had not caught up with me until that brief paralysis in 1967. My mother, as a twelve-year-old Russian/Jewish immigrant, had been too ashamed to continue attending school after being placed in an American kindergarten to become familiar with the language. There were no official schools teaching English as a Second Language in the 1930s. My father, a strange mixture of innocent, humanist, and untutored philosopher (I have never heard this eighty-four-year-old white man utter one racist slur), dropped out of high school, overwhelmed by the rush of insensitive adolescent humanity he encountered. He earned a GED and became a civil servant.

I, however, had been well on the way to assimilation—the recipient of both a fine education in University City, a suburb of St. Louis, and a scholarship to attend Washington University (WU), a well-known midwestern upper-class campus. I had it made, or so it would have appeared to most. But assimilation—not the whole-hearted inclusion of me and my constituent groups that would be the real test to democracy, but rather the denial of self in order to be part of the mainstream—really stared me in the face those two years at WU. I mean this quite literally, since the faces into which I was looking belonged to a large number of other Jewish students. We were seeing each other through a looking-glass; they would have been my future had I stayed on that path. I was already their past. It tore me apart no less than did the outrage of Vietnam and the lack of civil rights for African Americans. However, it was clear at that time that the latter issues were public ones, socially and politically unconscionable, while the former was seen by me as an issue I scarcely understood at any level, let alone the political.

Irena Klepfisz, "Secular Jewish Identity: *Yidishkayt* in America" in *Dreams of an Insomniac* (Portland, OR: Eighth Mountain, 1990), pp. 151, 159.

I was forty before I grasped that while I wanted "the good life," I need not be ashamed that I was unwilling to pay the price then demanded for attaining it: to forget/deny my constituent group, to allow others to shape my identity. The closest I ever came to hearing someone else describe what I experienced through temporary paralysis that spring day in 1967 (and my subsequent dropping out of school for the next seventeen years) was in Joyce Trebilcot's essay "Craziness as a Source of Separatism." She wrote:

> I wanted to participate in what was going on, but I simply could not, I was unable, I did not know how. I had the sense that there was a trick to it, something I had to learn. I now understand this nonparticipation not as inability, but as refusal: it is not that I could not take part, but that I would not. And the reason I would not is that I wanted to protect myself from the assault, from the intrusion, from the loss of my own will. So I think now that while I at that time experienced myself as being unable to do something I wanted to do, I was in fact taking good care of myself. I resisted in order to continue as an individual—in order not to be submerged, subjected, merged.*

After twenty years I could acknowledge that incident on the WU campus as something about which I could be proud. I want to note how even more difficult it may be for those with less privilege than I had—those without white skin privilege, or without a fine public education and a scholarship for more of the same—to stay attuned to their humanity, to not bear the burden of a devaluing assimilation, nor cooperate in their own oppression. In fact, while I believe my departure from WU was not a failure but the only way I then knew to not be co-opted into systems that denied my roots, I subsequently made other choices in which I temporarily submerged/closeted/denied the best parts of myself. Those are different stories, other routes I had to take to come to know a more honest, cohesive self.

As long as it took for me to reclaim this part of myself, my first-generation Jewish self—and trying to finish this piece has alerted me that

For Lesbians Only: A Separatist Anthology, eds. Sarah Hoagland and Julia Penelope (London: Onlywomen Press, 1992), p. 198.

the job is not yet done—it took even longer to salvage my mother's individual identity from amidst the debris of a very ethnic, immigrant Jewish family.

For some, the immigrant family resembles the AA model we have come to know as a dysfunctional family. In its effort to assimilate, that family cooperates in losing its history: no one talks about it in a valuing language, no one processes the experience of immigration, the native language is denied to subsequent generations, and the focus is on "fitting in." However, the family cannot fit in. The parents are shunned or patronized at the children's schools. *(Is that your grandmother? She talks funny. I think your mother called but I couldn't understand her accent.)* The few childhood friends who are allowed to visit may witness a loud, ebullient, bilingual family whose English sounds "broken" and whose customs are often different even though they both share cultural roots. Much depends upon the length of time the family has been in this country.

One might say I experienced a politicizing moment one Sabbath morning during my fourteenth or fifteenth year. My father, who worked a second job on Saturdays, could not attend a Bar Mitzvah at the reform congregation where his cousin's family were members. Instead of offering to drive my grandmother, mother, two younger sisters, and myself to the reception afterward, this wing of the family—wealthier than we were and more assimilated—left the five women in my family to wait for my father for over an hour on the temple steps. This "slight" let me know that we did not measure up for several reasons: my dad's second job (less because it was on the Sabbath than because it was necessary to our very existence), our lack of income and subsequent lack of "fashion," and our connections to an orthodoxy my grandmother and our extended family still adhered to. It also left me seething with anger that my mother and grandmother could be so discounted. Of course, as a teenage girl during the early 1960s, I hadn't a clue that my anger was justified or how to act upon it. In fact, such helplessness served to exacerbate the humiliation and shame I thought I felt only on my mother's and grandmother's behalf. I did not understand then that I would have been equally justified to feel anger on my own behalf and to have, somehow, shown some agency to rectify it.

Years later, as I began to reclaim myself, I found myself able to go back and understand—not revise—my herstory differently. To claim/reclaim myself as an activist, authentic, whole woman meant I had to also retrieve and reclaim my mother. I have revisited the trauma of my mother's life as an immigrant; as a strong, abrasive woman without an education who could not begin to understand her eldest daughter's soft-spoken literacy; as a woman without options and alternatives. This reaching back is not about forgiving my mother (though that may be a corollary experience for some) her (at times) narrow-mindedness, her mean-spirited verbal abuses, the belittling, and the too readily doled out corporal punishments.

These reclamations could not have happened for me without my coming out as a lesbian—without my consciously removing the last veil of yet one more layer of "other" I had suppressed. As soon as I came out, I found myself able to finally act on my own behalf, to do something with the anger and pain that I had long been experiencing. It was and is in a small but politicized lesbian community, within what was soon to be my accruing circle of friends, that I have been able to piece together the various conditions of my own birth—an eldest girl/lesbian child born to a working-class/immigrant/Jewish family—and to recognize how such a life can be representative of a larger picture, can illustrate class and ethnic/race analyses so that they are humanly recognizable and not only abstract concepts.

I cannot assess if it was luck or some more deliberate energy out of my own evolving consciousness that planted me on the doorsteps of that St. Louis lesbian community. What I do know is that if it were not for my own public coming out in this particular sphere/community, I would not have been able to break my silence around either personal or political concerns, or even to do work with others across lines of race, class, ethnicity, ability, sexual orientation. It was in the spontaneous discussions and planned gatherings around class and race that I glimpsed the interconnectedness of struggles of oppression. (The term *interconnectedness* may be misleading, but that is another conversation. Except to say that my focus today is to be part of creating an actively antiracist white culture. Understanding classism, sexism, and heterosexism is necessary to the antiracist work that is presently foremost in my life.) It was in those conversations that I developed a class analysis, that I discovered how my poor/working-class Jewish roots had differentiated me from mainstream society, that these were not only personal divisions but political and social ones as well. I learned, too, to affirm my resistance to societal pressures to assimilate.

As well, I came to know that regardless of my own sense of "otherness" around ethnicity, class, and sexual orientation, I had white skin privilege that I could not abdicate by merely refusing to identify as either white or American; that so doing robbed me of essential parts of my own identity; that if I were willing to do the work, I could find an antiracist/classist history and continuum into which my own identity does fit. I needed to participate in my own education to discern the myriad subtle ways my white skin privilege did and does benefit me. I needed to grasp how people of wealth and power use class and race to separate all of us. Without that knowledge I could not connect further to either my own past or future.

It was in a statewide battle to stop an antiqueer referendum that I saw firsthand how anti-oppression work, of whatever kind, cannot be done only in crisis, and that the failure to integrate various liberation struggles impedes any movement for real social change. For the most part, regardless of where or how or when we organized our Fight the Right activities, poor and working-class lesbians and gay men of color saw little point in joining with white lesbians and gay men, many of whom were finding out, for the first time, that they could be part of a system that would *not* work for them, *not* benefit them, in spite of their skin and class privilege. On the other hand, whatever the outcome of the struggle to stop the antiqueer referendum, it would little alter the lives of low-income lesbians and gay men of color who were already, and still are, being discriminated against because of race on their jobs, where they lived, when they went to apply for a loan or just shop at the mall.

I am still figuring out how to unify my various selves into a functioning, activist whole. It is undeniable that acknowledging my being a lesbian aloud has catapulted me much further along my journey than my silences around my sexuality ever did. Wiser amazon warriors have long understood this but perhaps, unconsciously, I had thought such silence could protect me. Opening only one door at a time while fearing another might shut in my face, I had never been able to speak out in my own behalf. Until I did so, I did not recognize how invested my own interests were/are in all liberation struggles. Until I did so, even my speaking out on behalf of others was often patronizing and ineffective because it appeared that I risked little. It was not until I could tell *my* story, to say I am a first-generation Jewish lesbian with white skin privilege, and at the same time recognize that none of my component parts or constituent groups are so sacred that they cannot suffer criticism, that I was also able to act with courage. To interrupt racism, anti-Semitism, classism, sexism, homophobia wherever I was, among family and friends, at work, in a political group whose intent is good but whose all-too-subtle white supremacist dynamic precludes effective work.

My uncle just called, as he does every few months. He goes by the name David Drake, a name he has used for over forty of his seventy-three years. It is his assimilated name, one he chose because he thought it would bring him more business, while offering some sort of cover to his Jewish heritage, deflecting anti-Semitism without his risking much to do so. My mother, his sister, would mock him nonetheless, calling him *dreck*, not Drake—the Yiddish word for *shit*.

My uncle just called, the one who used to be Harry Beitch, the Jewish boy who, shortly after arriving in this country, once lost a hard-to-come-by nickel an arm's length inside the wrought-iron fence of a church. He understood just enough to go home without that nickel when he found himself terrified at the thought of entering the churchyard to retrieve it. He understood he was not wanted there.

My uncle just called, the one who dyed his tightly waved, dead-give-away, dark hair a bright green one St. Patrick's day to "fit in," though to what no one could quite explain. My uncle just called, the one who, no matter what he calls himself, reminds me of where I come from. The one who, to this day, with all my self-probing and consciousness, still embarrasses me. I am his eldest niece; between us are what remains of shared memory that tells the story of who my mother was from child to adult, and still he embarrasses me. I want to believe it is because of his lack of consciousness, his refusal to change his own racist, sexist, homophobic behaviors. In fact, I fear the real reason may be more deeply layered than that. I suspect it is also because he is the loud, brash, Jewish "greenhorn" (a word of derision used often in my childhood home)

I have spent a lifetime trying to both understand and avoid. When he fails to call every three months or so, I call or find him to make sure he is alive if not well. Once a year, I invite him to share a holiday meal with other blood family members and my dyke family and friends, and I hold my breath that he will do nothing to embarrass, no, not himself, but me. Whatever ways I have demonstrated resistance to assimilation and disappearance (and I know these ways cannot be discounted), when compared to my uncle it is clear that I have, in some ways, done just that. He now is my mirror, a reminder to me that I am, in fact, not as peripheral, not as "other" as once I was.

For all my fine words, consciousness raising, and progressive rationale, I remain today embarrassed by one of my few living relatives, one of my links to where I came from, to who I am. I have processed in large part my own culture and class shock when first attending college. I have reclaimed some small parts of who my mother might have been. I live my lesbian life to some degree in the open. Yes, I am a Jewish working-class lesbian writer. That I am able to identify so definitively is part miracle and part constant struggle, and, no less than the social and political exertions in which such struggle is rooted, I find that my personal struggle with who I am is still, even if unexpectedly, raging.

Marlene Schuman is a fifty-two-year-old
first-generation white working-class Jewish
lesbian whose political voice will always
be very personal. Her life partner is a lifelong
activist involved in housing, women's, and
queer issues. Marlene teaches; her partner
inspects buildings. They fill their lives with
work, organizing, and writing. Marlene lives
the life she once only dreamed—as part
of a small but very conscious, always learning, progressive community of loving,
supportive lesbians.

A *great deal has been written on the subject of gay marriage, usually from the perspective of arguing for civil reform via legislative remedy. Very little has been written situating the issue in a broader historical and political context as Mab Segrest does here. She takes on this formidable task by using Hawai'i's landmark effort to legalize gay marriage to examine ways in which what is generally considered an assimilationist issue actually has links to anti-imperialist and antiracist struggles. Mab reminds us that constitutional amendments hard won by African Americans fighting slavery have given us the arguments being used to fight for gay civil rights today. With her customary insight, she offers a thumbnail history of the colonization of Hawai'i, links it to slavery in the South, and neatly stitches these struggles to gay liberation and the fight for sexual liberation.*

Hawai'ian Sovereignty/Gay Marriage: *Ka Huliau*
Mab Segrest

Aloha. I want to extend my deepest thanks for your invitation to participate in *Ka Huliau*/Linking Struggles. *Mahalo nui loa* from me and my *'ohana* to the People's Fund, to Rick and Cha and Ku'umeaaloha for your hospitality. I and my family are honored to be your guests. And *mahalo nui loa* to the state of Hawai'i from our lesbian family for the bold move in your courts on "gay marriage," which is stirring up so much commotion across the Pacific, and here as well I expect.

I have pondered since receiving your invitation if as a *haole* I can come to Hawai'i and not be merely one more of the six million tourists a year. That works out to thirty for every native Hawai'ian. I bring other questions as well. Why does this upholding of gay marriage happen here, and not another "state" in the U.S.? Is there something in Hawai'ian history—some link between gay marriage and Hawai'ian culture, gay rights and the struggle for sovereignty, or the labor struggles against the planter class, or women's struggles for equal rights, or the histories of peoples of color who make up the majority of the islands' people—to understand? I am excited to explore as many of these links as possible with you this weekend.

But for this talk, I want to focus, as a white person and a lesbian, on understanding the interweaving of sexuality, race, class, and gender within the context of anticolonial struggles in ways that allow us to more deeply link struggles—and spirits.

And, as long as we are thinking about marriage, how do we shape our commitments to one another—erotic, familial, communal, social, and economic—in an age when, once again, everything has been tossed up for grabs? How do we, linking struggles, claim the future?

I flew to be with you this weekend thousands of miles over the curve of the earth with my partner of twenty years, Barbara, and our ten-year-old daughter, Annie. How I get to you today is determined by where I

A version of this talk will be published in the author's forthcoming *Born to Belonging* (New Brunswick, NJ: Rutgers).

come from, who I am. I chart my way by my own relationship to my birth and chosen family and my land of the U.S. South, navigating my own historic tides, currents, trade winds in this season as the Pleiades sets.

Standing here in Honolulu, I acknowledge so many others who have come here for better or worse: Polynesians from the Marquesan Islands in their catamarans with sails woven from coconut fibers; Tahitians who conquered them centuries later, bringing divisions among commoner and royalty, women and men; Captain Cook who arrived in 1778 in one of the last spots on earth to be "discovered" by the West, breaking the *pono,* the balance; the missionaries who, coming to save souls, made fortunes, and the whalers and traders who followed, all bringing syphilis and other diseases for which the Hawai'ians had no immunity; the Chinese and Japanese and Portuguese and Filipinos imported to work the sugar plantations, deliberately set against each other by planters' practice of paying different wages to different nationalities (and, more recently, the arrival of Japanese developers); the men in French and British gunboats; and finally, the U.S. marines who overthrew the constitutional monarchy of Queen Liliuokalani in 1893 in an illegal coup, clearing the way for annexation by the U.S. five years later so that the 5 percent white minority came to control the economic and political resources of the islands. In my childhood in Alabama, it was a 10 percent white minority that controlled the 90 percent African American people and the land.

In this February of 1997, who am I to come to Hawai'i, and from where do I come? I come from a culture as rooted in practices of slavery as Hawai'i is in practices of colonialism, understanding that slavery was, among other things, a particularly virulent form of colonialism. Colonial practices required two things: ownership of land, and exploitable labor to extract its resources as private profits. In these respects, your history is sadly familiar to me.

Europeans encountered indigenous people whose spirituality could not conceive of humans *owning* the land, the water, the sky; and Europeans rapidly tried to destroy those cultures. When in 1492 Columbus landed in the Bahamas thinking he had found the trade routes to Asia that Cook and others later sought, he observed a communal people "astonishing…in their affection and kindness" in the moment that they met acquisitive, profit-driven Europe. Columbus cut to the quick of cultural differences in this huge moment: "I could not clearly understand whether the people possess any private property."[1] Likewise, Hawai'ian culture when Cook arrived, with its thousand-year-old system of Mālama 'Āina, caring for the land, had no verb for *to own*. In the 1820s, O.P. Emerson, one of the first missionaries to Hawai'i, made an observation remarkably similar to Columbus': "Among the common people themselves there was a loose, mischievous conception of the rights of private ownership. If one asked a friend for something he wanted, it was customary not to refuse the request for fear of being dubbed *pi* (stingy)."[2]

Columbus observed of the Arawak who swam out to his ship, unarmed, they were "well-built, with good bodies and handsome features.... They would make fine servants....With fifty men we could subjugate them all and make them do what we want." [3] Such attitudes had genocidal effects. Two years after Columbus' arrival in what is now Haiti, half of the 250,000 Indians were dead through murder, mutilation, disease, or suicide. In 1492, indigenous people in the Americas totaled at least 70 million; by 1650 they had been reduced to 3.5 million.[4] Similarly, European-introduced diseases decimated the Hawai'i population, 83 percent in the first forty-five years after contact, from 400,000-one million down to 40,000 in a little over one hundred years.[5] Such devastation brought huge grief, dislocation, and cultural and spiritual crisis that made Hawai'ians vulnerable to the Great Māhele, the introduction of private ownership through which colonizers quickly seized control of the island's resources. Forty years after the Great Māhele in Hawai'i, the United States government enacted the Dawes Severalty Act to make available what was left of communally owned reservation land at the end of the "Indian Wars" to white settlers, leading to a loss of 60 million acres in thirteen years.[6] In Hawai'i five years after Dawes Severalty, the political coup that established the new "republic" in 1893 was almost anticlimactic.

Under colonialism, exploitation of land and labor go hand in hand. In the Americas, indigenous people died from forced labor, or fought back in open warfare on familiar terrain, or died of diseases, so European settlers brought in Africans to work as slaves. Over 50 million Africans died in the slave trade, and millions of survivors faced two and a half centuries as chattel slaves in a culture whose religious, spiritual, economic, and political practices evolved to justify their brutal exploitation. In the county where I was born, settlers moved in African slaves five years after the Creek Indians were sent on a forced march West. Outside of official slave territory, investors found other means to similar ends. William Hooper, a Boston visitor to a sugar mill on the island of Kauai in 1835, noticed a small group of Chinese workers and wrote home to the New England businessmen who had sent him: "They have to work all the time—and no regard is paid to their complaints for food, etc., etc. Slavery is nothing compared to it."[7]

As a white person I can locate myself in this terrain by great-grandfathers who were settler colonists. But how do I locate myself as a lesbian? Let me return to your Supreme Court's stand on "gay marriage," which ricocheted through Congress and many states as Congress and state legislatures rushed to defend heterosexual marriage against our latest onslaught. I have not been so disgusted in a long time as in this past election season when even supposedly progressive politicians ran from gay marriage as well as from poor women and children on welfare. I guess that the relationship between Hawai'ian sovereignty and gay marriage is similar to the relationship between African American freedom struggles and gay civil rights. So, again, let me start on what to me is the more familiar terrain of civil rights.

Last year [in 1996] the Supreme Court in *Romer v. Evans* passed a landmark decision that finally gave gay and lesbian citizens of the United States constitutional status. The ruling came in response to Amendment 2 in Colorado, the prototype for an epidemic of ballot initiatives that would prohibit states or cities from extending lesbians and gay men protection against discrimination. The opposition argued that we wanted not "equal rights," but "special rights," and Justice Kennedy faced the issue head-on:

> We find nothing special in the protections Amendment
> Two withholds. These are protections taken for granted
> by most people either because they already have them,
> or do not need them; these are protections against exclusion from an almost limitless number of transactions and
> endeavors that constitute ordinary civil life in a free
> society.

Lesbians and gay men, the court affirmed, were not "strangers to the law." The Second Amendment was ruled to be a violation of the Equal Protection Clause of the Fourteenth Amendment.

When I celebrated this ruling last year, part of my gratitude went to the generations of African Americans and their antiracist white allies who struggled to abolish slavery and institute the Thirteenth, Fourteenth, and Fifteenth Amendments in the years immediately following the Civil War. These amendments brought the country closer to fulfilling its democratic ideals. The Thirteenth abolished human slavery. The Fifteenth prohibited denying suffrage on the basis of race, color, or previous condition of servitude. The Fourteenth defined citizenship for the first time as belonging to anyone born or naturalized within the U.S., guaranteed equal protection and due process, and made the Bill of Rights binding on the states. When lesbians and gay men took up our call for civil rights a century later, we inherited the legacy of this struggle against slavery and the "badges of slavery." When we are conscious of this legacy, we can link struggles. When we are not, we seem (and often are) guilty of racist appropriation.

When lesbian and gay lawyers argue the marriage question before the U.S. Supreme Court, as I am sure they some day will, they will undoubtedly cite *Loving v. Virginia:*

> The freedom to marry has long been recognized as one of the vital personal rights essential to the orderly pursuit of happiness by free men. Marriage is one of the basic civil rights of man, fundamental to our very existence and survival.

Thus in 1967 the U.S. Supreme Court struck down a Virginia law against interracial marriage.

We can also see in Southern history how cruelly this "marriage question" has played itself out. In 1859, the lawyer for an adult slave accused of raping a slave child argued:

> The crime of rape does not exist in the State between African slaves. Our laws recognize no marital rights as between slaves; their sexual intercourse is left to be regulated by their owners. The regulations of law, as to the white race,

> on the subject of sexual intercourse, do not and cannot,
> for obvious reasons, apply to slaves; their intercourse is
> promiscuous, and the violation of a female slave by a male
> slave would be a mere assault and battery. [8]

On the other hand, the rape by a white slave master of a black woman was no crime at all, but bore him more children and increased property. A slave master writing in 1856 to his white son about a black woman who was apparently his mistress and their children demonstrates this perverse intermingling of family and property rights:

> I cannot free these people and send them North. It would
> be cruelty to them. Nor would I like that any but my own
> blood should own as Slaves my own blood or Louisa. I
> leave them to your charge, believing that you will best
> appreciate and most independently carry out my wishes
> in regard to them. Do not let Louisa or any of my chil-
> dren or possible children be slaves of Strangers. Slavery
> in the family will be their happiest earthly condition. [9]

"No marital rights" among enslaved African Americans went hand in hand with the institution of "slavery in the family"!

Questions of race, gender, colonialism, and sexuality take us rapidly beyond civil rights, and to the limits of the U.S. Constitution as bases for democratic struggles. The Constitution in its first seventy-five years, after all, did allow human slavery; and in 1893 it did not stop Marines from overthrowing Hawai'i's constitutional monarch. The Fourteenth Amendment guarantees due process to protect "life, liberty and *property*." It is in that last word, *property,* that there's a Constitutional rub. The Declaration of Independence declared the inalienable rights "life, liberty and the *pursuit of happiness*." This passage from *happiness* to *property* is the passage of Hawai'ian history between Cook's arrival in 1778 and the Great Māhele in 1848 that ended the system by which ruling chiefs managed all land for the benefit of all the people. Instead, plots were parceled among commoners, ruling chiefs, royal family, and the government, dispossessing up to 90 percent of native Hawai'ians of their land and right to vote.

Your Aloha Spirit Law seems to invoke a higher principle than our Constitution. "The essence of relationships in which each person is important to every other person for collective existence" is the basis by which Judge Heely recently ordered the state to give back a billion dollars from its use of ceded lands, his last act before leaving the state! So much of the spirit of the law in the United States is still constrained by the idea that turned humans, including one's own children, and sacred land into "private property" operating for profit. Surely your Supreme Court's recent decisions on gay marriage come within the collective, relational spirit of Aloha.

It is on this slippery terrain of "native land and foreign desire," to use the title of a book on the Great Māhele, that I take my bearing as a lesbian. Last year, the World Council of Churches conducted a study process on Gospel and Cultures, and part of what they asked was, "When does the Gospel arrive as good news and when does it arrive as bad news in a culture?"

Missionaries in Hawai'i brought both good and bad news. The church as well, for lesbians and gay men, can be both very good or very bad news. The "good news" of the Gospel is a spirit of love that redeems the outcast, binds up the broken, lifts up the fallen, tends the poor and sick and pained. When Christianity arrives as bad news, it does just the opposite: breaks, casts out, divides. When Hiram Brigham landed with his missionary cohort in the 1820s, Hawai'ian sexual practices were an integral part of the cultural, spiritual, political, and economic life of this place. There were practices of *punalua,* in which two lovers could share the same mate, jealousy being discouraged and collective responsibility for children encouraged. Bisexuality, among men at least, was prevalent; *aikāne* were male lovers. I certainly hope the women were similarly engaged. In general, there was *moe aku, moe mai,* "sleeping here and there."[10] The Akua Lono, the god of fertility and sexuality, divided the calendar with Kū, the god of war. During Lono's four months there was feasting, celebration, dancing, sports. The absence of war, work, and sacrifice.

As a lesbian, I feel at home on Lono's terrain. I do believe that if I surveyed any particular group of homosexuals—*Do you want to sign up for Lono or Kū?*—97 percent of us would hunker down in the months of Lono and try to keep the party going for the rest of the year. I think the gays in the military thing was a peculiar aberration, a deliberate working against this grain. I know, like marriage, the campaign about the military was about economics, and for some people it was about patriotism. Lately, in discussions with heterosexual progressives, I get asked what gay culture is. It's a complex question. Partly I want to say gay people *are* culture: we recognize ourselves among the artists and shamans across cultures, although there are several homosexuals, I am sure, who are not talented or creative or particularly spiritual. We seem to have an affinity for Lono, Mardi Gras, gay pride parades, parts of which are downright scandalous.

Calvinist missionaries rapidly set about to introduce shame and guilt into Hawai'ian sexuality, as they simultaneously advocated for the institution of private property and the introduction of other European/white families to form a new colonial elite. The disruption of indigenous sexual practices was part of getting Hawai'i into the "missionary position" to get screwed in many other ways: conflating sexuality with guilt and shame; narrowing the range of sexual practices to heterosexual monogamous marriage. Was this good or bad news? Let me make clear that I am not talking here about heterosexual *relationships*, the *experience* of heterosexuality, but about heterosexuality as an institution enforced by legal, religious, and medical regimes, and by brutal random violence. From an anticolonial perspective, is enforced monogamous heterosexual marriage a Māhele of the body? The sovereign body, sovereign culture, sovereign government: is there not some principle here of self-determination in a context of our essential interdependence that also links Hawai'ian sovereignty and gay liberation?

The enforced nuclear family is part of institutional heterosexuality, as it is of sexism. Lesbian and gay relationships do not make sense within the framework of the nuclear family because it was constructed to exclude us. Many "welfare mothers" do not either because the nuclear family was also constructed to exclude people of color and the poor. That's what had all those politicians, Clinton on down, running this summer: an unwillingness to take on institutional heterosexuality, with its inherent sexism: one man in control of one woman and their children in one house equals a family. Perhaps it is this that so terrifies right-wing demagogues who bleat that gay marriage will end "six thousand years of Western civilization." I suspect that lesbian and gay families might fare better in cultures where, as in Hawai'ian, the word for *mother* and *father* also means *uncle* and *aunt*, or any member of one's parents' generation. And any *keiki,* child, is one's own child.

I want to emphasize that I raise these questions about marriage as someone in a twenty-year relationship, more than sixteen of which have been monogamous, and I don't foresee changing that agreement any-time soon. If the decision of the Hawai'i Supreme Court became law of the land, it would give me the possibility of access to a right "fun-damental to my existence and security." The custody of our child would be much more secure. Barb and I could be entitled to the benefits of the other's social security upon one of our deaths, which believe me we will need. Whatever we can scrape up of retirement would pass to the other without taxes taking out another chunk of it. We would sig-nal to our families and much of the rest of the world, in ways they under-stand, the primacy of our relationship, our intent to be life partners, including sharing of physical passion and spiritual discovery, a com-ing together of increased consciousness. Such a ruling, especially, would put lesbian and gay committed relationships on a par with het-erosexual committed relationships—as psychologically, spiritually, economically equal. That is exactly where I think they should be.

However, I am cautious about a tendency within the lesbian/gay/bi/trans community that sees gay marriage as a way to normalize our desire, so that it is no longer "foreign," without realizing that within Western culture, there is a way in which all desire is foreign desire. Freud was very clear about this: Western civilization is based on the repression of "instinct" (by which he meant sexual desire). So any desire lies outside of "civilization." Oppressed people (various people of color, women, the poor, homosexuals) are understood as heathen, savage, barbarous, subhuman because we are seen to be more sexual.[11] Freud called this process *projection.* Of course, various talk show hosts are working tire-lessly to fill in the gap between culture and desire with endless conver-sations about infinite forms of sexual acts and identities. In the meantime, Christian Coalition-type groups are toting their latest video versions of subhuman gay desire around these islands right this minute build-ing a backlash to gay marriage. On the one hand, they argue that we are inherently promiscuous. On the other, that we want to destroy West-ern civilization by getting married. It's that old double whammy, artic-ulated by the slave/master/lawyer: *Our laws recognize no marital rights between them./Their intercourse is promiscuous.* What you do not hear them talking much about a-tall is what *they* do in bed.

When lesbians and gay men do not recognize this schism between culture and desire, we underestimate the resistance to our assimilation and the dangers of the culture into which we are assimilating. Or we declare ourselves *forever queer—get used to it,* and unassimilable. For me, a gay marriage civil rights strategy must also be accompanied by a broader discussion of culture and desire. Sexuality (outside of procreation) has an integral place in the culture's balance. What are the cultural/sexual/social/economic arrangements that are worth our linking struggles to build so that none of us is cast permanently as outsider?

Should gay marriage become legal in Hawai'i (and I realize that's still a long shot), the gay community nationally needs to think long and hard about how lesbians and gay men who choose to come to Hawai'i to marry can join with and support progressive struggles here, not become just a homo version of hetero honeymooners, or some new incarnation of gay tourism gone berserk. (I can see it now. Lesbians float over on Olivia cruises, choosing between getting hitched on the beach or the lava flow. For the guys it's that ritzy hotel with the dolphins in the pool....)

So how do we, linking struggles and spirits, claim the future? What kind of relationships do we want to have, anyway? We are answering that in many, many ways this weekend. Let me come back again to this question of marriage. When the North Carolina legislature "outlawed" gay marriage last summer, part of the lesbian/gay community planned a wedding ceremony on the steps of the legislature. No genuine preachers being available, they asked me to preside. I tried to explain to the zillion cameras and the legislators peeking through the doors that the wedding vow—*to have and to hold, for better or worse, richer or poorer, in sickness and in health*—is a social contract for everybody. If the legislature does not protect the rights of workers to safe jobs with decent pay, or provide healthcare and insurance for everyone, or protect the most vulnerable among us such as women and children on public assistance, then all our relationships suffer. Because we are all interdependent.

Barb and I once again asked ourselves that question—what relationship did we want to have—a couple of years ago when we had our fifteenth anniversary celebration, which actually came at seventeen years because it took us that long to get up the nerve to do it. We invited two hundred friends, hired a band, and told them to bring a lot of good food. Then we set about to figure out what we wanted to promise each other. We affirmed our process, over the years, of "me becoming you becoming me" and the commitments that, as we follow them, keep our friendship vital.

> *I promise*
> *to honor the spirit in you,*
> *to protect your freedom as if it were my own,*
> *because it is:*
> *to seek abandon and play,*
> *to honor our bodies' pleasures,*
> *to speak anger freshly, share pain,*
>   *allow comfort and release.*
> *I promise to create joy*
> *in the tasks of a shared life.*
> *I promise to nurture your love for Annie.*
> *I promise to come to find you in the present's*
>   *blinking eye*
> *which is the only moment we ever have.*
> *And when I do not do all these things,*
> *perfectly, every time*
> *I promise to forgive myself and gently*
>   *to begin again.*

It's probably not such a bad formula, either, for linking struggles.

Notes:

1. The Columbus Letter of March 14, 1493 (Chicago: The Newberry Library, 1953), 10, quoted in Virgil J. Vogel, *This Country Was Ours: A Documentary History of the American Indian* (New York: HarperCollins, 1992), p. 34.

2. Lilikala Kame'eleihiwa, *Native Land and Foreign Desires* (Honolulu: Bishop Museum Press, 1992), pp. 9, 204.

3. Quoted in Howard Zinn, *A People's History of the United States* (New York: Harper & Row, 1980), p. 1.

4. Eduardo Galeano, *Open Veins of Latin America: Five Centuries of the Pillage of a Continent*, trans. Cedric Belfrage (New York: Monthly Review Press, 1973), p. 50.

5. Kame'eleihiwa, p. 20.

6. Nell Painter, *Standing at Armageddon: The United States, 1877-1919* (New York: W.W. Norton, 1987), p. 163.

7. Quoted in Ronald Takaki, *Strangers from a Different Shore: A History of Asian Americans* (Boston: Little, Brown & Company, 1989), pp. 32-33.

8. Quoted in Catherine Clinton, "'Southern Dishonor': Flesh, Blood, Race, and Bondage" in *Our Joy and Sorrow* (New York: Oxford University Press, 1991), p. 66.

9. James Henry Hammond, quoted in Clinton, p. 62.

10. Kame'eleihiwa, pp. 43, 44, 47, 160.

11. Sigmund Freud, *Civilization and Its Discontents*, trans. and ed. James Strachey (New York: W.W. Norton, 1969).

Mab Segrest *is an organizer and writer who lives in Durham, North Carolina. She is currently coordinator of the Urban-Rural Mission (USA), part of the URM network of the World Council of Churches. She is also the author of* My Mama's Dead Squirrel: Lesbian Essays on Southern Culture *(Firebrand) and* Memoir of a Race Traitor *(South End), which was the 1994 Editor's Choice (Lambda Book Awards) and was named a Myers Center Outstanding Book on Human Rights in North America.*

In *this forceful essay, Barbara Smith discusses the necessity for lifelong activism. She delivers a concise explanation of the differences between reform and liberation work, and the reasons for navigating between the two. Her eye is focused firmly on the prize—"radical social change"—and her lens is that of a black lesbian socialist. She uses the work of other black lesbians in particular to discuss what a commitment to activism looks like. Starting with the collective that issued the groundbreaking Combahee River Statement in 1977, she fast-forwards to the contributions of a number of black lesbian activists today. Their jobs may have changed but their work has not. These are women whose vision and dedication to the often unglamorous work of grassroots activism frequently goes unrecognized.*

Invaluable here is her discussion of the disturbing synergy between homophobia—including internalized homophobia—within the black community, and the unexamined racism of the predominantly white male reform-minded activists in lgbt organizations. These distinct strains combine to thwart what Barbara Smith argues, and I would agree, is the best hope for real revolution: the leadership of lesbians/women of color, in particular women who are out of the closet and whose grassroots vision for linking struggles is critical to the lgbt liberation movement.

Doing It From Scratch: The Challenge of Black Lesbian Organizing

Barbara Smith

For Audre Lorde and Pat Parker

Like many activists, I have been frustrated by how little written material there is about what it takes to do political work. I wanted to address that need when I wrote this article in 1995 for a black lesbian anthology in which it ultimately did not appear. "Doing It from Scratch" complements the dialogue, "Black Lesbian/Feminist Organizing: A Conversation," which I did with three other women in 1982 for *Home Girls: A Black Feminist Anthology.*

As I grow older, I am more and more convinced that coming of age in the 1960s was one of the luckiest coincidences of my life. I graduated from high school in 1965 and from college in the class of 1969. The incredible intensity and political ferment of that decade perfectly coincided with the time when I was personally discovering who I was, testing my intellect, leaving home, exploring my sexuality, and meeting more and more people who cared about the same things I did: writing, art, and making political change.

I am well aware that the sixties often take on the proportions of a myth, a myth which does injustice both to the achievements and the failings of that era. From the vantage point of the 1990s, however, I realize that one of the sixties' greatest gifts was providing a living, breathing sense of radical political possibility for those of us who were open to embracing it.

Simply switching on the television or picking up a newspaper could furnish that day's object lesson about this society's incredible contradictions, its moral and material wrongs. The useless carnage in Vietnam; the violence that whites visited upon black human beings who wanted to do outrageous things like attend school, ride public transportation, and vote; and eventually not being able to distinguish news footage of Newark and Detroit burning from Soweto and Saigon all served to raise popular consciousness and to heighten a sense of urgency. Current events provided dramatic illustrations of a system on the edge, a country in grave need of repair.

My political education and commitments were profoundly shaped by this history. The iconoclasm and hopefulness of those times inspire me still. One of the most important things I learned was that actual power lies in the hands of "ordinary" people who come together to challenge authority and to make a difference; that effective grassroots organizing can transform consciousness, policies, laws, and most importantly, the quality of individual people's daily lives. I learned that the measure of successful organizing lies not in the size of a group's budget, but in how clear its goals are, how consistently its members carry out the tasks they have taken on, how deep their analysis goes of what is really wrong with this system, and finally how much they care about and love other human beings. The political ferment of the era gave me a school for life.

I often explain that the reason I am an activist is that for me not being one is tantamount to saying, *Yes massa, yes boss, whatever you say. It's fine with me that your heavy foot is planted directly on my neck.* While it certainly takes courage to speak out, and any organizer who is really doing the work sometimes gets scared, to me the alternative of unchecked racism, homophobia, sexual and class oppression is a hundred times worse.

The only activity that has ever altered oppression and transformed disenfranchised people's powerlessness is collective grassroots organizing. The abolition of slavery, the overturning of Jim Crow, the victories of the labor movement, ending the war in Vietnam, the ongoing struggles against racism and imperialism, and the fight for lesbian, gay, and women's liberation are all examples of what people can achieve when we band together to take control of our lives. On the other hand, getting politicians to listen, passing needed legislation, creating positive media images, and individually earning a decent living at a workplace that would not have hired you a generation ago are the result of effective organizing, not the ultimate goals of liberation itself.

The former examples have revolutionary potential because of how they alter power relationships in the society and challenge the status quo. The latter examples are essentially reforms, which although beneficial and needed, do not get to the root of our problems and transform the system. The so-called democracy that we have under capitalism can accommodate numerous reforms without diminishing the power of the ruling class. As a socialist and an alert black woman, it is clear to me that it is not possible to achieve justice, especially economic justice, and equality under capitalism because capitalism was never designed for that to be the case. When I do political work, it is always important to be able to distinguish between issues and actions that have the potential, ultimately, to change the system, and those that address symptoms of oppression more than causes. The assaults from the present system necessitate that most activists work for reforms, but those of us who are radicals understand it is possible to do so at the very same time that we work for fundamental change—a revolution.

Recognizing capitalism's fundamental limitations and inequalities, I have no illusions that individual financial success (which I have never experienced) is a substitute for real freedom because I am not merely concerned about what I possess. Of course I want to be able to pay my bills, but I also want to live in a world where no one and nothing suffers because of violence, exploitation, and poverty. I cannot really be free if I live in a context where wrong is being carried out in my name, and as a U.S. citizen, this government's inhumane domestic and foreign policies constantly place me in this undesired position, unless I counter them by speaking out and fighting back. The financial success of a few, even if they are members of racially and/or sexually oppressed groups, is not justice. It is merely privilege.

I have brought the practical lessons and the passionate optimism of my political awakening in the sixties to my organizing as a black lesbian feminist. Activism, like the deepest learning, or an art form that one hones for a lifetime, can stay with you forever if you keep it alive through constant use. Because I still work for peace, I cannot forget going to New York one Saturday in the spring of 1967, marching to the United Nations to protest the Vietnam War, and hearing Martin Luther King, Jr. speak out against the war at a time when most blacks still saw it as a white issue. Nor will I forget being on the streets of Chicago during the Democratic convention in the summer of 1968, when the Chicago police rioted and brought the war home. Because of my devotion to black women's freedom, I will never forget meeting Fannie Lou Hamer at a basement party in Cleveland in 1965 following a rally at which she had spoken. What struck me most about her was how much she resembled the women in my family who I would return home to later that night: her Southern voice, her ample figure, her difficulty walking, and her great kindness to me simply because I was young.

I have received an incredible amount of joy from activism. I suppose it is in my nature always to question, to want to shake things up, to be generally "contrary" as my grandmother would have put it. It gives me great pleasure and a feeling of pride to hear, for example, that Indian peasants rebelled in Chiapas, Mexico, on the day that the North Atlantic Free Trade Agreement (NAFTA) went into effect or that black lesbians and gays had the courage to organize the Bayard Rustin memorial contingent at the thirtieth anniversary of the 1963 March on Washington. I feel good whenever I hear that those who are not rich, not white, not male, and not straight have stood up to our enemies and triumphed. Whatever the outcome, the ultimate victory lies in the fact that they chose to stand up.

Because of where I have come from I find it difficult to accept that many black lesbians who are so multiply oppressed are not involved in organizing on behalf of their own liberation during this period. As we wrote in the Combahee River Statement in 1977:

> The most general statement of our politics at the present time would be that we are actively committed to struggling against racial, sexual, heterosexual, and class oppression, and see as our particular task the development of integrated analysis and practice based upon the fact that the major systems of oppression are interlocking. The synthesis of these oppressions creates the conditions of our lives. As Black women we see Black feminism as the logical political movement to combat the manifold and simultaneous oppressions that all women of color face.

Although we acknowledged the difficulty of organizing as black women against myriad forms of systematic oppression, we nevertheless asserted:

> We might use our position at the bottom, however, to make
> a clear leap into revolutionary action. If Black women
> were free, it would mean that everyone else would have
> to be free since our freedom would necessitate the
> destruction of all the systems of oppression.*

Obviously black women, including black lesbians, have a remarkable tradition of struggle. But the great potential for vibrant political leadership embodied by the work of Combahee and the unprecedented, energetic coalitions of a variety of feminists of color at the beginning of the 1980s seem to have all but disappeared in the 1990s. Of course there are lesbian of color activists who are doing wonderful organizing on a range of issues in the United States and Canada, and it is gratifying that many of them are also younger women. Nevertheless, my impression is that the majority of black lesbians are not politically active, and this includes women who only a decade ago would probably have become dynamic organizers. I do not pretend to know all of the reasons why more black lesbians do not get involved in doing political work, but I am aware of several roadblocks that seem to prevent people from becoming active.

Probably the most serious deterrent to black lesbian activism is the closet itself. It is very difficult and sometimes impossible to organize around black lesbian issues, such as homophobic violence, child custody, and right-wing initiatives, when you do not want people to know who you are. Not only does staying closeted keep women from becoming involved in specifically lesbian activism, but I have seen it deter them from being politically involved in any issue. In Albany, where I have lived for the last ten years, very few black lesbians are out and politically active, which means that they not only avoid lesbian and gay activities, but they also steer clear of feminist organizing, antiracist organizing, antiwar organizing, et cetera. I have often wondered if they avoid political involvement completely because they are afraid that if they are seen participating in any progressive cause, it might make them more visible as lesbians.

The repercussions of being out can indeed be quite serious, but I

The Combahee River Collective Statement: Black Organizing in the Seventies and Eighties (New York: Kitchen Table: Women of Color Press, 1986), pp. 9, 15.

have found that the benefits of being honest, of loving one's self, of building a supportive community where you can be all of who you are, and the empowerment and sense of freedom that come from not being in hiding, far outweigh the negatives.

Another roadblock for potential black lesbian activists, which results from being closeted, is a lack of visible models of what effective black lesbian (and gay) organizing looks like. To this day, black women ask me how to get in touch with the Combahee River Collective, which disbanded in 1981. Clearly, the collective's words communicate a practical vision that continues to inspire. I wish that I could fully convey to them what it was like to do black feminist and lesbian organizing in the mid-1970s when we certainly had no specific role models. As one of our cofounders, Demita Frazier, said at one of our early meetings, "This is not a mix cake. We have got to make it up from scratch." Not only did Combahee do consciousness raising and political work on a multitude of issues, we also built strong friendship networks, community, and a rich black women's culture where none had existed before.

I believe that another serious roadblock to activism is the ideological content of much of current theory, especially in the academy. Black lesbians who have been in school recently have often been exposed to the airless, inaccessible abstractions that dominate literary studies, women's studies, and queer studies. The varieties of academic theory that are most popular have little to say about collective struggle and less to say about the inhumane material conditions that motivate people to want to make change.

Despite the largely incomprehensible arguments that proponents of such theories offer when challenged about the political usefulness of their ideas, most of these modes of thought are frighteningly effective in maintaining the political status quo. Very little is said about why and under what conditions people begin to move, about how successful movements happen. One criterion I often rely upon for assessing the revolutionary content of ideas and actions is to ask the question originally posed by the visionary poet and activist Sonia Sanchez, which is, "But how do it free us?" Sanchez is asking about collective strategies, not individualized solutions. When most popular theoretical models are interrogated in this way, they do not have much to offer.

Other deterrents to effective organizing are the negative attitudes and behaviors that substitute for activism among some black lesbians and gay men themselves. These individuals operate with unfortunate, even dangerous misperceptions of what organizing actually is. Their actions ignore one of the most basic principles for a successful organizer: she must have a sufficient capacity to work with other people so that a job can get done without emotionally annihilating those with whom she works. Sometimes it seems that people actually measure the success of their activities and the righteousness of their politics by how thoroughly they can attack and tear down the efforts of others. In short, how lousy they can make others feel.

Humor, cooperation, reliability, humility, and kindness work better than arrogance, cruelty, manipulation, and divahood any day. Real leaders know this. They also know that being in the limelight or up on the stage is a by-product of effective organizing, not the goal. The best organizing is not ego driven, power tripping, or top down. It is egalitarian, fair, humane, and damned hard work.

In assessing reasons for the diminishing of dynamic black lesbian organizing during this period, it is crucial to take into account the overall political climate in which we must operate—the blows to progressive organizing that all of our movements have experienced in the eighties and the nineties. Reactionary politics not only have dominated the government for more than a decade, but hold more and more sway among the population as a whole, as illustrated by the huge popularity of media hatemongers such as Rush Limbaugh and Howard Stern. The increasing power of the well-organized right wing makes this a difficult and challenging time to be an activist. The problems we face—such as drugs, homelessness, and violence—seem so overwhelming and complicated that cocooning and focusing on one's personal life and career appears much easier than figuring out what to do politically. In this situation, the lack of visible models of successful activism becomes particularly debilitating to movement building.

Our lack of political activism is dangerous at a time when the right wing is flourishing and has placed homophobic campaigns against lesbian and gay rights at the top of their agenda. In the last two years, the white pseudoreligious right wing has specifically targeted communities of color nationwide with their hate-filled, protofascist message. They are successfully passing homophobic initiatives or rescinding existing gay rights legislation in cities throughout the country, and all too often doing so with the help of black ministers, black church members, and black voters. This is the first time in history that some segments of the African American community have made alliances with groups that have always been our enemies. The Right's divisive tactics are exemplified by the vicious propaganda film, *Gay Rights, Special Rights,* which is explicitly aimed at black audiences.

In most of the places where the Right has run these campaigns, black lesbians and gay men have not visibly mobilized to counter their attacks. Often the right wing has had complete carte blanche in targeting the black community in a particular locale because black lesbians and gays have not previously organized around any issue. When national right-wing groups begin to mobilize in their hometown, they are unprepared to respond to a crisis situation that requires organizational infrastructures and strategic political expertise impossible to acquire overnight. In most cases, countercampaigns against the Right are led by white gays and lesbians who have little idea how to communicate with and work effectively with members of the black community. The racism, white solipsism, and elitism that traditionally dominate the mainstream white gay male political agenda spell absolute disaster when what is at stake is changing our own communities' attitudes about issues of sexual orientation and civil rights.

I see the need for specifically black lesbian-led organizing more than ever. Not only do we have the potential to counter homophobic and heterosexist attacks within the black community, but we also can provide much needed leadership in all kinds of struggles. Despite the challenges I have outlined, there are, in fact, black lesbians who are engaged in incredibly effective organizing all over the country. Knowing that these courageous women exist plays a major role in keeping me sane. When I feel discouraged and alone I think of them and am heartened that there are other sisters out there doing the work.

There are sisters like Skye Ward in the Bay Area, who was a founding editor of the black lesbian magazine *Aché* and is now doing groundbreaking work in the African American community to counter homophobia and attacks from the right wing; Stephanie Smith, who coordinates the Lesbians of Color Project of the National Center for Lesbian Rights and is organizing against the right wing both locally in the

Bay Area and nationally; Kathleen Saadat in Portland, Oregon, who has been a black lesbian feminist activist for two decades and who worked exhaustively to defeat the Oregon Citizens' Alliance's Proposition Nine; Cathy Cohen in New Haven, who did organizing against police brutality in Ann Arbor, Michigan, and who co-founded New York's Black AIDS Mobilization; N'tanya Lee, who works with People Advocating Change in Education (PACE) in New York City, an organization which played a pivotal role in the struggle to establish the Children of the Rainbow curriculum and which is now developing a school curriculum about lesbians and gay men of color; Tamara Jones in Brooklyn, who is currently working to build the first organization for Caribbean American lesbians and gay men; Tania Abdulahad in Washington, D.C., who was a founder in the 1970s of Sapphire Sapphos and who has done years of organizing to challenge violence against women; Mandy Carter of the Human Rights Campaign Fund, who worked on Harvey Gantt's historic campaign against Senator Jesse Helms in North Caroline in 1990 and who now coordinates a national project cosponsored by the National Black Lesbian and Gay Leadership Forum to mobilize the black community against the right wing's homophobic initiatives; Ivy Young of the National Gay and Lesbian Task Force in Washington, D.C., who is a long-time political and cultural organizer and who coordinates the Task Force's annual Creating Change conference; Pat Hussain, who was a national coordinator for the 1993 March on Washington for Lesbian, Gay, and Bi Equal Rights and who is now working to develop strategic lesbian organizing in the South; and Candice Boyce, Maua Flowers, and many other women in New York City, who founded and are still committed to African American Women United for Societal Change, the oldest black lesbian organization in the United States. Of course there are countless sisters I have not mentioned, but whose political energy is apparent even in these hard times.

I want to pay particular tribute to black women in Albany, the "home girls" with whom I do political work. Sheila Stowell coordinated the first Grassroots Organizing Track at the 1994 National Black Lesbian and Gay Leadership Forum Conference with Suzanne Shende from New York. This two-day series of keynotes and workshops offered an explicitly progressive political focus at the conference and established a base for an ongoing activist presence. Mattie Richardson is the associate publisher of Kitchen Table: Women of Color Press and in her less than two years in Albany has worked for reproductive rights, organized against homophobia and the right wing in the black community, run writing workshops for women who are HIV positive or who are living with AIDS, and been an active member of the Feminist Action Network (FAN).

I always describe Vickie Smith as a natural organizer because of the quality and quantity of the work she does. She had played a key role in the Capital District's Coalition Against Apartheid and Racism, served on Albany's Police/Civilian Relations Commission, done AIDS organizing in the black community, was actively involved in our area's organizing against the Gulf War, was a co-founder in 1989 of FAN, and has provided transforming leadership as president of the board of Holding Our Own, Albany's women's foundation. One of Vickie's longtime dreams, finally realized in 1993, was to bring the Lavender Light gospel choir to Albany. Not only was the concert a highly successful cultural event, but it was consciously organized as a unique opportunity to bring various constituencies together, especially the African American and lesbian and gay communities.

Albany, New York's state capital, is a small, conservative city, which means that the organizing we do here must overcome some of the same obstacles that challenge activists who work outside of east and west coast urban centers. Before I moved here, I had never tried to do political work in so inhospitable a context. But through the years we have continued to do whatever we could to link issues and communities and to offer an alternative vision to the electoral and legislative campaigns that dominate the politics of this city's racially exclusive white lesbian, gay, and women's communities. Soon after I moved to Albany I realized two things. First, that you cannot have everything: for example, a lower cost of living and less hectic lifestyle at the same time as the stimulation of an intellectually and politically diverse big city. Second, I learned that you have to brighten the corner where you are, which meant to me that I had to do the most effective and needed political work I could in the situation where I was. The conditions for making social and political change are never perfect; if they were, you would not need the change to begin with. Serious activists know that they are a part of the struggle for their entire lives, which means that success must be measured with a very long yardstick. Committed organizing guarantees not just a lifetime of very hard work, but the most incredible triumphs. Nelson Mandela's election to the presidency of South Africa after decades as a political prisoner is a stellar example.

Personally, despite my initiation into organizing during the remarkable political ferment of the 1960s, I cannot explain all of the reasons I became so committed to political work. Sometimes students ask me if my parents were activists. I smile at the image of the women in my family, who spent almost all of their time working so that our family could survive, being "activists." But then I remember their daily discussions about what was in the news, their conversations about race and black history. I recall how seriously they took voting, a right which most of them only began to exercise as elders after moving up North. My grandmother worked at the polls regularly and attended ward meetings. My family was also very active in our church, which played a significant political role in Cleveland's black community during a period when blacks were excluded from participation in the city's government and civic life. Obviously, I learned some important lessons about struggle at home, for which I am eternally grateful.

I have also learned most of what I know about organizing from working with other activists. When I was growing up it was activists and writers whom I most admired, and since it was the civil rights era, many black activists were clearly heroic. There are two black lesbians whom I was privileged to learn from who made a great difference in my life: Audre Lorde and Pat Parker. Not only were they out as lesbians in their writing in the early 1970s, but they were incredibly political women who did not have the illusion that it was enough for them just to pursue their individual artistic careers and let the rest of the world go hang. Both Pat, who died of breast cancer in 1989, and Audre, who died of breast cancer in 1992, were people I could count on for inspiration, and in Audre's case, as we were personal friends, direct support.

In the early 1980s there was a black feminist writers' conference in Eugene, Oregon, that all three of us attended. On Saturday afternoon we were going around the room discussing how we defined black feminism and saw our work. I will never forget what Pat said. She stated that she saw herself as a revolutionary. That although this was a word people used to say all of the time in the sixties and seventies, we did not hear it much anymore. She told us that what she was working for as a black feminist and lesbian was a revolution. What Pat said reminded me of how highly we had defined the stakes just a few years before. I vowed to myself from that day on not only to use the word *revolution* when I describe my political goals, but always to be conscious in doing the work that this is what we are, in fact, fighting for.

The contradictions, privation, and inhumanity of these times tell me that we need a revolution more than ever. And who better to forge it than radical lesbians of color?

Clint Steib/Washington Blade

Barbara Smith *was co-founder and publisher of Kitchen Table: Women of Color Press. She is the author of* The Truth That Never Hurts: Writings on Race, Gender, and Freedom *(Rutgers), and has edited three major collections about black women:* Conditions Five: The Black Women's Issue, *with Lorraine Bethel;* All the Women Are White, All the Blacks Are Men, But Some of Us Are Brave: Black Women's Studies, *with Gloria T. Hull and Patricia Bell Scott (Feminist Press); and* Home Girls: A Black Feminist Anthology *(Kitchen Table). She is co-author with Elly Bulkin and Minnie Bruce Pratt of* Yours in Struggle: Three Feminist Perspectives on Anti-Semitism and Racism *(Firebrand), and is one of the editors of* The Reader's Companion to U.S. Women's History *(Houghton Mifflin). Her articles, essays, literary criticism, and short stories have appeared in a wide variety of publications. She has been writer in residence and taught at numerous colleges and universities for over twenty-five years.*

This

essay links the movement for lgbt liberation to the fight for reproductive freedom, and connects both to a larger economic assault on the poor, on women, on children, and on people of color. Urvashi Vaid challenges Planned Parenthood's role, urging that organization to move from a reproductive rights focus to taking a "renewed and fearless leadership role in the revitalization of...a grassroots, multiracial, co-gender feminist movement." But she could easily be talking to the lgbt movement, which is just as stalled as the women's movement, delivering social services in a paternalistic system of them and us that forever keeps them dependent and us in control of the resources, framing the policies. Just as Mattie Richardson calls for a re-visioning of both the women's and lgbt movements on issues of class, sexual freedom, and race, Urvashi urges our national organizations to seriously rethink the underpinnings of their public policies.

Sex, Love, and Birth Control in the Twenty-First Century

Urvashi Vaid

Inviting a lesbian activist to speak about sex, love, and birth control is a bit like asking a priest…both know more than you might think about the subject. It is one of the ironies of history that the movement I come out of—the gay, lesbian, bisexual, and transgender movement—focuses far more on love and birth today than it does on sexual freedom. Indeed, some of the staunchest defenders of traditional idealized romantic love, marriage, commitment, and monogamy are gay men and lesbians; and a vast baby boom of childbearing, adoption, and parenting is underway among gay and lesbian couples. Now, I am all for equality, and to me that includes the right to marry for same-sex couples. But I am also a feminist, deeply aware of the bias embedded in the institution of marriage, and I am an Indian woman deeply suspicious of cultural mandates that define a marital relationship as superior to any other. Call me old-fashioned, but I prefer to live in sin with my girlfriend of ten years.

Having established my qualifications to address the topics at hand, I want this afternoon to appropriate the prescriptive posture of the cleric —and not the chic posture of the lesbian—to talk about the organizing that we who are advocates for reproductive freedom must do to continue the journey of women's liberation that we celebrate today.

Specifically, the next century requires us to recenter our work for sexual and reproductive freedom around the fact that public policy related to sex, love, and birth control is tied to economic decisions and to who has political power. I agree with Frances Kissling (Executive Director, Catholics for Free Choice) and Faye Wattleton (past chief executive of the Planned Parenthood Federation of America)—we need to revive a liberation-based movement in the twenty-first century if we want to defeat the threats to women's equality and to sexual and reproductive freedom that we now face. The second challenge of the future is more conceptual. It requires us to broaden our understanding of sex, love,

Adapted from an address originally delivered at the Planned Parenthood "Mapping the Future of Choice" conference in January 1998.

and birth control so that we see them as issues of sexual freedom, not just personal choice. To that end, in the next century, feminist organizations, gay, lesbian, bisexual, and transgender groups, traditional reproductive service providers, faith-based progressives, and sex educators must all forge a much closer link as a movement for sexual and reproductive freedom, because sexuality and gender, sexism and homophobia are inseparably linked.

Let me elaborate on these two points.

Economic Realities, Political Power, and a Reproductive Freedom Movement

In a recent review of Seymour Hersh's dishy book about JFK, Gore Vidal suggested that our interest in the sex lives of famous people in many ways diverted us from focusing on the issues of how money and power operate to allow some people the kind of privilege Hersh details. Gore Vidal is right. Economic realities more than sex define the lives of most Americans. Indeed, while sex will always entrance and distract us, in many ways it is losing its potency: today money is the ultimate aphrodisiac. Mainstream America pants over the endless articles about the lives and tiny teeny thoughts of billionaires and millionaires as palpably as it pants over pornography. The *Wall Street Journal* long ago displaced *Playboy* as the arena for male fantasy. Greed has replaced lust, and the market (it's down it's up, it's up it's down) has displaced the site where sex occurs—the bedroom, the barroom, the back seat of a Volkswagen—occupying more of people's daily attention. We live in interesting times.

In their informative book, *Intimate Matters: A History of Sexuality in America* (University of Chicago), historians John D'Emilio and Estelle Freedman suggest that economic changes drive sexual changes far more than the other way around! D'Emilio indicates, for example, that the combined impact of industrialization, the mobility of labor, and the social dislocation of millions of men and women in the World War II era allowed for the emergence of a gay and lesbian subculture and identity. In other words, while gay behavior always existed, in a sense capitalism helped create gay identity in the twentieth century. Similarly, the technological advance of the Pill allowed women to control pregnancy, even as such advances created a whole new set of health hazards and problems.

Given this historical truth, do economic-based decisions shape public policy about sex and birth control today? Emphatically yes. Two examples illustrate this point.

The first is historical. While access to contraception indeed liberated women from childbearing, we must remember that population control policy also had a more sinister dimension that today's welfare reform recalls: a history of justification rooted in the idea of eugenics—that certain classes and races were fitter and as a matter of public policy ought to be encouraged to reproduce while others should not. The welfare reform bill passed by Congress and endorsed by the Clinton Administration has embedded in it age-old population control measures designed to regulate the sexual lives of poor or low-income women: the bill provides greater funds to those states which reduce "out of wedlock" births. Control women's bodies, the federal government has said, and we will reward you at the same time we cut programs for the poor and taxes for the upper-middle class. In fact, the agenda of corporate capitalism—lower taxes and privatized public services—is being achieved through the demonization and targeting of poor and politically disempowered women of all colors. And we all know that the targeting of women has an explicitly sexual and reproductive component.

A second example is evident in the growing backlash to women's work outside the home. Anxiety about the domestic economy's ability to sustain job growth underlies this backlash. Today, right-wing pundits and think tanks openly question whether having women in the work force in large numbers is good for families: women's entry into the job market is being blamed for everything from men's low wages to the rise in teenage pregnancy to the decline of moral values. Whom does it benefit to have a public policy that women should stay home and raise the children? Women at home/men at work means that companies don't have to worry about messy policy issues like childcare, equal pay for equal work, sexual harassment in the workplace, job training and more.

Economic policy choices—or to use an old-fashioned term, ideology—guide public policy decisions about sex, love, and birth control all the time. Given this truth, we need a sexual and reproductive freedom movement that, first of all, has its own economic policies and platform it is seeking to enact; and second, has the political clout to guide public policy from a prowoman, pro-human rights perspective. Unfortunately, such a movement does not yet exist.

We face a different landscape than our predecessors did in the 1800s or the 1920s or the 1950s or even the 1980s. Today, more women have individual autonomy than ever before. We won the right to vote, and our vote matters. Lots of smart women are in political office or leadership positions in social justice organizations. More men identify with feminism than ever before. We have created a whole body of history, analysis, and theory. We boast a solid national, state, and local organizational infrastructure of women's organizations. We have won many elements of legal equality and the right to redress. We have a large and growing pool of young women and men not invested in the old sexist double standards, or the old sexual order, for that matter. We have at least a rhetorical understanding that we have to take on racism inside our organizations and economic policy outside in order to significantly affect women's lives. There is a wide-ranging infrastructure of social justice groups working on the full spectrum of issues. In other words, we are not all alone in our work for women's equality.

That is good news.

On the other hand, we have a political movement that is not cohesive, or powerful, that still does not tap the full potential of women's political power. Violence against women is incredibly pervasive and intolerable. We have a domestic women's movement that is far too timid to make an economic critique of the destructive market-driven policies that most threaten women. The voice of our movement's organizations is not spreading to broader classes and kinds of people, and as a result, fewer and fewer women and men identify as feminist even as they identify with the goals of equality for women. Support for reproductive choice remains strong, but susceptible to the manipulative politics of the Right. Racially and classwise, we operate in virtually segregated organizations—where our clients and constituents are a different race and class than our organizers, staffers, funders, or leaders.

We have feminist organizations that are insular and isolated from fresh ideas, and from the energies of younger women, low-income women, or the women of color whose lives so much of their policy work is about. We do not have powerful legislative lobbies in every state or even at the national level. Instead of seeing ourselves and each other as part of a broad-based feminist movement for economic and social change, we are so specialized that our work seems to be a series of narrow, single-issue problems—abortion and reproductive choice, violence, domestic violence, sexual harassment and so on. Don't misunderstand me: these are all issues critical to the health and lives of women, but our lack of a far-reaching, grassroots, militant feminist movement hurts us at the very instant that we need to link women's problems to broader policy solutions.

Major mainstream groups like Planned Parenthood must play a renewed and fearless leadership role in the revitalization of such a grassroots, multiracial, co-gender feminist movement. Imagine if Planned Parenthood prioritized the rebirth of such a women's liberation movement and brought to it the same resources, skill, and imagination that you have brought to planning this conference! We would be in great shape. The future may require some women's groups to merge with others, for new ones to be formed, for think tanks to really focus on the platform and specifics of how we implement reproductive choice for all women and teach sex education and responsibility to all boys and girls. We may need to create state-by-state political constituencies for women's equality, sex education, birth control, and healthcare. It will require the emergence of candidates—men and women—who see that this is not a single issue vote, not all about abortion or not, but a multifaceted movement that cares profoundly about the quality of the culture in which we raise our children, that has values of responsibility and love, of tolerance and honesty, that values the lives of poor and working-class women as much as it values the lives of the middle class and the wealthy. An explicitly electoral or political role is perhaps one that some in this organization will argue about—but I think it is imperative. For without such a presence, every one of the gains we have won thus far remains vulnerable and reversible.

A final aspect of this revitalized women's movement has to involve the very women and girls, boys and men that your clinics and counseling programs serve—the 70,803 clients who visited Planned Parenthood of New York City in 1996 alone, for example. The notion of social service agencies as social workers must be replaced by the vision of service providers as participants in a movement for social transformation. Are we willing to be fierce advocates for young girls, for young women with limited incomes of all colors, for black women, Puerto Rican women, or immigrant girls and women who do not speak English well? What if, in the next century, Planned Parenthood chose to focus 50 percent of its resources on the education, organizing, training, and advocacy of poor and limited-income women? How would that change our movement? How would it affect your funding base? The kind of positions you take?

In a sense, to do so would require Planned Parenthood to make the implicit more explicit, to transform itself organizationally to better reflect and to organize the constituencies it serves today. I want to urge you to make this explicit transformation because I see this as more than a rhetorical shift: we need strong, loud lobbies for girls and women who are poor—of whatever color, who are working class, who are middle class, who are currently voiceless in the political process. Choice for young girls needs to mean more than the ability to delay pregnancy. It ought to mean the ability to have a sense of self big enough to allow for all sorts of life choices.

Reproductive Freedom and Sexual Freedom

My second hope for the future is that Planned Parenthood will ally itself far more closely with the gay, lesbian, bisexual, and transgender movement; and that it will speak out more forcefully on all matters of sexual freedom, sexual expression, and sexuality. Four links bind the movement for lgbt liberation with women's liberation: (1) there is an intimate connection between homophobia and sexism; (2) there is an intimate connection between sexism and gender rigidity, and between the gay and lesbian liberation movement and gender nonconformity; (3) there has long been among feminists a critique of the limitations and pathologies of the traditional, patriarchal, nuclear family and a commitment to its reconstruction into a more egalitarian unit; and (4) both movements have worked hard to achieve and protect full sexual, reproductive, and personal autonomy and choice for all women. Not all who identify as feminists agree with what I am saying, and you should know that not all gay people agree that we should be closely linked to the reproductive freedom movement. But the progressive wings of feminism, of gay and lesbian liberation, have long articulated these four connections.

In a succinct book titled *Homophobia: A Weapon of Sexism* (Chardon Press), the author, organizer Suzanne Pharr, makes the point that in a culture in which women and men have unequal power and unequal freedom, sexism is enforced through homophobia. Men and women are required to prove their heterosexuality again and again or risk the stigma of being labeled homos. Proving you are not a gay man requires men to prove they are heterosexual, as efficiently as they can—which is by following convention and objectifiying and conquering women sexually, and boasting about it afterwards. Proving you are a real woman—in the military—requires you to put up with unwanted sexual advances by men or run the risk of being "reported" to investigators as gay. Sexism is enforced through homophobia.

Another set of issues connect feminism to lesbian and gay liberation: a critique of gender roles as we currently know them. Feminist academics have successfully explained that gender roles are as much a cultural construction as they are rooted in biology. Feminists have worked hard to try to define the ways our biology as women does not limit us to performing gender-specific roles. Issues of gender are very important to gay people as well. For one, a central key to homophobia is persecution of all those who are gender nonconformists—the sissy, the tomboy, the butch. Whether you are gay or straight, if you are any of these types, you have a school playground story of teasing and ridicule to tell.

Ironically, it is the Right that understands the importance of gender to both feminism and the lgbt movement, often more than many of us do. For example, in the months leading up to the UN's Fourth International Conference on Women held in Beijing in September of 1995, the antifeminist Right made a concerted effort to remove the term *gender* from all UN documents and policy statements. They sought to replace *gender* with the term *sex*. Why? Because, they argued, *gender* was a "radical feminist" plot to impose acceptance on all societies of five genders: male, female, gay, lesbian, and transgender. As if! I mean as if we even had that level of sophistication to have that as an agenda.

Luckily for us, because of the hard work of the international women's human rights movement, the Right failed in Beijing and the term *gender*—with its broader meanings for women's freedom—stayed in the document. But my question is this: If the Right can see that there are profound practical implications to feminism's argument that what it means to be female and male is as much a product of culture as it is of biology, then why don't we?

The third way that the lgbt movement, and at least the radical wings of feminism, have been linked is in arguing that nuclear families are not necessarily the sole or the best forms for human relationship or child-rearing. This remains a brave assertion to make in the face of two decades of family values rhetoric. Indeed, few gay leaders or feminist leaders take on the old notions of family and say we don't think it works. We don't defend single-parent families. Few feminist or mainstream leaders oppose the homophobic anti-adoption or antifoster parenting policies that more and more state legislatures are enacting. With our uneasy silence, we allow a public discourse on family that is full of misinterpreted data: blaming women for leaving the home to take jobs when they have no other economic choice; blaming the entry of women in the labor force for the decline in men's wages, rather than seeing the fault lying with a corporate production system that is willing to uproot companies and level towns in order to boost the profits of its managers; blaming single-parent families for the poverty of children in them, rather than faulting the economic system; seeing divorce as the problem rather than a symptom of the deeper problem; attacking the idea that child sexual abuse in the family exists, by attacking repressed memory syndrome (as the Right does).

The final link I want to raise is the question of sexual and reproductive freedom. Framing the issue as *freedom* rather than *choice* broadens the set of concerns a feminist and reproductive health movement is implicated in. I think Planned Parenthood and all reproductive freedom activists have a vital stake in issues of sexual freedom. We are witness today to pitched battles in schools over sex education and the content of those curricula; over what books should be in school libraries; over whether sexually explicit images can hang in public spaces; over whether music and popular culture should be censored; over whether arts institutions should receive funding to support plays like Tony Kushner's *Angels in America*. We are seeing the defunding of scores of organizations whose only misstep was to champion an artist who did sexually explicit work. The statistics on the rise of HIV infection among young people cry out for stronger sex education programs aimed at high school, college age, and sexually active youth. Debates about promiscuity and disease, moral corruption and sexual freedom rage as vigorously today as they did at the turn of the last century. The calm and experienced voice of Planned Parenthood needs to forcefully engage in these debates from your unique vantage point of counseling and serving hundreds of thousands of women and men who are sexually active. We need public leadership that is not hysterical, not puritanical, but frank and pro-sexual freedom.

Conclusion

The Planned Parenthood of the future ought to be an organization that is actively engaged in these arguments and questions. It should be a partner with the gay rights movement on many things. And it should be a leader in the articulation of policies, educational strategies, and practical outreach programs aimed at achieving a world in which women are truly free to be sexual agents.

If silence on questions of values or questions of sexual freedom was necessary at one point, or politically expedient at another, let us be clear that in the next century, it is not adaptive. It is essential that we are vocal in our struggles for sexual and reproductive freedom. Let our labor in the future be for a creative feminist movement that defends and expands freedom, love, and choice for all. Let our labor in the twenty-first century boldly counter the narrow and fear-based sexual policy proposals of the Right. Let it teach young people to respect and cherish their sexuality and their bodies. Let it organize a wide circle of men and women, boys and girls with a hopeful, positive, inclusive, and loving sexual politics of liberation.

Urvashi Vaid is an attorney and community organizer whose involvement in the gay, lesbian, bisexual, and transgender movement spans nearly twenty years. She is the Director of the Public Policy Institute of the National Gay and Lesbian Task Force and the author of Virtual Equality: The Mainstreaming of Gay and Lesbian Liberation (Anchor Books), which won the Lesbian/Gay/Bisexual Book Award from the American Library Association in 1996. She is the recipient of numerous awards and honors including a Rockefeller Residential Fellowship from the Center for Lesbian and Gay Studies at the City University of New York. She was born in New Delhi, India, and lives in New York City.

What

does it mean to be a queer American? Are we "just like everybody else" or do we have a unique contribution to make to the rich stew that is American culture? What are the costs to individual gay people, and to American society at large, of queer assimilation? Carmen Vazquez distills two years of speaking and writing about queer liberation to make a strong case for the existence of a uniquely queer soul. The queer spirit, she argues, plays a critical role in the sexual health of the American spirit. She links sexual liberation to other struggles for social justice and takes lgbt political leadership to task for selling our queer souls in a "deal with the devil." She articulates a bold and necessary vision for twenty-first century activism.

Citizen Queer
Carmen Vazquez

I will be using the word *queer* a lot in this essay. I do this for two reasons. *Queer* is an inclusive term for lesbian, gay, bisexual, and transgender people. It is also a term that an entire generation of our youth has been empowered by. I honor them and their spirit of inclusiveness when I use the word. You should also know that I have a different and fond cultural affinity with *queer*. Among Puerto Ricans, *queer* roughly translates into *maricon* or *maricona*. If you hear the word with hatred on the street, it is an insult and possibly dangerous. It is also, however, a word used to describe people who are slightly kooky or somewhat rebellious and mischievous. So, I have fond memories of being called *mariconcita,* or *little queer,* with love and affection by my mother. I bring that affection to the English use of the word.

I have been blessed many times over in my life as an activist by the thousands of people I have had the privilege of working with in the struggle for progressive social change. From Puerto Rico to Harlem to San Francisco and back to New York City are only the broad strokes. In between, there are many, many places where I have been nurtured and challenged. In Yakima and Seattle, in Eugene and Portland. In Los Angeles and San Diego. In Salt Lake City and Phoenix and Scottsdale and Santa Fe and Denver and St. Louis and Chicago. In Dallas and Houston and San Antonio and Austin. In Detroit and Ann Arbor. In Milwaukee and Minneapolis. In Atlanta and Tallahassee and Miami and New Orleans, and in Jackson, Mississippi. In Philadelphia and Washington, D.C. In Albany and in teeny little Clinton, New York. In New Jersey and Connecticut.

I have seen the length and breadth of America, and its ordinary, everyday queer people are good and generous and searching. I see us struggling for a balance between surviving the assaults of a homophobic world and finding the courage to confront it. I see us searching for a way to act on our intuitive understanding of our connection to other oppressed people. But I also see and hear a gay "leadership" that does not sound or look very much like most queers, a gay leadership determined to cast off the historically progressive character of a movement once dedicated to liberation. I challenge the notion that attaining "equal rights" in a society that forsakes social and economic justice is worth our while. I assert liberation as the mission of all those "little queers" from Puerto Rico to Yakima who know we haven't anything to lose but our souls. And we are not giving them up.

Sex and sexual liberation are at the heart of my vision for queer liberation. It is not possible for me to get to the essence of how I experience race, class, and gender oppression without looking through the prisms of my sexuality and my sense of spirit. This is because I am alive, barely fifty, and still most sexual. I am a citizen of America, where the public discourse on sex is so omnipresent and overwhelming that even a president can get drawn into the vortex of its seamy but never-ending appeal for the American public. I am also a lesbian, a fact that all of my enemies and some of my peers would like me to deny, disguise, or hide. But it is not possible for me to do this. I can no more disguise or hide my sexuality than I can my humanity. I am queer to the core. I celebrate the body queer. I celebrate the uniqueness of our gift to the human spirit, our self-conscious affirmation of the individual right to desire and pleasure for their own sake.

The regulation of sexuality and the commodification of desire are powerful political tools precisely because sexuality and desire are essential to the spirit of what we call human consciousness, or soul. Being human means we know the difference between reproduction and connection with another human being for the sake of transcending oneself, for the sake of love and communion, and nothing else.

That should make queerness a highly integrated spiritual state, an automatic ticket for a ride to heaven if one were to believe in such a place. It should make our sexuality not immoral but inviolate.

The state has no role—no business—in how we order our desire, our sexuality, and our spiritual life. The people in charge of what I call the state are the people who control wealth and its distribution. They are well aware that sexuality cannot be ordered or totally controlled. When vilification, scapegoating, moralizing, and legal strategies fail to contain or repress the out queer, the state requires our acquiescence. We get seduced with the possibility of belonging. The state offers safety in exchange for domesticity; citizenship in exchange for being clean and white and pliant; a "place at the table" in exchange for a sanitized sexuality. It is a bargain the state has tried to strike with countless immigrants. We are just the most recent, and possibly the most complex, of the people U.S. capitalism has tried to absorb because we really do come from everywhere. How we respond to the seduction of belonging and its attendant dangers depends on how we define our mission as a movement and our understanding of how our upbringing in a culture dominated by a Christian, white, male, heterosexist world view shapes our allegiance to or rejection of the status quo.

I believe a politics of liberation requires that we articulate who we are as individual queer souls with an affinity for what oppression and exploitation mean to poor people, people of color, women, and all the people who keep being left out of the "clean" body politic, or continue to be defined as "less than" the ideal citizen in contemporary American politics and culture.

The voices of people committed to a politics of liberation, however, are heard with decreasing frequency. As we approach the next Christian millennium, our public images and what we espouse as an agenda for our movement demonstrate less affinity for justice than for the desire to be "normal" at any cost. It is the "virtually normal" strategy for how we will attain equal rights and acceptance in the heartland. The strategy will fail. Individual autonomy in human sexuality is not the norm in America. No matter how we dress or redress ourselves, growing up to be Citizen Queer is not an acceptable option in America.

I remember my friend Steven and his sweet stoned self singing in a New York Jewish lilt he could never quite disguise about "The Last Pioneers," a song he wrote and promoted as the gay national anthem. The song paid tribute to outcasts, to old gay life, to queens and butches, to the ones who just won't/can't pass. I was always moved by the song, by Steven's melancholy and defiance, by his vision of us as a people exploring a new geography, a universe of desire. Most of all, I was inspired and grateful that he gave us lyrics with which to think of ourselves as a people. It was the closest I ever came to hearing queer gospel music, a call to sisterhood and brotherhood in our struggle together against the bigotry and violence in our lives, a call to solidarity where the most despised among us can be our heroes.

Current gay civil rights strategy calls for us to embrace white middle-class heteronormalcy. We are no longer to challenge the absurdity of living in a culture that reveres individualism while telling us (as it has told countless other "misfits") that the price for its tolerance is lockstep conformity with a Madison Avenue image of "happy Americans" that has as little to do with the reality of how most Americans really live as Disney World does. So wounded are we by the denial of belonging, by the loss of family, community, and a right to faith in whatever we understand to be god, that we accept the absurdity and the illusion that we can belong to America's family if we are "good."

It's a bargain with the devil. As America faces the next millennium bereft of community, as more and more working people are left to struggle from one paycheck to the next, as the extreme right wing moves relentlessly toward consolidation of political power, we are accepting their terms. Bad move. The liberated queer soul is possibly the best of what human imagination has yet to conjure. If, in the end, those who would eradicate us from human existence win, it will not be because they have anything better to offer the human race. It will be because we stopped believing that we, without makeover, are special, unique, and worthy of dignity.

What a pity that would be.

Imagine no poetry by Sappho or Emily Dickinson or Langston Hughes. Imagine no music by Tchaikovsky or Bessie Smith or Cole Porter or k.d. lang. Imagine no art by Michelangelo or Keith Haring. Imagine no essays by Audre Lorde. Imagine a world without the grace and courage of Martina Navratilova on the tennis court or Greg Louganis diving for Olympic gold. Imagine no butch or femme, no drag on Halloween. No transpeople splendor. Imagine no Eleanor Roosevelt. Imagine no novels by James Baldwin or Dorothy Allison, no plays by Tennessee Williams or Paula Vogel. Imagine Macy's windows unadorned by queer sensibility.

I will not exchange my sexuality for citizenship. I will not embrace a sexless visibility or a virtual sexuality. I will not let America off the hook because it is having an anxious moment here, a flaccid period of post-New Deal, post-World War II, and post-Communism that produces eleven-year-old boys who carry arms and kill their classmates because they don't know what to do with being lonely, rejected, unloved, and untouched. I don't want to be mainstreamed into an America that no longer knows how to hold and comfort its grandchildren or how to create and maintain the safety of community. I will not let America ensnare me in its seduction of belonging, not when the truth of America is that there isn't anything to belong to: its workers are transients, its factories have gone overseas to exploit people poorer than us, and the only thing that matters is that which gets counted on Wall Street.

The real tragedy of America is that it places more value in and devotes more resources to an investigation of a president who lies about a consensual sexual affair than it does to prevent children from killing each other. That America has no use for lesbian, gay, bisexual, transgender people. Either queers join in coalition and alliance with others seeking justice, or we will be destroyed.

At OutWrite '97, a lgbt writers conference, I was on a panel that posed the question: How should we respond to the enemy, the abuser, the extreme Right? I think the question is disingenuous at best. As people raised in an overwhelmingly Christian culture, we are conditioned to respond to the question with: *Love thy enemy. Love him or her because there, but for the grace of God, go I. She is mere flesh and blood. From dust unto dust. They are no different from you and me except, perhaps, for an idea here and there.*

Well, maybe.

And maybe a few dollars here and there. The color of your skin, your gender, your sexual orientation, and your wealth matter greatly to the pursuit and attainment of success in America. The complexities of race, class, gender, and where you sit on the economic ladder create differences among us, differences that place us on one side or the other of privilege and power. To say otherwise, to say, *We are just like everybody else,* has no meaning in a progressive context. The phrase, as used by queers in pursuit of mainstream "respectability," has enormous class and race bias attached to it.

Which *everybody else?*

Difference matters. I confess a genuine attraction to the idea that there is more in common between the abuser and the abused than we are ever willing to admit. More empathy would certainly make better human beings of us all. But I don't think that empathy requires us to lose sight of those very material realities we call race, class, and gender. I think the search for what ultimately can bind us one to the other in humanity, as one people with a resplendent rainbow of souls, will only reach fruition if we look, unblinking, at the very real divisions and understand how they do make us different and unique and worthy of our stripe in that rainbow.

I don't think *Love thy enemy* was ever meant to obscure our differences from each other or to relieve us of the responsibility for articulating and defending a vision of social justice. Although I may have much in common with the bat-wielding slum kid who is out to bash my head in because I'm queer, I have nothing in common with Pat Buchanan or Pat Robertson. To collapse the two Pats with the slum kid is dangerous. At the same time, to glamorize the working class and demonize the Right is also dangerous.

Ideology serves the interests of class and the political forces that privilege one class over others. An ideology that promotes competition, profit, racial superiority, cultural superiority, authoritarian institutions, and a global marketplace as the site of freedom only serves the interests of global corporate conglomerates. An ideology of cooperation, equitable distribution of wealth, racial equality, cultural diversity, and democratic institutions serves the interests of the oppressed. To ignore the role of ideology in sustaining or resisting institutional oppression and class privilege is foolish and dangerous.

My father was not a good man. He was an alcoholic, a wife beater, someone who disciplined his children by having them kneel on tile floors, arms outstretched for as long as he told you to. When our arms gave out, he used his belt to lash across our arms, back, and legs. We lived on welfare for years, and if he got to the check before my mother did, there wasn't going to be much money for food. On one particularly awful Saturday after a welfare payment, he got all dressed up: black dress pants creased to a razor's edge by my mother, his favorite hound's-tooth checked black-and-white sport jacket, starched white shirt, and those short ties with swirls of burgundy, from the forties, that I myself fancy these days. He was a handsome man. He left for his party—and left us without food. My mother sent me to the Chinese grocer across the street to get a pound of rice and a quart of milk. We would have rice soup for dinner. But even the rice soup was not to be on this Saturday. The grocer said my daddy hadn't paid the bill for more than a month and he couldn't afford to keep giving his store away. There were people in the store, and he talked loud enough for them to hear. I burned with shame, a shame that seared right through my hunger. I left the store crying because there would be no dinner tonight, and I hated my father with a depth of passion that made me tremble.

Over the years, my rage at my father only grew. He died in a veteran's hospital in Puerto Rico in 1980. I did not go see him. My initial response to his death was numbness. Nothing. I didn't care. The world was better off without him. But in the weeks and months that followed his death, I found myself grieving for a man I hated. I was dumbfounded. Memories of him kept creeping up on me. Memories of baseball games and of riding on his shoulders, laughing, somehow became mingled with memories of violence and hunger and rage. I talked with my mother about him and heard stories I had never heard or had long buried. How he drove a truck full of soldiers over a mine in a South Pacific island during World War II. He was the only survivor. He was found in a ditch, ribs and wrist fractured, covered with blood and surrounded by the body parts of the men he was driving to the carrier that was to take them home. He was broken in body and spirit. He was never the same man.

Time passed, and slowly my rage gave way to compassion and to sorrow, to sadness over the waste of a life. In death, my father gave me the capacity to have empathy and compassion. My life changed forever. I understood that the abstractions of feminism or any other political vision are meaningless if they are not grounded in the heart of living, in love for people broken by racism or the violence of poverty and the despair of loss.

I share my father's death because I believe it is vital to distinguish between a personal process of growth that allows us not to demonize our parents, siblings, and friends who have turned away from us, and the institutions and conservative social movements that use queer, immigrant, and welfare scapegoats to feed fear and mistrust.

Without a vision of social justice that can join our different experiences of oppression, without an absolute and unwavering commitment to building coalitions and community with each other, we defeat each other and any possibility of radical change in America.

These days there is a great deal of public discussion about Sex Panic! both in our own and in the mainstream press. Sex Panic! is the name of a group of people—all genders—that has developed a response to what we see as an institutional and cultural assault on queer culture and sexuality. In loud and public opposition to Sex Panic! are the usual radicals of the Right, but also individuals known to mainstream America as gay activists. People like Larry Kramer, Michelangelo Signoreli, Gabriel Rotello, and Andrew Sullivan. These are high-profile men, all published authors, one of them an individual of considerable personal wealth. All are white men. All are critical of a "promiscuous" gay culture that they argue kills gay men.

The complexities of a dialogue about sexual politics and what that dialogue might mean to the queer soul are enormous and require much more thought than I have room for in this essay. I address it because I am furious with how this discussion is framed in public and because it offers a good example of what I assert about the importance of distinguishing between ideologies and political systems, between identity politics and social change movements, between individuals and institutions.

For starters, most of the Sex Panic! discussion is a "he said/he said" dialogue. *She* is not present in this pissing match. This is true despite the fact that the state's overt repression of women's sexuality (birth control prohibitions, abortion, suppression or outright censorship of women's erotica) all predate anything remotely resembling a gay movement. When women are referenced by critics of Sex Panic!, we are touted as the ideal (read: monogamous and faithful, not promiscuous) modern gay men should aspire to. It is much like the old Madonna/whore dichotomy of Christian lore, except that now the promiscuous gay men are the whores while lesbians and monogamous HIV-negative men are the Madonnas.

Sexism aside, what most infuriates and astounds me as I listen to the conservative voices in our own movement who denounce Sex Panic! is the posture these men assume as rational, scientifically informed individuals motivated only by love of their brethren. We who support the notion that individuals have a right to engage in consensual sexual activity free of state harassment, we who believe that the best way to keep young queer men and lesbians of all colors and IV users from becoming HIV infected is to provide them with the resources and emotional support necessary to negotiate safer sex and clean needles, we are accused of being delusional and motivated by political ideology. Well, I am as motivated by a progressive social justice political ideology and vision of liberation as they are motivated by a conservative political ideology and vision of tiptoeing into the mainstream clean and unseen. They want post-gay. I want queer and present. Loud and proud. They want assimilation. I want liberation.

Silly me. I keep forgetting that their politics need not be referenced. Theirs are the politics of the land, of the mainstream, of power and privilege. I forget that the visibility of "good" gay people in mainstream media and entertainment is actually about the invisibility of the rest of us. It is about invisibility for most of us because the ones you see on TV, the ones with op-ed pieces in the *New York Times,* are cleaned-up gays. No messy ones, no sir. No "radicals," no queers critical of our system of government or class, no one dwelling on the shrinking safety net for the poor and how they are dying in the midst of the greatest economic upturn this country has seen in thirty years. Nope.

We get *Ellen* and her spiffy clean house in LA. Did you ever notice that it is always clean? Did you ever notice that everyone is white and no one struggles with his or her finances, with paying the electric bill or buying groceries? I suppose since she doesn't work she can keep up with the place, but how does she pay the mortgage without a job?

I liked *Ellen.* I watched the show faithfully. I think it is both historic and personally valuable that a lesbian was on television almost every Wednesday night for two years, and maybe some blonde, blue-eyed kid in Ohio saw herself reflected in *Ellen,* and maybe it will save her life. I just don't want that child in Ohio to be the only kid who sees herself reflected on television or the local gay rag. I want kids in the Bronx and in Brooklyn and in East LA and in rural Mississippi and in East Cleveland and South Chicago to be saved too. I want us not to forget that this is a movement rooted in liberation that grew on the backs of people who struggled and died for racial and gender equality, for peace and for economic justice.

Someday, I want to step into the austere and grand silent passion of an ancient Catholic church in Isola Madre in Northern Italy. I want to kneel and breathe in centuries of hope and prayer and incense. I want to light a candle to warm and illuminate cold stone walls and I do not want to ever fear what might happen to me when I step out from the shadows of that church dressed in the cloth of a man. That day I will be free.

In the wilderness of hate-filled hearts, distinctions between toney A-gays on Fire Island and Greenwich Village, effeminate boys in Wyoming, butch dykes in Brooklyn, and black female-to-male sex workers in the alleys of any American city are not relevant. We all die the same way. We are all hated the same way. We need not waste our time re-creating hierarchies of the most oppressed or the most hated. What we must do is take off the hoods. We must stop pretending that our assimilation into this culture will tame the hate-filled hearts. We must stop pretending that laws alone can end oppression and systemic, institutional discrimination. We must envision and create a just and clean and safe world. If we do that, *normal* will not matter. We will be free.

Carmen Vazquez, a self-described Butch-Puerto Rican-Socialist, is director of public policy at the Lesbian and Gay Community Services Center in New York City. She is a former board member of the National Gay and Lesbian Task Force and the OUT Fund for Lesbian and Gay Liberation, a project of the Funding Exchange.

Firebrand Books is an award-winning feminist and lesbian publishing house. We are committed to producing quality work in a wide variety of genres by ethnically and racially diverse authors. Now in our fourteenth year, we have over ninety titles in print.

A free catalog is available on request from Firebrand Books, 141 The Commons, Ithaca, New York 14850, 607-272-0000.

Visit our website at www.firebrandbooks.com.